Manifest
Technique

THE ASIAN AMERICAN EXPERIENCE

Series Editors
Eiichiro Azuma
Jigna Desai
Martin F. Manalansan IV
Lisa Sun-Hee Park
David K. Yoo

Roger Daniels, Founding Series Editor

A list of books in the series appears
at the end of this book.

Manifest Technique

HIP HOP, EMPIRE, AND VISIONARY FILIPINO AMERICAN CULTURE

MARK R. VILLEGAS

UNIVERSITY OF ILLINOIS PRESS
Urbana, Chicago, and Springfield

Publication of this book was supported in
part by funding from the Franklin & Marshall
College Office of College Grants Resource Fund
administered by the Office of the Provost.

An earlier, condensed version of chapter 1 was
previously published in the *Journal of Asian American
Studies*. An earlier, condensed version of chapter 3
was previously published in *Amerasia Journal*.

Library of Congress Cataloging-in-Publication Data
Names: Villegas, Mark R., author.
Title: Manifest technique: hip hop, empire, and visionary
    Filipino American culture / Mark R. Villegas.
Description: Urbana: University of Illinois Press, [2021]
    | Series: The Asian American experience | Includes
    bibliographical references and index.
Identifiers: LCCN 2021005206 (print) | LCCN 2021005207
    (ebook) | ISBN 9780252043789 (cloth) | ISBN 9780252085772
    (paperback) | ISBN 9780252052682 (ebook)
Subjects: LCSH: Filipino Americans—Social life and customs.
    | Filipino Americans—Ethnic identity. | Hip-hop—Social
    aspects—United States. | Filipino Americans—Music—
    Social aspects.
Classification: LCC E184.F4 V56 2021 (print) | LCC E184.F4
    (ebook) | DDC 973/.049921—dc23
LC record available at https://lccn.loc.gov/2021005206
LC ebook record available at https://lccn.loc.gov/
    2021005207

For the loud, yet unheard

Contents

On Constant Replay

In 2010, the Filipino American hip hop group the Native Guns released the song "Handcuffs" to honor the memory of twenty-two-year-old Oscar Grant who was killed by a transit police officer in Oakland, California, on New Year's Day. Grant was handcuffed, pinned down, punched, and shot in the back at point-blank range. The execution-style killing was followed by local protests, spurring renewed national attention to police violence against Black people. After chanting the names of African Americans recently taken at the hands of the police, Kiwi raps:

> We sick of just yellin "No justice, no peace"
> Déjà vu, 1992, pause and repeat
> All the tension been buildin, it's gotten to a peak
> It's a Molotov party, and we brought our own drinks.

The Native Guns' musical catalog is part of a broader cultural response to police violence, adding to hip hop's reputation of documenting and communicating the practice of racial profiling. At the time, "Handcuffs" was their latest contribution to seemingly permanent problems in U.S. policing. As if our world is a piece of film caught in a loop, like the replayed, fuzzy camcorder footage of Rodney King being beaten, Kiwi intimates that little social progress has been made over decades of police abuse, protest, riots, calls for peace, promises . . . and repeat. The images of rage and revolt in "Handcuffs" could apply to any number of episodes of police violence against African Americans before Oscar Grant and after.

In 2012, the *Seattle Times* invited Filipino American emcee Geologic (who at the time performed as Prometheus Brown) to write a guest column on a rash of gun violence in Seattle. Instead of an essay, Geo wrote "May Day," a song that criticizes society's double standard of attitudes on gun violence and policing, which shifts depending on the race of victims and perpetrators and on the neighborhood where violence occurs.[1] "May Day" pricks at the conscience of Seattle, which prides itself on its supposed cultural liberalism but maintains residential segregation. In the hook, Geo reveals a north/south divide in Seattle, with the latter being more Black, brown, and working class and thus invisible, and the former being more white, wealthy, and thus deemed by some to be worthier of protection:

> Shots fired in the South End, nobody cares
> Shots fired in the North End, everybody scared
> Nothing they can do for us that we can't do ourselves
> Point the finger at the mirror instead of somebody else.

It seems that we must be constantly reminded of the tension between American society's inherent violence and its more acceptable mythologies of freedom and egalitarianism. For the past few decades, hip hop music has articulated this tension with precision and harrowing clarity. "Handcuffs" and "May Day" serve as cultural markers inserted in the long game of memory work. The constant replay exhibited in hip hop music shows us that memory is fragile. It is not made of stone or steel. Memory takes work, stewardship, and social movement.

The politics of the Native Guns and Geo are not isolated or exceptional; they emerge from interconnected, collaborative, and intergenerational Filipino American hip hop cultural communities. *Manifest Technique* examines the ways in which Filipino Americans inhabit and perform multiple, messy, and often contradictory expressions in hip hop, which I claim represent a vernacular culture rooted in colonial dispossession. By defying the racial tropes espoused in Spanish and American white supremacy, Filipino Americans have been connecting with a larger universe of racial dignity in spaces of hip hop.

We as Filipino Americans have been engaged in protracted wars over memory and meaning. Che, a Black Filipina American vocalist of the eclectic and visionary hip hop group LOVE Culture in Jacksonville, Florida, was active as an artist-organizer in the successful movement to remove Confederate monuments, symbols that stood for white dominance and permanence. This Black-led movement signaled an urgent call for freedom from white supremacy; it was a war over memory and meaning: white supremacy is not invincible. Che and her comrades toppled the monuments. Yet, statues still dot public squares across the United States inscribed with tall tales of the nation "gifting" freedom to the Philippines, such as the Admiral George Dewey Monument in the heart of San Francisco's financial district.

But blocks of granite do not write, dance, or sing. People do. *Manifest Technique* exhibits the creative knowledge Filipino Americans exude. Our culture demonstrates we are a mighty and resilient people—and we are so because African Americans have might and resilience. The pages in this book testify to the fact that Filipino American decolonization is indebted to Black freedom struggle—in fact, Philippine independence has been intimately linked to Black resistance since African American soldiers banded with Filipinos during the Philippine-American War.

"No justice, no peace" is not just a protest chant; it is a motto reflecting the painful inevitability of constant replay. Our artists are restless, always at the helm of leading us toward new possibilities. At its best, hip hop offers a space to envision a future that is race conscious, pro-Black, and absolutely beautiful.

Acknowledgments

Single-author books are deceptive—writing a single-author book, I quickly learned, is far from a "single" endeavor. It requires a massive team of supporters, mentors, and thinkers. I take pride that this project (as with all academic projects) is inherently collaborative. This book would not have been possible without the encouragement and friendship of the artists, activists, and educators who offered their time to chat with me. I don't have space to name everyone, but I've met with you at cafés, conferences, classrooms, festivals, and online. From the bottom of my heart, thank you. Let's keep building.

Huge shout-outs to the following folks who keep me alive and thriving: To Leo Esclamado, my funky and talented Duval brother from another, who keeps me grounded in reality and has brilliant ideas. He reminds me that joy is not only fundamental but elemental. To Teishan, from Verano Place to P.A., we have been through a lot together. May our next adventure be full of pawpaw fruits. To Joseph Alvaro, this project began while we spun on the cold concrete of his garage. A.D.B. always. Hours of windmill practices and the blood, bruises, and rug burns are the roots of my research. And I still don't got mills. To Jonathan Calvillo, whose keen eye, tireless work ethic, and lyrical wisdom keep me going. To Ray San Diego, who gave honest feedback and is always willing to hear my ideas. To Vince Laus, who always believed in me and is like family. To Sharon Quinsaat, from joining our Filipino grad student group, to hosting Vince and me in La Union, to our journeys to our respective campuses, I am grateful for her advice and tsismis.

The first time I met Roderick Labrador, he wore a giant smile. This is how I know him: he has an effortless ability to balance scholarship with gravity and a spirit of happiness. Rod has provided valuable guidance, input, and a listening ear. Kuttin Kandi has always been a source of fire for me. She was there in the beginning sketches of my research, always keeping me questioning and improving. Kandi keeps me—keeps us *all*—sharp.

I am grateful for the thoughtful and friendly guidance from the University of Illinois Press team, especially Martin Manalansan and Dawn Durante. Thanks also to the reviewers who kindly helped me improve this project. This project was completed with the gracious assistance from the Franklin & Marshall Office of College Grants Resource Fund. I appreciate my colleagues in the Department of American Studies at F&M for their warmth and inspiration: Carla Willard, Alison Kibler, Dennis Deslippe, Gabriel Mayora, David Schuyler, Louise Stevenson, Ann Wagoner, Cristina Pérez, and Eric Usner. Special recognition to Barbara Altmann for her encouragement, Laura Shelton for her care and guidance, and Jennifer Conley for her consultation. The motivation from my students gave me life throughout the writing process. To my writing groups and dear friends across campus, thanks for providing a caring, loving space. Special big ups to the good folks in POCA.

I want to recognize my friends and long-time collaborators in the Association for Asian American Studies and the American Studies Association: Rick Baldoz for his encouragement and feedback; Elliott Powell, who has supported me immensely and whose work inspires me; Faye Caronan for her wisdom and advice; Oliver Wang, who was an important ally very early on and continues to be a valuable collaborator. All my thanks for the guidance and care from Sarita See, Antonio Tiongson, Jr., Allyson Tintiangco-Cubales, Dawn Mabalon (rest in power), Robyn Rodriguez, Theo Gonzalves, Michael Viola, Emily Lawsin, Gina Velasco, Dana Nakano, Anthony Ocampo, Brian Chung, Valerie Francisco-Menchavez, Angelica Allen, J. Lorenzo Perillo, Victor Viesca, Sylvia Chan-Malik, Marisol LeBrón, and Tracy Lachica Buenavista.

My advisors, mentors, and colleagues during my time at UC Irvine gave me the tools and confidence to initiate this book: many thanks to Christine Balance, Linda Vo, Glen Mimura, Sohail Daulatzai, Bridget Cooks, Jim Lee, Dorothy Fujita-Rony, Claire Jean Kim, Miguel Abad, Elaine Andres, and Erica Cheung. I want to recognize my colleagues at UCSD Ethnic Studies, Cal State Long Beach, and Cal State Fullerton. I am especially grateful for Linda España-Maram and Natalie J. Graham. This book developed out of initial research at UCLA's Asian American Studies Center and Department. The following people helped me at those exciting, early stages: Melany de la Cruz-Viesca, Irene Soriano, Valerie Matsumoto, Lucy Mae San Pablo Burns, H. Samy Alim, Victor Bascara, Cheryl L. Keyes, Anna Alves, La'Tonya Rease Miles, Paul Nadal, and Mike Gonzales.

Infinite respects and appreciation to Bambu, Krish, Kiwi, Hopie, Ruby Ibarra, Odessa Kane, and Manila Ryce. Special acknowledgment to Jeff Chang, who encouraged me to write on this topic decades ago. I told him someday someone should write a book on Filipino Americans and hip hop, and he said it should be me. To Mark Pulido—the mayor—one of the first dudes I met when I moved back to Southern California. He connected me to an amazing Filipino American community. Mark's energy gives me energy. To Isaiah Dacio, for his dedication to the scene and big heart keeps us all motivated. To Delrokz, Mikeydisko, Sha Boogie, Rob Nasty, Chris Woon, Arnel Calvario, Kimmy Maniquis, Anna Sarao, Brian Redondo, Stephen Bischoff, Eric Sanford, and Nate Nevado for their talent, insight, and important advocacy. To Ricardo Cofinco for the dope cover art. To Geo, for his enthusiasm for my ideas. Our chats sparked foundational aspects of this project. To Freedom, who has always been a tremendous source of support and knowledge. And I can't forget the kind folks in the isangmahal arts kollective.

Before academia, I was involved in a number of arts organizations, where I learned to work with wonder: FilAm ARTS, Festival of Philippine Arts and Culture, and Visual Communications in LA and the Exhale crew at the University of Florida. I want to recognize Malini Schueller, Sharon Wright Austin, Dawn-Elissa Fischer, and Tanya Koropeckyj-Cox for their impactful mentorship. Very special shouts to my amazing community in Lancaster, especially Sir Oliver the Aardvark, the Sanctum crew, and Somos Lancaster. I dream about my parents and siblings every night. Despite being far, they're close to me. Salamat sa inyong pasensya. I inherited the houzer style from my brother, Thom (MAC Vibes!). Denice, te agradezco por tu amor y apoyo. Me ayudas a ser una mejor persona. Salamat, mahal.

Savage Folklorists
in Your Empire

Small Stages, Big Networks

In 2008, the Jabbawockeez dance crew captivated MTV *America's Best Dance Crew* audience members with their street-certified moves. Eight years later, Jabbawockeez choreographer Phil Tayag and pop crooner Bruno Mars dazzled in one of the largest Super Bowl halftime show viewerships in history. The same year, the Jabbawockeez stunned fans at the NBA Finals halftime show in Oakland, California. Bruno Mars and the Jabbawockeez represent an arrival of Filipino American talent to the mainstream stage. But, long before the solidification of the few Filipino Americans who "made it" to the upper echelons of the entertainment industry, there flourished Filipino American hip hop dancers, DJs, graphic artists, party promoters, and fans who would never receive such international acclaim.[1] Even if they would never grace big stages such as the Super Bowl or the NBA Finals, Filipino American contributors formed an important expansive, organic, and bottom-up cultural infrastructure that helped produce the world's most renowned Filipino American talent. *Manifest Technique* acknowledges the multigenerational presence of a sprawling Filipino American hip hop cultural network composed of small stages of cultural production.[2] Given Filipino Americans' participation in hip hop since its embryonic days (and in pre–hip hop cultural scenes such as funk, disco, popping, strutting, and mobile DJs), documenting spaces and moments of Filipino American hip hop cultural production is long overdue: the dynamic hip hop talent found in the Rock Force Crew, Renegade Rockers, Rock Steady DJs, and legion of mobile DJ crews in the San Francisco Bay Area; Johnny's Quest, the Beat Junkies, Legend Entertainment, and Jalan

Productions in Southern California; DJ Nasty Nes, isangmahal arts kollective, BOSS Crew, and Massive Crew in Seattle; the Neptunes and Kuya Tribe in Virginia Beach; Joe Bataan and the Fifth Platoon in New York City; the Little Green Apples, City Street Breakers, and Main Ingredients in Florida—this list is modest. But the purpose of this book is not to give shout-outs to unheralded pioneers and practitioners. Given their nearly four decades of commitment to hip hop, the genre, I contend, has been Filipino America's most important but often its most overlooked cultural aesthetic.

Within local spaces of intense and sustained creative energy, Filipino Americans have been crafting worldviews and political possibilities through hip hop. This book observes the narratives, music, embodiments, and visual expressions emerging from Filipino Americans' localized hip hop cultures. My hometown of Jacksonville, Florida, exemplifies a node in the geographically disparate locales of Filipino American hip hop performance. A sketch of my hometown gives readers a sense of hip hop's importance in less-familiar Filipino American cultural centers.

Jacksonville is a navy community populated by families who have migrated from other navy towns. Our links to the armed services shaped our residential patterns, schooling, careers, political habits, and relationships. Navy kids from a large Filipino American community can relate: the Junior Reserve Officer Training Corps in my high school was effectively a Filipino American club. Navy bases functioned as conduits for hip hop cultural networking. Most of my friends had roots in Virginia, California, Hawai'i, Japan (host to a large U.S. Navy base), and Washington State. The mix of fashion, music sensibilities, and dance styles seemed to be grounded in our immediate locale, but we also glanced in the direction of other cities where we had lived. My schools were very racially mixed, in terms of both the census-based demographics (Jacksonville is one-third African American) and the racial diversity within families. Due in large part to overseas military contact, being mestizo with a white, African American, or Latino father and a Filipina mother was (and still is) quite common in Jacksonville. In this environment, young Filipino Americans in my city engaged in hip hop culture. Constantly migrating bodies, styles, and reference points informed our understanding of the world and shaped our expressions. In the 1990s, regional African American musical vernaculars like Miami bass made up our musical diet. After all, the bass legends 69 Boyz, 95 South, and Quad City DJs came out of Jacksonville. New York hip hop and Bad Boy Records also dominated the radio waves until Master P, No Limit Records, and southern rap took over the nation beginning in the late 1990s. At parties, young Filipino American DJs were spinning dancehall reggae many years before reggaetón (dancehall's heir) became more popular in the early 2000s. Filipino kids from other cities would also introduce us to new music, such as mixtapes from the predominantly Filipino American DJ crew the Beat Junkies and CDs from the vibrant Filipino American freestyle and R&B music industry in Northern California. VHS tapes also traveled: my brother would show off footage of Filipino American hip hop dancers performing at car shows. My friends put on repeat a fuzzy, over-dubbed tape of breakers (also called b-boys or b-girls) from Seattle. Tapes of B-Boy Summit battles were also bootlegged among aspiring Jacksonville breakers.

Within this environment in the U.S. South, where Filipinos are relative newcomers, we created public and private spaces through hip hop expressions. Pinoy breakers flexed moves on the navy base basketball courts, in single-family home garages, and on the multicolored tiled floors of Jacksonville's Regency Square Mall. One humid summer afternoon, crosstown rival crews engaged in an epic battle at the Orange Park Mall. Before the homeroom bell, the drum section of our high school band threw down beats for dancers getting in an early morning sweat. With some skillful tweaking of a loose door, we would trespass into the fitness room of a luxury apartment complex to practice windmills. In church halls and living rooms, Pinays rehearsed their hip hop routines for the next debut, a party to celebrate a Filipina's eighteenth birthday. Long before Filipino Americans "made it" on the stages of *MTV's America's Best Dance Crew, American Idol, So You Think You Can Dance* or on YouTube, these were the small stages where we performed ephemeral acts that built durable cultural foundations. Before those rare flashing moments on TV in which "you felt that tremor of recognition," to quote journalist Jeff Chang's description of Filipino Americans' exciting but fleeting visibility, we recognized one another as talented and dedicated practitioners of hip hop without being compelled to reflect on the cumulative magnitude of our cultural productions.[3]

For young, second-generation Filipino Americans, what was my Jacksonville in the 1990s could for them have been the Navy communities in Virginia Beach, San Diego, Honolulu, or Bremerton. Across the country, concentrations of Filipino Americans were producing everyday culture with forms of hip hop practices that were our dominant mode of expression and affiliation. Aside from navy communities, urban locales like Queens, New York, and Jersey City, New Jersey, fostered lively hip hop scenes where Filipino Americans were key participants. The rhythmic lyricism of award-winning poet Patrick Rosal reawakens memories of DJ and b-boy culture of his hometown in multiracial New Jersey.[4] On a large scale, Filipino American youths of those decades were finding themselves and each other through hip hop. The 1980s and '90s were a special moment in Filipino American history for its diversity of young Filipinos: children of the first cohorts of post-1965 professional immigrants mixing with military brats and with descendants of agricultural workers who arrived during the U.S. colonial period. This period saw Filipinos from a range of socioeconomic classes, including from what I call the Filipino American military class. There was also large-scale diversity of linguistic groups (perhaps even more than during earlier Filipino agricultural worker cohorts), Philippine regional affiliations, religions, and skin colors and hair textures. Within this context of fluid and bewildering Filipinoness, hip hop was for many of us our common expression. In any one of our Filipino American communities, hip hop brought together different kinds of Filipinos into a shared space of socialization, camaraderie, rivalry, sexuality, and pleasure. Cheryl Cambay explains the meaningful ways she and her peers in Southern California in the late 1980s and early '90s embraced hip hop, "utilizing our love of dance, music, and creativity as a way to be heard and seen. We were representatives of Filipino American youth of our time."[5] Recalling her first predominantly Filipino American party in New York City, DJ Kuttin Kandi was surprised to encounter so many young brown people just like her: "Just witnessing the way the long line full of young brown people like me went around the block to get into the club just to dance to Hip Hop had me excited and taken aback. I had no idea that this many Pilipina/o Americans existed in New York City nor did I know there were any Pilipina/o Americans who were just like me, who loved Hip Hop."[6] These spaces opened up opportunities to learn artistic skills, such as DJing. After her encounter with a thriving Filipino American party scene, Kandi trained as a DJ (more accurately, as a turntablist) and soon began winning championships and awards. As products of their local multiracial hip hop scenes, exceptionally skilled Filipino American hip hop practitioners, such as Kandi, shook the larger world of hip hop and popular U.S. culture: the avant-garde turntablists in the mid-1990s, politically charged lyricists of the mid-2000s, and virtuoso choreography dancers late in the first decade of the new millennium and in the early 2010s. With our bodies, art, and music, we shared a cultural vernacular that continues to pervade among current generations of Filipino American youths, with the children of parents who came of age in the 1980s and 1990s becoming today's internet and television celebrities.

This book was born from local stages. The multitude of voices that trained on these stages form a rich cultural reservoir that shape the creative expressions of the artists, thinkers, and culture leaders examined in this book. *Manifest Technique* provides a critical reading of these expressions by tracing the ways Filipino American hip hop performances labor to remember the racialized histories of the Filipino body. Mediated through hip hop performances, Filipino Americans have been contributing to crucial forms of Filipino racial knowledge. Hip hop culture, I argue, operates as a local and popular site for Filipino Americans to investigate their racial position in history and the world, expanding the opportunities for practitioners to author their own representation. I refer to these sets of cultural practices as a Filipino American hip hop vernacular, or a cultural grammar emanating from the material conditions inherited from U.S. and Philippine history. The title, *Manifest Technique*, puns the ideology of manifest destiny, which since the nineteenth century has professed the United States' divine right to expand and acquire territory.[7] *Manifest Technique* flips the rhetoric of British writer Rudyard Kipling's 1899 "The White Man's Burden: The United States and the Philippine Islands." In that poem, Kipling charges the United States with bearing the responsibility to civilize and uplift the savage and lowly Filipino through divinely ordained violent imperial conquest.[8] Instead of deeming Filipinos as passive victims of the United States' heavy burden of annexation, this book elevates colonized people as brilliant agents of their own future and as cultural vanguards who cleverly flex everyday techniques of resistance against dominant power.

Filipino Racialization and Hip Hop

This book is anchored in Filipino Americans' cultural labor in mobilizing memory and knowledge. Since the 1980s, a Filipino American hip hop vernacular has narrated a multivalent, historically situated, and bottom-up cultural language of Filipino subjectivity. Fueled by hip hop's cultural resources that uplifts the dignity of Black people, Filipino Americans' immersion in hip hop has influenced ongoing Filipino racial self-construction. I am inspired by Nitasha Tamar Sharma's concept of global race consciousness, which she applies in her study of South Asian American hip hop cultural producers. Global race consciousness refers not to an understanding of race as biology or phenotype but as critical knowledge of the invention of racial categories by Western Europeans.[9] Sharma observes South Asian Americans' thoughtful critique of ethnic authenticity, anti-Blackness, and model minority expectations. She demonstrates a cultural mutuality and political collaboration among African Americans and South Asian Americans in hip hop, a kind of defiance in the face of traditional middle-class stereotypes for South Asians in the United States. My analysis investigates Filipino Americans' various acts of defiance. I place the vernacular nature of Filipino American hip hop expressiveness within a larger legacy of Filipino decolonization. These decolonial expressions are important because U.S. hegemony was built on colonial conquest and, it should not be forgotten, the United States still possesses colonies and continues to assert violence with its global presence.

Filipinos' modern racialization is inexorably linked to an entangled, serialized history of western colonization, wherein which people in the Philippines having been racialized for four centuries as childlike, uncivilized, and inferior. A racial caste system governed Philippine society under Spanish colonialism, which occurred between the sixteenth and nineteenth centuries. People were ordered by proximity to Europeanness, with Spanish-born Peninsulares occupying the most privileged status and non-Christianized and darker-skinned indigenous people relegated to the lowest rungs. Then came the Americans. *The Forbidden Book: The Philippine-American War in Political Cartoons* provides an archive of the ways in which the U.S. public racialized Filipinos as primitive during the onset of U.S. colonization in the archipelago in the late 1890s. Featured in *The Forbidden Book*, the front page of the *Boston Sunday Globe* in 1899 illustrates the intended transition of the archetypal Filipino from savage to civilized under white U.S. tutelage. The representative Filipino in this cartoon is racialized as Black.[10] The racialization of people in the Philippines and Filipinos in the diaspora offer important references in unpacking Filipino American racial discourses. As her fourth-grade classmates viewed a documentary on the Tasaday tribe isolated in the remote jungles of the Philippines, writer Grace Talusan recalls her white peers taunting her as possibly being as primitive as these stone-age people. (The "discovery" of the Tasaday was later exposed as a hoax, the display of primitivism a paid performance.)[11] In her memoir, *The Misadventures of Awkward Black Girl*, comedian Issa Rae quips that Filipinos are the "Blacks of Asians" and suggests that they are therefore less intelligent than other Asians.[12]

During the same centuries that the Philippines was colonized by the Spanish and Americans, Black people were tormented under white supremacist colonialism, slavery, and apartheid becoming, in the words of scholar Paul Gilroy, "expelled from the official dramas of civilization."[13] The *Boston Sunday Globe* cartoon exemplifies how newly colonized Filipinos and post-Reconstruction-era African Americans were similarly racialized, both targets of violent white racism masked as benevolence. In the continental United States, white racist domination of post-Reconstruction America meant the lethal disciplining of African American bodies and communities. This program of racist domination migrated to the colonized Philippines. Vince Schleitwiler uses the "black Pacific" as a placeholder term for the "mythic preserve" in which African American and Filipino bodies were both subjected to simultaneous U.S. racial uplift and sexual violence during post-Reconstruction.[14] Flowing racial logic during this period is evidenced in the 1896 *Plessy v. Ferguson* ruling, which sanctioned racial apartheid across the continental United States, soon followed by the Treaty of Paris in 1898, which effected the annexation of the Philippines. In a trans-Pacific racist echo, Filipinos were inaugurated into U.S. civic status as dark savages. During the Philippine-American War, which began in 1899 as Filipinos resisted their new colonizers, Filipinos were called the epithets "niggers," "black devils," and "gugus" by white soldiers, military wives, and officers.[15] Nerissa S. Balce uses the term "necropolitics" to describe how the U.S. colonizing state synthesized bloody violence and more "tender" civilizing methods to conquer and control Filipinos. This management of life and death over abjected bodies flowed between the unleashed prevalence of lynching of Black people happening domestically and the bloody war on Filipinos abroad.[16] The African American public was mostly anti-imperial, with the Black press having developed a "bond of sympathy" for Filipinos' struggle for independence.[17] Simultaneously, the Filipino revolutionary army was aware of lynchings in the United States and implored Black soldiers in the islands to reconsider their allegiance to America. Many African American soldiers in the Philippines, called buffalo soldiers, defected from their segregated regiments to fight for the Philippine Revolutionary Army.[18] Given colonial fascination with dark-skinned indigenous people in the Philippines, Filipinos were overrepresented as Black in U.S. wartime illustrations and photographs.[19] Also during this time, diverse Filipino bodies were medically examined under the scope of eugenics to verify their biological inferiority. Compounding early wartime racialization, Blackness was again assigned to Filipinos with the large-scale arrival of male workers to the U.S. continent two decades later, when Filipinos brazenly mixed with white women. Supposed beneficiaries of American civilization, for twenty years Filipinos were taught by U.S. teachers of the virtues of egalitarianism, yet, as assimilated colonial subjects living in the United States, were brutally punished for crossing what W. E. B. Du Bois prophetically called the "color line."[20] Filipino men during this moment were victims of both anti-Filipino and anti-Black racism; white women in the taxi dancehall scene who dated Filipino men were referred to as "nigger lovers."[21] As transgressors of white respectability, Filipino zooters, along with their African American and Mexican American peers, were terrorized by white servicemen during the Los Angeles zoot suit riots of 1943.[22]

Given the above examples of incipient U.S. imaginings of Filipino bodies, proximity to Blackness must be acknowledged as a way Filipinos have been racialized.[23] Negotiating Blackness as a racial signifier, therefore, is important in understanding contemporary Filipino American cultural politics. Early twentieth-century moments of colonial encounter traveled through a series of paternalistic and neocolonial relationships that developed into more contemporary manifestations of U.S. racialization of Filipinos and, in turn, Filipinos' own counter-discourses. For Filipino Americans, hip hop as a cultural resource should not be regarded as counterintuitive or peculiar. The following chapters show that hip hop has instead been vital in communicating inventive expressions of Filipinoness. With Blackness and Black people constituting hip hop's primary racial politics, the genre consults a long-range knowledge of racial domination that counters white supremacy's fundamental debasement of the Black body. *Manifest Technique* traces hip hop's linkages between contemporary popular cultural practices and a long history of colonial and racial violence applied to "uncivilized" people. For more than forty years, hip hop has been key in reenvisioning African Americans' spiritual dignity through its embrace of Islam as a response to colonial culture in white Christianity. More popularly, hip hop has served as a venue to witness the seeming permanence of racist police violence. Importantly, the genre has served as a popular medium to express joy, imagination, and pleasure in the face of structured erasure, marginalization, and death. Filipino Americans have labored as inventive accomplices in these hip hop political aesthetics, which in turn has aided in their own Filipino self-making. In exploring this process of self-making, I hope this book makes abundantly clear Filipino Americans' indebtedness to African American politics and cultural production.

Currently, Filipinos in the United States are typically associated with a triumphant immigrant narrative awash in model minority valorization. Data from 2017 show Filipino Americans' achievements since 2000 in key areas of demographic well-being, such as high levels of educational attainment and median annual household income.[24] Filipino socioeconomic integration in the U.S. economy, though, does not bury the historical fact of U.S. colonization of the Philippines; in the face of American exceptionalism discourses that obscure U.S. colonial occupation, Filipino socioeconomic integration must be understood as direct outcomes of material and ideological integration of U.S. institutions, militarization, and labor recruitment in the Philippine colony. In centering imperialism, this book provokes the understanding of otherness as formed from the racial violence of white supremacist colonial ideologies; current Filipino American assimilationist discourses need to be understood as emerging from a lineage of the early twentieth-century U.S. colonial program of benevolent assimilation.

For the Record: Synapses as Knowledge

Hip hop has been a key popular cultural arena in which Filipino American practitioners contemplate, decode, and evoke knowledges of Filipinoness. For many, hip hop has been a primary motivator of Filipino memory, despite this memory's fragility and elusiveness. Ultimately, in scrutinizing the multiple and malleable vantages of "Filipino" in hip hop expressions, this project of memory recuperation serves as an impetus to understand race and ethnicity in the United States not simply in terms of liberal multiculturalism, which distributes power horizontally and ahistorically, but through the critical lens of structural domination, which recognizes power as vertically applied and historically rooted.

At the same time the investigation of Filipino Americans in hip hop re-cuperates Filipino racial memory, it also forces a reworking of official hip hop cultural knowledge. Clustering in West Coast metropolises, Filipino Americans refocus the significance of the West Coast within the global hip hop cultural narrative. Hip hop lore privileges New York City, where hip hop cultural pioneers are exalted as inviolable. To be clear, in many ways New York's hip hop hegemony is well-deserved. However, obscured in hip hop's regional hierarchy are hip hop aesthetics emerging outside of the city's purview, such as the iconographies of Too $hort's pimpology and Digital Underground's funky flamboyance, both unique to the urban history and cultural ecology of Oakland, California.[25] What vehicle in hip hop is more iconic than the customized West Coast lowrider? What would hip hop dance be without Don Campbell's joyful locking from Los Angeles? Nurturing crucibles of its own Black cultural productions, West Coast metropolises developed music (e.g., funk), car culture, slang, fashion, and dance forms (e.g., boogaloo, popping, strutting, and locking) now casually branded as hip hop. Young Filipino Americans were also collaborative participants and leaders in many of these pre–hip hop expressions.[26] As central innovators in what morphed into West Coast hip hop culture, Filipino Americans calibrate hip hop's regional multiplicity by drawing attention toward vibrant Black cultural productions in cities like San Francisco, Oakland, and Los Angeles (a calibration that also rings true when considering the hip hop influences of Chicanos and Samoans). This doesn't mean New York City hip hop is less significant; I am simply suggesting that the West Coast is often overlooked when considering official hip hop cultural origins.[27] In his 2007 hit "Hip Hop Lives (I Come Back)," KRS-One, a hip hop luminary who staunchly defends a South Bronx hip hop cultural foundation, proclaims hip hop's cosmic universalism and role in social movement. Significantly, the music video for this song features cameos of a number of West Coast Filipino American artists, including Mike "Dream" Francisco (as a mural), Rocky Rivera, Bambu, and DJ Rhettmatic.[28] As implied in the video, Filipino Americans were vanguards in the West Coast's multiracial hip hop spaces, advancing and spreading hip hop culture before and outside of the genre's commercial mainstreaming. An epistemological reevaluation of the West Coast's influence—bridging the gaps in hip hop lore—both reclaims the uniqueness of West Coast expressions within larger, interconnected hip hop cultural circuits and uncovers Filipino American collaborations in Black popular culture.

But this book is not a tribute to the West Coast. Rather, *Manifest Technique* testifies to the labor required to bridge the gaps from the margins of official memory; it outlines how young Filipino Americans have shaped the broader contours of hip hop while self-fashioning creative modes of Filipinoness. I give examples of how these hip hop performances operate within the following arenas: the cultures of militarization that form the spatial and cultural apparatus of hip hop among Filipino Americans, alternative modernities through Islam with which practitioners find spiritual and political redemption, inventive forms of racial embodiments and abstractions in what I call Afro-Filipino futurism, and modern embodiments among hip hop dancers who have built liberating communities of belonging. But, how does one attempt to theorize complex processes of Filipino racial discourses emanating from the expressions in dance moves, rap lyrics, and crew allegiances?

In their performances, Filipino American hip hop practitioners have been prolific albeit often unheralded authors of Filipino racial discourse. My study consults recent scholarly literature that regards performance as offering crucial modes of knowledge. In analyzing the Filipino performing body as a critical object of study across multiple moments of U.S.-Philippine imperial relations, Lucy Mae San Pablo Burns "situates Filipino/a performing bodies within the contexts of nation building and community formation, and highlights the imbrication of Filipino/a racialization with histories of colonialism and imperialism."[29] Burns allows the body to function as a kind of archive of Filipino American history. Diana Taylor's concept of repertoire is key to the study of Filipino performance. According to Taylor, repertoire "enacts embodied memory: performances, gestures, orality, movement, dance, singing—in short, all those acts usually thought of as ephemeral, nonreproducible knowledge." Like the varied performances throughout the Americas of which Taylor is concerned, the multiple modes of expressions in a Filipino American hip hop vernacular "functions as an episteme, a way of knowing, not simply an object of analysis."[30] So, too, does Burns's work stand "in solidarity with Taylor, not only foregrounding the ongoing, 'shared history of power relations and cultural domination' but also in celebrating the acts of survival and imagination that undergird such histories."[31] Also focusing on a Filipino performative episteme that offers what Taylor calls "vital acts of transfer," Theodore S. Gonzalves demonstrates Filipino American college student cultural show dancers' "lateral" (rather than "literal") practice of remembering alternative times and locations that counter "official" accounts.[32] In this way, he contends, these students' nostalgic pining for authentic Filipino national identities are also imagining sideways substitutions for these identities. Here, Gonzalves belies his earlier denouncements of Filipino Americans' participation in hip hop as "not even necessarily terribly interesting" by affording cultural show dancers with substantive and multivalent embodiments where they otherwise seem to perform frozen and essentialized versions of Filipino culture.[33] Like these college students' counterintuitive pronouncements of memory, Sarita See examines Filipino American performance and abstract art, maintaining that performance "does not yield evidence so easily or directly. It does not precede knowledge but rather shapes knowledge."[34] Taylor's repertoire and its threading throughout the works of Burns, Gonzalves, and See help reinforce the links that imagine hip hop performance as a knowledge-producing repertoire, which provide the spiritual, community, and aesthetic resources with which Filipino Americans transfer vital knowledge for a circuit of histories and embodiments.

Yet, in these acts of knowledge transfer, any official record of a Filipino American hip hop vernacular is almost always elusive. U.S. exceptionalism's amnesia of colonial violence colludes with the erasure of culture, bodies, and history that occurs due to the subordinating of more ephemeral culture (oral and kinetic expressions) into what are considered to be savage forms of knowledge. If so-called civilized people can build architecturally sound monuments and temples, record their sacred universe, and inscribe the coherency of an "original" nation, then Filipinos can only be deemed savage for their painful lack of documentation and absence of a precolonial archive. Aside from notable cases, such as the Laguna Copper Plate discovered in 1989 documenting a debt-release record inscribed centuries before the arrival of the Spanish, the people in the Philippines came into civilizational purview, as it's said, only after Spanish contact and after the thorough process of Hispanicization that resulted in the erecting of what was seen as more permanent cultural artifacts, such as the Philippines' renowned circuit of Catholic churches.[35] The tangible archive of Filipino culture, then, is much indebted to Spanish conquest. Further damning, in western anthropology, Filipinos are not seen to "*have*" culture, but they are to be displayed *as* culture for world's fairs and natural history museums.[36]

Despite its ephemeral qualities, a Filipino American hip hop vernacular creates a thriving and expansive culture that responds to the exigencies of colonial and civilizational erasure, standing as a testament to a vibrant Filipino presence in the face of supposed invisibility. Rather than arresting a Filipino American cultural repertoire, the exigencies of imperial erasure enables and punctuates it. Invisibility, then, should not be regarded as marking Filipino Americans with cultural deficiency. Instead, the discourse of invisibility offers an abundance of cultural and temporal resources that contribute to their imaginative and transformative projects of Filipino American subject making. Critical scrutiny of the politics of visibility refocuses epistemologies of Filipino and Filipino American cultural production.[37] Accordingly, a consideration of Filipino American hip hop practitioners' expressions beyond an assurance of visibility allows for a more dynamic understanding of culture as an active production rather than as a static essence that freezes Filipino American culture. Filipino American hip hop practitioners are creative collaborators and artistic vanguards in Filipino American culture and in a larger hip hop cultural universe. In the afterlives of colonial violence, their expressions produce new knowledge and reconstruct historical memory. As See writes, "there is precious little recognition of the variety of sophistication of the cultural forms that have withstood the violence of American forgetting and that continue to proliferate in the twenty-first century."[38] In resisting "American forgetting," the gaps that make up Filipino culture can be reimagined as neurological synapses: the emptiness in between memory actually facilitates the crucial transference of knowledge and creativity. Within these gaps, then, Filipino American cultural forms flourish. The supposed lack of Filipino culture and history enables memory as a practice, what Juan Flores, who investigates Puerto Rican knowledge production through hip hop, calls "putting-on-record" or "the gathering and sorting of materials from the past in accordance with the needs and interests of the present."[39] This book is concerned not so much with a cataloging of the contributions of Filipino American artists within hip hop. Instead, it is the prevalence of erasure that I find productive. Cultural practices abound despite a lack of documentation and permanence. The varieties of creative expressions emanating from Filipino American culture thrive because of their present-tense nature. In this way, a Filipino American hip hop vernacular works as an agentive mode of expression as much as a project of remembering. The savages are the folklorists, the authors of history.

Even though the synapsis and action-oriented nature of Filipino American culture facilitates creative acts of remembering, formal scholarship still largely relies on a set of written publications to advance arguments. *Manifest Technique* therefore draws some material from *Empire of Funk: Hip Hop and Representation in Filipina/o America*. The anthology, which I coedited with DJ Kuttin Kandi and Roderick N. Labrador, attempts to fill in the void of printed material on Filipino American hip hop cultural practices in an effort to address the problem of erasure while at the same time unsettling the practices of colonial documentation. For example, that book curates Filipino American hip hop performance by centering the voices of practitioners themselves and by appreciating their expressions on a broad scale: women, gay, and queer voices are highlighted; the contributors hail from California, New York, New Jersey, Hawai'i, Washington, Virginia, and Florida; they represent various hip hop craft makers as dancers, emcees, graphic artists, DJs, poets; and their ages span a wide range. *Empire of Funk* includes a range of views and expressions that establish the complexity of Filipino American hip hop performance. *Manifest Technique* offers a theoretical lens to make intelligible this "empire of funk," a title that alludes to imperialisms' imbrication in Filipino American creative expressions.

Vernacular Presences

For hip hop, 1992 was a big year. Seminal albums dropped, including Dr. Dre's *The Chronic*, the Pharcyde's *Bizarre Ride II the Pharcyde*, Ice Cube's *The Predator*, Pete Rock and C. L. Smooth's *Mecca and the Soul Brother*, and Kriss Kross's *Totally Krossed Out*. The rage leading up to the Los Angeles riots in 1992 and the attempts at healing after the riots are well-documented in the music of NWA, Ice Cube, and Boogie Down Productions. Hip hop called for peace and expressed visceral rage, which shocked U.S. (and global) listeners but finally aroused awareness of urban racial inequality and the problems that result.

For young Filipino Americans, 1992 was also a big year. Active in hip hop's broader universe at the time, including as leaders rallying for peace in the ashes of post-riots LA, a generation of Filipino American youths took the reins in hip hop innovation throughout the United States.[40] Already a decade immersed in hip hop culture (and disco, funk, jazz, and older forms of Black American music and dance before that), they laid permanent groundwork to a larger Filipino American hip hop cultural network.[41] The internationally renowned dance company Kaba Modern and the all-star DJ crew the Beat Junkies pioneered, respectively, hip hop dance and turntablism communities

FIGURE 1. Legend Entertainment flyer for a party at Samerika Hall in Carson, California, occurring on the eve of the 1992 Los Angeles riots. Designed by Allan De Guzman. Courtesy of Thom Villegas, from his personal archives.

in Southern California in 1992. Alex Aquino established the Universal Zulu Nation, a hip hop organization, in San Francisco. The avant-garde DJ crew Shadow Posse formed and were featured together with Knuckle Neck Tribe dancers in the Bay Area's public-access television show, *Home Turf*.[42] Filipino Americans' contributions to hip hop, such as the works of graffiti artist Mike "Dream" Francisco, the Shadow Posse (who later became the Invisibl Skratch Piklz), and the dancers of Knuckle Neck Tribe were recognized in the 1992 year-in-review issue of the *Source* magazine, one of the nation's most prominent hip hop publications. As president of the Samahang Pilipino student group at the University of California, Los Angeles, Mark Pulido organized Unity Jam in 1992, bringing together Filipino American dancers and DJs from across California to party for peace as gang violence plagued Filipino American communities in the Los Angeles area. The success of this event prompted Pulido to run for president of the university's student government, which he won. (Years later, Pulido was elected mayor of Cerritos, California.)

FIGURE 2. Flyer for Unity Jam, a call for peace through hip hop. Designed by Mark Pulido. Courtesy of Mark Pulido.

Aside from these Filipino American innovators making noise in the early '90s, astute hip hop enthusiasts will cite important Filipino American hip hop artists who contributed to the culture since the early '80s. DJ Nasty Nes, partner to Sir-Mix-A-Lot of "Baby Got Back" fame, is credited with starting the first West Coast hip hop radio show.[43] Legendary Latin soul crooner Joe Bataan pressed the early rap record "Rap-O-Clap-O" before the Sugar Hill Gang's iconic "Rapper's Delight."[44] The list of impactful Filipino American hip hop artists can go on. Apl.de.Ap of the group the Black Eyed Peas is often celebrated for being the first Filipino American emcee to make it big globally. Grammy Award–winning Chad Hugo, partner to celebrity singer and music producer Pharrell Williams, boasts unquestionable influence on hip hop beat making and is credited with elevating the music's sound.[45] Just as important as this list of artists are the unrecognized Filipino American practitioners and fans who promote events, share music, show off dance moves, recite spiritual philosophy, create hip hop groups, and buy merchandise. Hip hop endures as a vernacular culture among recent generations of Filipino Americans because of its large-scale horizontal appeal and mobility; it is largely quotidian, percolating largely from Filipino American cultural spaces; it is a shared repertoire that circulates without a decided commitment to permanence or

BAY AREA OLD SCHOOL REVIVAL

Back To The Future

BY BILLY JAM

"Hip-hop has been so fucked with and watered down," says Alex Aquino of FM20, a San Francisco rap crew. "That's really why people are going back to the roots of where it came from." Between those too young to experience b-boy culture the first time round and those driven back to basics by rap's commercialism, there is a definite revived interest in the full range of hip-hop culture beyond the latest chart-topper in the Bay Area. Fliers for breakdancing contests started popping up. Graffiti became more prominent. And there has been a renewed interest in old school DJ skills.

Q-BERT, DJ MIXMASTER MIKE AND DJ APOLLO (L-R) OF FM20 DISPLAY THE SKILLS HEARD 'ROUND THE WORLD

What makes this more like a renaissance than just a revival is the direct link to old school culture. Q-Bert, Apollo and DJ Mixmaster Mike, the DJ mixmaster team of FM20 , were christened The West Coast Rock Steady DJs by New York's Crazy Legs who gets crazy props every time he visits the Bay Area. The South Bronx's Phase 2 and his magazine I.G.T. have inspired many Bay Area graffiti artists. And, no less significant, the Zulu Nation's West Coast membership has swelled over the past year.

MIXING & SCRATCHING

"People these days have forgotten about DJing. In concerts and in videos, you see people just fakin' it. And you see a lot of rap groups out there that don't even have a DJ in back of them," exclaimed FM20's DJ Mixmaster Mike, shaking his head. During the New Music Seminar in New York last June, Mike won the DJ Battle for World Supremacy contest. A few months later, he and the other two West Coast Rock Steady DJs, Q-Bert (last year's DMC champ) & DJ Apollo, won the DMC National Championships which took them off to London for the world finals.

All of this they take in stride, being more interested in boosting awareness of hip-hop culture than boosting their own egos. "Being a good DJ takes more than having speed and style and knowing your beats and breaks. You've got to know who invented scratching, like **Grand Wizard Theodore** in the Bronx and all the other pioneers of hip-hop."

GRAFFITI

Berkeley graffiti artist **Razer-1** of the **KTD** crew is a good example of someone who is *true to the game.*

FIGURE 3. The *Source* magazine highlights the Invisibl Skratch Piklz and Knuckle Neck Tribe in 1992.

mainstream legibility; and it is a way of inhabiting the world, a recognition not measured by graphs and surveys but felt in their everyday lives.

Despite a number of breakthrough artists and more anonymous hip hop practitioners, Filipino Americans in the U.S. popular imaginary may not be thought of as the first or the most influential people in hip hop. As the third largest Asian American demographic in the nation—and the largest in some states, including California—who have had a more than a century-long migratory, cultural, and juridical relationship with the United States, Filipino

Americans certainly hold demographic and historical significance.[46] But in the recent past and in this moment, their cultural significance remains disproportionately unrecognized. In hip hop culture, this discrepancy between statistical representation and cultural representation is especially stark. For example, the triumphant arrival of Asian Americans in mainstream hip hop dance culture in the late 2000s benefits from the erasure of Filipino American cultural labor, despite such labor having helped set the stage for Asian American visibility in hip hop. Salima Koroma's 2016 documentary, *Bad Rap*, reaffirms the elusiveness of Filipino American cultural labor in relation to the struggles for Asian American representations in hip hop, which in the film's case is coded as East Asian American. After opening with forty-six seconds acknowledging West Coast Filipino Americans' foundational contributions to hip hop, the eighty-minute documentary recounts the obstacles encountered by Asian American artists in the rap industry. After that brief nod toward Filipino Americans, they disappear throughout the rest of the film. The filmmakers effectively obscure Filipino Americans' representation in hip hop, even though the Native Guns and the Blue Scholars and other Filipino American recording artists had already made an unprecedented splash among multiracial audiences before the profiled artists in *Bad Rap* were emerging. Despite the scale of Filipino American participation in hip hop, their cultural contributions remain perpetually diminished.

For many outside observers, the cultural synapses that help propel creativity and memory making among Filipino American hip hop practitioners are rendered irrelevant, thus erasing their presence and contributions in very real moments. For example, in a 2007 *L.A. Weekly* article "The Fil-Am Invasion: Embedded with the Hip-Hop Movement That's Taking Over Hollywood," the author marvels at the novelty of the presence of Filipino American DJs performing in the area.[47] His "taking over" language suggests that Hollywood belongs to someone else and Fil-Ams are invading, even when Filipino American DJs have been immersed in Hollywood's club scene—in fact in numerous crevices of Los Angeles nightlife—for two decades prior to that article.[48] Filipino Americans involved in the clubbing scene were not surprised at all by the extent to which Filipino Americans have asserted their presence. The comments section of the *L.A. Weekly* flooded with letters by L.A.-based Filipino Americans involved in the scene who wanted to set the record straight. DJ Icy Ice, a veteran of this scene, comments about the *L.A. Weekly* article in my short documentary film *Legend* (2008): "We have so many talented brothers and sisters within our community that represent out there, but they're not being heard. They're not being exposed out there. We're like that invisible community there. So, it's hardly an invasion now. It's just an invasion in that writer's mind."[49] For some performers, Filipino American presence in the DJ scene is "common sense." In the dance world, this "common sense" of Filipino American hip hop involvement also rings true for those who have closer knowledge of hip hop culture. In *B-Girling in a B-Boy's World* (2010), a short documentary on Filipino American b-girl Sharon "Sha Boogie" Mendoza, the dancer opens the film saying, "You always knew if you were gonna go to a dance competition that there would be a dope Filipino crew that was gonna be in the finals or win the thing. It was just always an understanding from, I don't know, I guess from years of being in the scene. Filipinos have always put it down." Of the Jabbawockeez dance crew, who won the first season of the dance competition show MTV's *America's Best Dance Crew* in 2008, Sha Boogie remarks: "When they got on TV they put on the masks. People were forced to recognize the way they danced as opposed to them being Filipino. But when they took off the masks and everybody saw they were Filipino, most of the dance community was just like, 'duh.' We already know them, and we already knew how dope they were."[50]

Certainly, whether Filipino Americans routinely "represent out there" or regularly "put it down" does not guarantee the legibility of Filipino bodies in hip hop. They have been "putting it down" for so long but have never "stood up" tall enough to be seen. In order to flourish, a vernacular does not need the sanction of legibility—or celebrated recognition of the firsts or the big names. Filipino Americans have been speaking this vernacular regardless, asserting a presence despite a pervading condition and discourse of invisibility.[51] As a way of living and performing, a hip hop vernacular is not exclusive to pioneers and celebrities; it is instead fueled and mobilized by a shared, quotidian practice.

As a popular, mostly youth-driven expression, a Filipino American hip hop vernacular eschews an elitist, enlightened, top-down cultural agenda, aligning with this quotation by popular music scholar Russell Potter: "particularly in the case of black cultures, where there has been, as Paul Gilroy hints at, a vernacular ethics, a vernacular history, and a vernacular version of 'modernism,' it is vital to recognize that there are material inheritances—such as slavery—whose reverberations need not be recorded by a seismograph in a sealed laboratory, but can be and are felt in the everyday life of black diasporic cultures." In one of the earliest academic books on hip hop, Potter describes hip hop culture as postmodern: it deconstructs grand universalities, transgresses the boundaries of "high" and "low" culture, and pleasures in fragmentation.[52] The racialized histories reinvoked in hip hop—the material inheritances of centuries of slavery and colonialism—circulate horizontally among practitioners. It bears repeating that it is precisely because certain language and performances are expressed in everyday life that a Filipino American hip hop vernacular has become so enduring and expansive. The notable Filipino American hip hop artists mentioned earlier represent only a tiny sample of performers, fans, and organizers who were instrumental in promoting a Filipino American hip hop vernacular's sustainable base through their creativity, community building, and love of the craft. Perhaps a Filipino American hip hop vernacular could not have thrived to the extent that it has without these noted leaders, innovators, and firsts. Maybe their influence as role models and cultural vanguards was that substantial. Although it would be noble to catalog these figures' contributions, this book is more interested in the broad nature of a Filipino American hip hop vernacular. More pervasive than the cultural productions of a dozen or so male Filipino American performers, the larger phenomenon of a Filipino American hip hop vernacular stretches out as a network whose support by an often-uncelebrated set of participants such as women, fans, and queer folks has helped sustain it.

Even more, outside of navy kids' migrations and cultural exchanges, the counterintuitive beauty of a Filipino American hip hop vernacular is exemplified in many Filipino Americans' own unrecognition of their connection to a nationwide Filipino American hip hop cultural network. Although largely clustered on the West Coast, Filipino Americans' participation in hip hop needs to be understood as a much broader phenomenon. A Filipino American hip hop vernacular, as a global circuit, does not locate San Francisco or New York as the core of Filipino American hip hop experience.[53] For this vernacular, "movement, relocation, displacement, and restlessness are the norms rather than the exceptions."[54] In this vein, Filipino Americans have often only modestly recognized themselves as being part of a much larger phenomenon; instead of mutual appreciation of one another's connectivity, performers have for a while been rapping, dancing, writing, and DJing in their own dispersed, diverse, local pockets. This unrecognition, of course, follows a power relationship, with larger Filipino American metropolises possessing enough cultural capital to ignore smaller scenes. For example, despite military connections and other migratory networks mentioned earlier, many practitioners in San Francisco, California, have been for the most part unaware of the thriving Filipino American hip hop sites in Bremerton, Washington, or Virginia Beach, Virginia. This phenomenon that has thrived without centrality or strong connectivity yields an amorphous yet durable cultural edifice.[55] A Filipino American hip hop vernacular operates as a capacious expression, where knowledge is mobilized by the circuits of the local and global, the past, present, and future.

Unholy Authenticity: Masculinity, Multiplicity, and Flexible Politics

For my friends and me in Jacksonville, the Universal Zulu Nation (UZN) was foundational in the way we understood and respected hip hop culture. Founded in 1973 in the Bronx, New York, to unify gangs and encourage an environment of positive and creative energy, the UZN soon spread its motto of "peace, love, unity, and having fun" around the world through hip hop. For us, the UZN cofounder Afrika Bambaataa symbolized the essence of hip hop culture for his funky, otherworldly, post-radical style of cool. Through fashion, sonics, and rhetoric, Bambaataa's syncretic aesthetics combined gang culture, Afrofuturism, Islam, and Egyptology. Afrika Bambaataa and the Soul Sonic Force's pioneering song "Planet Rock" celebrated youthful energy and global unity, providing a fitting soundtrack to our parties almost twenty years after the song's release. "Planet Rock's" steady and portable electronic beat (derived from the music of the German artists Kraftwerk) constituted a sonic staple for songs featured on mixtapes floating around Jacksonville. My favorite mixes were "Planet Rock" blended with sped-up slow jams. Commercial hip hop artists shared this sonic affinity: throughout the 1980s and 1990s, various genres like gangsta rap, Latin freestyle, and Atlanta and Miami booty bass created anthems using looped "Planet Rock" samples and renditions. Proving versatile, "Planet Rock" emblemized both the UZN utopian ideals *and* the rambunctious sexuality of booty bass music.

Like many hip hop fans, I upheld the UZN and Bambaataa as purveyors and protectors of real hip hop; it kept the culture close to its aesthetic and political roots by not selling out to the glitz and nihilism of so-called commercial hip hop. The UZN provided a nostalgic, Bronx-centric hip hop authenticity, a type of static reverence that Gonzalves complicates in Pilipino Culture Nights. I romanticized this type of hip hop, of course, as I feverishly enjoyed commercial hip hop's repurposing of "Planet Rock." In 2016, hip hop fans' admiration for Bambaataa and the UZN was thrown into a tailspin. After a series of sexual abuse accusations against Bambaataa became public, the New York–based UZN Supreme World Council resigned from their leadership position. At first, the council attempted to deny and deflect the allegations, but the horrid details of the abuse were too believable and the council's response too dismissive. Furthermore, influential hip hop voices inside and outside of the UZN's inner circle even spoke about conspiratorial efforts to tarnish the name of Bambaataa and the reputation of hip hop, that the legacy of the UZN and hip hop outweighs Bambaataa's supposed committed crimes. "Our leadership has to be untouchable. . . . Some of us are infallible," commented

KRS-One, a revered Bronx emcee and fervent Bambaataa defender.[56] To many observers of the unfolding drama, it had become abundantly clear that Bambaataa and the UZN were perverting their "peace, love, unity, and having fun" code. Given the disarray of the UZN, what was to become of the first family of hip hop culture?[57] More importantly, if these allegations eventually prove to hold merit, what about achieving justice for Bambaataa's victims (whether or not they have come forward), who cannot press charges because of New York's statute of limitations? As soon as the scandal became public, hip hop community leaders Rosa Clemente, DJ Kuttin Kandi, and Julie-C took charge in advocating for the victims of sexual abuse, reminding us that victims should be the hip hop community's main concern. In an open letter, they write, "Hip Hop as we came to know it by our pioneers is a movement and a culture, not a structure . . . While one such as Afrika Bambaataa has done many good deeds and organizing work in our communities; it doesn't mean he's sacrosanct. No one should be above accountability."[58] Hip hop, these leaders remind us, should not be a structure that confines us, and the idolatry afforded to one person or group is detrimental to marginalized people such as LGBTQ folks and victims of abuse and rape. Whether KRS-One likes it or not, no one is "infallible." Looking toward a future-facing solution, they continue, "this is an opportunity for a rebirth of Hip Hop in the millennial age, one that creates foundational changes in individuals, interpersonal relationships, communities, and organizations while invoking our founding principles of peace, love, and unity. We owe it to ourselves to preserve the legacy of Hip Hop culture by remembering that this is bigger than Hip Hop." While recognizing hip hop's legacy, Clemente, Kandi, and Julie-C challenge the hip hop community to critique and resist power, instead of uphold and preserve it. Author and former UZN member Adisa Banjoko refers to the UZN leadership's culture of secrecy and cover-ups as the Hip-Hop Vatican.[59]

Yes, hip hop's community leadership must be more open and democratic and eradicate patrimonial leadership. This book is inspired by this sentiment. Bambaataa's severe transgressions and the actions of his defenders illustrate the hip hop's crises of masculinity, sexuality, and orthodoxy. Even if the criminal justice system fails to convict the accused, justice in hip hop will still prevail if practitioners embrace a large-scale cultural shift to actively rejecting toxic masculinity. The Bambaataa scandal reveals a collapsing of hip hop's cultural contradictions that seek purity while embracing chronic sordidness.

To ardent followers of hip hop culture (specifically, Bronx-centric hip hop culture), the Bambaataa scandal represents a crisis in hip hop's identity. For all of its machismo and New York toughness, how can this movement be led

by a pedophile? Are other leaders in UZN or other hip hop organizations victims or co-perpetrators? This scandal is reminiscent to the rumors of sex and
material exchanges occurring in San Francisco during the rise of the Filipino
American mobile DJ scene in the 1980s. Mark Bradford, a large-scale party
promoter and an influential kingmaker for DJ crews' reputation, was well-
known for his sexual interest in Filipino boys. Bradford, who was white, older,
and wealthy, gave DJ equipment and other goods to Filipino teenage boys in
exchange for sex. Bradford was found dead in 1992 in an unsolved murder
case.[60] As with Bambaataa, the origin stories of the Filipino American hip
hop scene is riddled with sexual assault. Both the Bambaataa and Bradford
episodes reveal layers of contradictions in hip hop culture: how can hip hop
be manly if its influential figures are *gay*? I ask this question rhetorically in
order to emphasize the point of hip hop's gendered and sexual expectations
falling short of reality. The above criminal scenarios make acute hip hop's
sexual contradictions. This crisis, so articulated by Clemente, Kandi, and
Julie-C, can yield a shift in hip hop's heteropatriarchal power over women,
LGBTQ folks, and victims of sexual abuse.

Hip hop culture encompasses the good, bad, and scandalous. Hip hop
inherently presents a complex field of power. In this way, I suggest "Planet
Rock" is a sonic symbol of hip hop's multiplicity: elements of Bambaataa's
most popular anthem appear across a whole political spectrum of hip hop
over thirty years, from the righteous rage of Public Enemy to the raunchiness
of 2 Live Crew. Scholarly critiques on hip hop must also be open and allow
for a variety of vantages; they must not simply relegate hip hop's cultural
production, representations, and consumption as either conservatively color-
blind or radically anticolonial. This book unpacks a multiplicity of politics
in Filipino American hip hop performances. As hip hop culture is rife with
contradictions, so too are Filipino American hip hop performances.

Manifest Technique explores the multiplicity of practitioners' messages,
allowing their creative performances and modes of belonging to speak—as
funky, contradictory, romanticized, and mystifying as they may seem. In an
interview, Theodore Gonzalves expresses his skepticism of Filipino American
involvement in hip hop. Calling the phenomenon a "fetish," he observes: "You
can travel to Los Angeles and find Filipinos participating in hip-hop, which
has absolutely nothing to do with politics. . . . It's just that hip-hop ensnares
middle-class white kids that have actually popularized the music to the rest of
the world."[61] Gonzalves's opinion of Filipino Americans' participation in hip
hop is plainly evident if by "politics" one expects only a defined (or encaged)
set of actions and ideologies. Gonzalves is implying that the participation
of middle-class white kids in hip hop is equal to (or perhaps more valuable
than) Filipino Americans' contributions. Antonio T. Tiongson Jr. expands this

idea of politics in his critique of Filipino American hip hop DJs' deracialized, color-blind claims as members in the "hip-hop nation."[62]

As much as Filipino American hip hop participation has been criticized as not valuable or as anti-conscious, scholars also overpromote it as inherently politically leftist. In one of the first scholarly publications to examine Filipino American hip hop cultural production, Lakandiwa M. de Leon responds to the "cultural limbo" of Filipino American youths who are not taught Filipino culture or history by their parents, who themselves harbor a "colonial mentality," and who apply strategies of social erasure in the United States. For de Leon, hip hop and gang culture in Los Angeles provided an alternative for Filipino American youths to their parents' worldviews: "By inspiring Filipino youth to envision new possibilities, the DJ scene and broader hip-hop culture provide role models who have created an original, distinct, and positive culture for Filipino American youth." De Leon's chapter pioneers critical inquiry into Filipino American hip hop performance and its linkages to Philippine colonial history. Yet, for de Leon, hip hop culture seems to operate according to a pure resistance model that equips Filipino Americans to "fight racism."[63] As de Leon aptly demonstrates, politics-as-resistance in Filipino American hip hop performance has given scholars credence to champion a Filipino American cultural legibility premised on antiracist and leftist politics.

Filipino Americans' important cultural labor in politicized social agitation should without a doubt be acknowledged. The seminal documentary, *Beats, Rhymes, and Resistance: Pilipinos and Hip Hop in Los Angeles*, recounts the contributions of Filipino American DJs, graffiti artists, spoken-word performers, and emcees in expressions of decolonization and consciousness-raising in the late 1990s in the hip hop cultural hotbed of Los Angeles.[64] The spirit captured in the documentary reflects the concurrence of Filipino Americans' prominent roles in Los Angeles' multiracial, four-elements-focused, and politically visionary community space the Foundation Funkollective. Also at the same time, avant-garde groups like Seattle's isangmahal arts kollective exemplify Filipino Americans' aesthetic experimentations and commitment to multiracial coalition-building. Victor Viesca connects the upheaval of the Los Angeles riots in 1992 to the activist and cultural work of Kiwi and Bambu of the group Native Guns. He writes: "Their instrumental use of rap music as a consciousness-raising tool suggests how hip hop is being used to organize youth in the twenty-first century. . . . Kiwi, Bambu, and the Filipino American youth with whom they work do not separate the tradition of U.S. black liberation from global anti-imperialist movements, but rather see them as part of the same struggle."[65] *Sounds of a New Hope*, Eric Tandoc's documentary, chronicles Kiwi's journey from street life in Los Angeles to transnational community organizing. For Kiwi, hip hop works as a key cultural tool to motivate social revolution among lumpen proletariat Filipinos in the Philippines. Also highlighting Filipino American emcees' role in consciousness-raising, Michael Viola rightly situates the music of the Blue Scholars as counter-pedagogy to colonial and neoconservative education. Of hip hop as a musical genre, he writes: "Hip-hop artists often speak 'in active participation in practical life' revealing people's present needs for adequate food, shelter, and security. Furthermore, hip-hop is an important musical outlet that possesses the ability to leave a lasting imprint in the hearts and minds of the struggling."[66] For Viola, the Blue Scholars "use their music as an organizing tool to reclaim history, challenge what is viewed as 'natural,' and engage with the masses in charting alternatives to capitalism." Similarly, Anthony Kwame Harrison emphasizes the "oppositional thrust" of hip hop among Filipino Americans in the Bay Area. Harrison focuses on Filipino American hip hop practitioners, who express a "Filipino hip hop script" that helps in a "reawakening of Filipino consciousness" in light of social obscuring and the lasting impact of colonialism.[67] Artists like Kiwi, Bambu, the Blue Scholars, and those in Foundation Funkollective and isangmahal have demonstrated an irrefutable commitment to radical social change and have contributed to hip hop's "oppositional thrust."

In sum, problematic, apolitical, and über-political are qualities that circulate within a range of hip hop expressions among Filipino Americans. These qualities may be specific to certain locales, contexts, and hip hop elements (color blindness in DJing versus politics-as-resistance in emceeing, for example). Yet, this book complicates academic discourses that risk caricaturing participants. It values the vernacular attributes of hip hop performance and does not wish to either categorically dismiss performers' expressions nor simply valorize "proper" political subjects. The latter specifically risks replicating the political propriety and elitism of late nineteenth century Philippine nationalists who welcomed a defined political subject into their aspired nation while abjecting those who diverge from a pure Philippine national narrative.[68] In vernacular culture, there is not one script nor is there no script. "Politics" should be considered in a messier, more capacious framework by provoking hip hop's more varied, complex, and contested meanings for practitioners who inhabit multiple positionalities and cultural stakes. Subjects' narratives are not simple, nor are they always legible (nor do they necessarily desire to be). For example, the readily identifiable politics of the Native Guns' verbal assault on George W. Bush's Iraq War in their album *Barrel Men* resonates differently with the more ambiguous politics of emcee Hopie being abducted by aliens in her music video "Space Case." There is value in the varied and agile politics of performers' artifacts, texts, gestures, and bodies in motion. In this way, the application of "politics" takes on more flexible roles.[69]

Treating Filipino American performance as a vernacular invites a critical distance that suspends essentialisms while interrogating the discursive purposes of difference. Understood as generating epistemological value through its discourses of difference, "Filipino" for Filipino American hip hop cultural producers has been politically endowed, such as its historical usage among nation-aspiring Philippine elites versus its value among more contemporary Filipino leftist nationalists who congeal together disparate Philippine populations such as Muslims and indigenous people. The ways in which the narrations of "Filipino" are authored in hip hop imaginaries illuminate processes of Filipino American subject making where terms of difference are always contested, where boundaries are already scandalized. Yet, "Filipino" is not an arbitrary construct; for more than a century, it has been a category that has responded to the racial vortex of colonialism.

Savage Standing: On Becoming Filipino

In August 2013, Filipino American emcees performed sold-out shows in San Francisco and Los Angeles. Bambu headlined in both cities, summoning veteran and up-and-coming Filipino American emcees and an army of fans. In anticipation of the shows, flyers circulated throughout social media sites such as Facebook and Instagram. Several versions of the flyer were disseminated, some with just one artist facing side-profiled and unsmiling (as in fig. 4) and others with multiple artists boxed in by panels posing in the same fashion. Two artists in the collage were not Filipino American: Reverie is Latina, and Artie McCraft is African American. In all versions, the photos are staged to give the impression that the artists are posing for a mug shot, complete with a blank canvas in the back and a harsh flash aimed directly at the subjects, accentuating the shot's documentation effect. The camera records the details and shapes of the artists' nose and jaw structure, as if their unsmiling features can be measured and compared.

The flyers recall the photos taken by white American colonial administrators and scientists at the outset of American rule in the Philippines, as seen in the Bilibid Prison photos (figs. 5 and 6). A primary function of colonial photography in the Philippines was to organize a variety of people into "racial types," all of which were shown to be subordinate to the white body.[70] Pearlie Rose S. Baluyut writes that "under American colonial rule, the photographs of the Philippines and its people were regarded as ocular templates of truth—scientific records of both the ideal and the stereotype."[71] Photography served as a technology that secured a sense of white American modernity, which was constituted by contrasting itself to the so-called primitiveness of America's subaltern others. Along with the grand spectacle of the St. Louis World's Fair

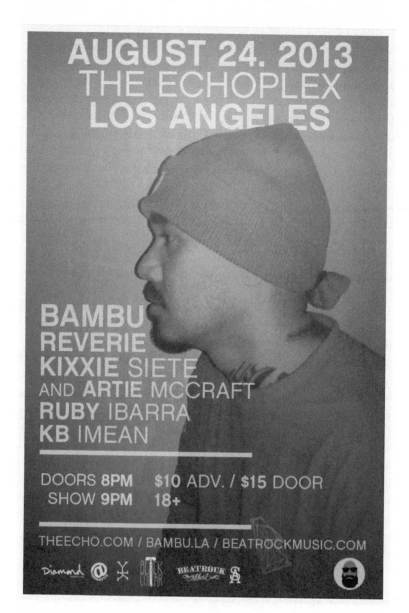

FIGURE 4. Flyer for Bambu concert in Los Angeles.

in 1904, which exhibited in its Philippine Reservation the warm-body spoils won in the Philippine-American War, photography gave visual evidence to a white American public of the need for racial uplift of "primitive" people in the new colony. Yet, colonial photographs are not simply stagnant documents. As part of an archive of U.S.-Philippine relations, they are artifacts that contribute to continuing discourses on these relations. The editors of *Confrontations* write: "Loquacious and never silent, photographs are versed narrators that tell many stories and, simultaneously, pose historical riddles. As such, they no longer remain as objective, unchanging evidence of history, but are encounters in the making."[72] Baluyut displayed this "loquaciousness" in her *(Dis)embodied Filipina: Fashioning Domesticity, Weaving Desire* exhibit (2009) in the Pacific Asia Museum in Pasadena, which critiques the binary of primitive versus modern in juxtaposing items invoking primitivism, such as nude anthropological photos of women in the Philippines, with those that are seen as modern, such as the Maria Clara *terno* dress.

The concert flyers for Bambu and company rewrite a colonial history's creation of the savage Filipino body. Like Baluyut, they visualize a Philippine-U.S. imperial encounter. The flyers recast the artists as physiological racial types who are objects of surveillance, criminalization, and spectacle but who are also hip hop stars to be celebrated on stage. Where colonial photography offered an early twentieth-century U.S. viewing public evidence of Filipinos' inability for self-governance, the artists playfully portray themselves as cultural icons: they are "most wanted" as hip hop artists. The emcees' noms de plume written on the flyers assert a counter-identity responding to their colonized names and bodies. Furthermore, the paneling of the artists gathered into a single flyer organizes the artists to gaze upon each other, as if they are standing in a circle of mutual acknowledgment. Therefore, while they mirror the scientific objectification documenting the colonized, criminalized, nonwhite racial Other, the flyers perform sly work in repositioning the artists' agency by satirizing the absurdity of colonial documentation.

American exceptionalism, as a discourse that whitewashes the sins of U.S. imperial violence, ironically obscures history along with formerly hypervisible, photographed bodies that were objects of colonial gaze. A Filipino American hip hop vernacular establishes a process of naming Filipino bodies in history while asserting a Filipino presence in the here and now. Where the "savage" Filipino body is seen as devoid of history, culture, and a place in modernity, a "loquacious" Filipino American hip hop vernacular defiantly announces U.S. empire's well-kept secret: the savage has always been present, always watching, listening, and doing.

As diasporic bodies resulting from imperial encounter, Filipino American hip hop performers utilize strategies of memory making through their

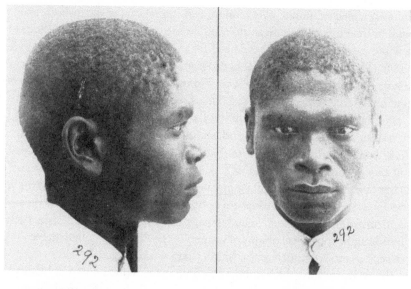

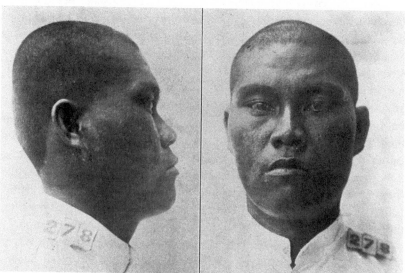

FIGURES 5 AND 6. Colonial mug shots from Bilibid Prison. Although the source text gives photos of eighty men and boys with data on their provinces of origin, "span of arms," "length of head," "height of nose," and "breadth of nose," it fails to give their names. Photographer unknown. Photos from Daniel Folkmar, *Album of Philippine Types* (1904).

music, record scratches, movements, and murals, as well as in the communities they create, the knowledge they speak, and alternative ways they author their souls in the universe. A Filipino American hip hop vernacular cites the aftermath of U.S. and Spanish colonization, whereby descendants of racial subjugation cultivate the ongoing project of articulating a Filipino postcolonial subjectivity.

Whereas "Filipino" once applied to people of Spanish ancestry born in the archipelago, during the late 1800s, elite nationalists appropriated "Filipino" to describe members of an emerging Philippine nation. With the curtailing of Philippine national development due to U.S. colonial occupation, "Filipino" became sanctified under the administration of U.S. colonial statecraft, becoming reserved for "fit" and "modern" racial and ethnic groups in the proto-nation. The fractured and wounded trajectory of Philippine nation-state building contributes to contemporary iterations of Filipino culture. Since the civic category "Filipino" developed out of U.S. colonial statecraft as much as it emerged out of earlier anticolonial consciousness of elite, exiled, mestizo Philippine nationalists, "Filipino" remains a contested category proceeding along a larger historical arc of racist practices.[73] As such, Filipino Americans, as with other racialized and colonized groups in the United States, exceed the categorical strictures adopted in U.S. liberal multiculturalism that situates racial difference as well-defined and horizontal in a field of power. Filipino American hip hop expressions testify to the historical and geographic excessiveness of Filipino bodies. Rather than treating "Filipino" as constituted by a timeless, coherent, and homogenous Philippine nation, performers express the tentativeness, incompleteness, and gradients of Filipinoness. Just as "Filipino" began as a racial project useful for Philippine nationalists or U.S. colonizers, Filipino American hip hop performers continue a legacy of exploring "Filipino" as a racial project but in service of understanding their own belonging inside and outside of the modern nation. In a Filipino American hip hop vernacular, the dynamics of racial power come into relief, particularly a historical memory recalling the influence of Spanish and U.S. colonialism. In this way, a Filipino American hip hop vernacular isn't simply a whimsical experiment with varying identities made possible by Filipinos' racial ambiguities. Quite the opposite: it provides a grounded, history-laden language of postcolonial memory. Traditionally, hip hop's political imperatives embrace a "knowledge of self" mantra that helps reclaim the dignity of African Americans whose history, homes, names, and relationship to the sacred were destroyed by the violence of white supremacy. Hip hop's tools for racial reclamation has been essential in the exploration of a Filipino racial project. A Filipino American hip hop vernacular is not simply the voice of group X rebelling against their parents or seeking resistance against oppression. Rather, it is a cultural practice inserted within the ongoing racial project of Filipino emergence; it is a recent iteration of Filipino postcolonial culture.

The Playlist

The chapters of this book roughly follow a path that begins with the material and then continues to the imaginative. First, "Currents of Militarization, Flows of Hip Hop: Expanding the Geographies of Filipino American Culture" examines how the geographic vastness and the cultural politics of a Filipino American hip hop vernacular are made possible through the United States' century-long pivot to Asia and the consequential migration of Filipino communities in military bases worldwide. This geographic and cultural arrangement sets the stage for understanding Filipino American culture's material and structural contexts. Filipino American hip hop performers testify to these contexts in their political articulations emerging from a Filipino American military class. Specifically, I analyze the lyrics and biographies of Filipino American hip hop artists Geologic and Bambu, whose biographies and poetics exemplify the significance of militarization in the lives of Filipino Americans. This chapter aptly ushers in *Manifest Technique* given that U.S. militarization and war in the Philippines greatly defined the formation of "Filipino" as a racialized and colonized subject determined by universalizing projects of U.S. white supremacy. A careful consideration of this Filipino status flows throughout my remaining chapters.

Building from the structural foundations in militarization that made the scale of Filipino American hip hop cultural production possible, the next two chapters elaborate on the insurgent and imaginative worlds created by Filipino American hip hop participants. Specifically, I examine how the intimately linked spiritual, cosmological, and racial codes in hip hop contribute resources for the ongoing processes of Filipino subject-making and the fostering of counter-modernities for Filipino American hip hop performers. "'Civilize the Savage': Toward Islam, Filipino Origin, and the Golden Age" reveals how Filipino Americans' encounter with Islam is mainly through hip hop. In examining the narratives and visual art of Filipino American hip hop artists Geologic, Bambu, Rocky Rivera, Odessa Kane, Freedom Self-Born Allah Siyam, Manila Ryce, and the Digital Martyrs, I argue that Filipino Americans' recuperation of Muslims in the Philippines is a modified version of late nineteenth-century Philippine nationalists' quest for a Filipino race and civilization, an early quest that decidedly disavowed Muslims and privileged Hispanicized Filipinos. Through their "return" to Islam, Filipino

American hip hop performers exemplify the fragmented and contested nature of Filipino ethnic and racial authenticity. Chapter 3, "Nation in the Universe: The Cosmic Vision of Afro-Filipino Futurism," observes Filipino Americans' extraterrestrial and cosmic imagination, a mode of performance that consults hip hop's links to the 1960s Black Arts Movement and the science fiction genre Afrofuturism. Some Filipino American hip hop artists embrace alternative worlds of civilization and temporality to counter Filipinos' historical suspension from civilization and the modern nation. In particular, I study Filipino Americans' understanding of their roles in the Universal Zulu Nation, hip hop's first cultural organization and an arbiter of hip hop authenticity that exudes cosmic and fantastical cultural politics. I also focus on the eccentric and otherworldly sonics and visuals of the Invisibl Skratch Piklz and Hopie. Building on earlier themes, chapter 3 demonstrates how the spiritual, cosmological, and racial allegories in hip hop inspire Filipino knowledge creation, unraveling "proper" political subjectivity through these performers' funky and alien representations.

The final chapter, "Postcolonial Bodies, Modern Postures: Erasure and Community Formation in Filipino American Hip Hop Dance Culture," scrutinizes Filipino American hip hop dancers' posturing of "modern." Filipino American hip hop dance culture both critiques and acquiesces to modes of visibility and acceptability. In this way, I claim, the use of "modern" to construct themselves as dancers is an act of punning—wordplay—by Filipino American dancers. The chapter focuses especially on the popular discourses surrounding the rising visibility of the dance group Kaba Modern, whose mainstream appearance on season one of MTV's *America's Best Dance Crew* in 2008 set internet fan sites on fire. The scandal involving the absence of Filipino Americans on the six-member MTV Kaba Modern team gestures to requisite Filipino American erasure in service of a larger Asian American mainstream arrival, where exhortations of "Asian pride" meets an uncomfortable congruence with Filipino American dancers' complex racialization. Through their queer performances and forms of affiliation, I read Filipino American hip hop dancers as embodying racial power relations in ways that liberal multiculturalism fails to represent. Remembering Filipino American hip hop vernacular dance culture as a continuation of a longstanding and intimate engagement with the United States instead of an inauguration into it narrates the terms of modern Filipino American embodiment not as a linear immigrant "coming-to-voice" but as structured vertically by colonial power. An appreciation of this historical relevance in Filipino American hip hop dance culture offers a fuller vantage of race and racism in shaping various iterations of the "modern" in modern dance.

CHAPTER 1

Currents of Militarization, Flows of Hip Hop

Expanding the Geographies of Filipino American Culture

On October 11, 2011, U.S. Secretary of State Hillary Clinton's op-ed "America's Pacific Century" in *Foreign Policy* signaled President Barack Obama's desire to rebalance U.S. economic and military interests away from Iraq and Afghanistan and toward Asia.[1] On April 28, 2014, helping to fulfill the president's geopolitical "pivot to Asia," the United States and Philippine governments signed the Enhanced Defense Cooperation Agreement (EDCA), calling for an increased U.S. military presence in the former U.S. colony. The agreement allowed U.S. troops, warships, and aircraft to share existing Philippine military infrastructures—rent-free—for a ten-year period, authorizing a large-scale U.S. military presence not seen since prior to the closures of Subic Bay Naval Base and Clark Air Base in 1992. The EDCA purported to improve response times for natural disasters in the region and to provide greater security during a heightened time of maritime disputes in the South China Sea between the Philippines and China.[2] As the Trump administration inherited Obama's pivot to Asia in intensifying U.S. military dominance in Asia in the name of regional security, the Philippines found itself in a familiar twentieth-century drama: the capitalization of U.S. foreign expansion in exchange for the abridgment of Philippine sovereignty. The drama of the Philippine and U.S. presidential administrations rehearsed on the stage of regional struggle: China has been aggressively asserting control of the South China Sea, which holds strategic geopolitical importance among several nations, thus testing the assurances of U.S. hegemony in the region.

Despite the United States assuming a role as regional protector, Philippine president Rodrigo Duterte's position regarding the EDCA was famously erratic. Early in his tenure, Duterte lambasted U.S. influence in the Philippines and threatened to seek a "divorce" from the United States in order to explore a previously unimagined alliance with China—which Duterte immediately retracted.[3] In 2019, as Chinese aggression in the region escalated, Duterte renewed his commitment with the United States despite his series of public flip-flops on the matter of Philippine allegiance.[4] Further adding to the geopolitical circus, in 2020, Duterte unilaterally scrapped the 1998 Visiting Forces Agreement (VFA), which served as a prelude to the EDCA in permitting the presence of U.S. military personnel in the Philippines for "joint exercises." Yet, also in 2020, betraying the president's tough posturing against the United States, Duterte's regime secured a $2 billion U.S. Department of Defense weapons sales package and continues to enjoy millions of dollars in U.S. military aid used to violently repress poor people, environmental activists, labor organizers, and indigenous people in the name of counterterrorism programs, Duterte's notorious and sketchy war on drugs, and Covid-19 pandemic order violations.[5]

Long before Duterte's chaotic efforts at geopolitical realignment, imperiling the fates of the EDCA and VFA, the Philippines was bound to its former colonizer in colonial and neocolonial relationships. This partnership—formed in the aftermath of the Philippine-American War in the early 1900s, reaffirmed after Philippine independence in 1946, and solidified during the Cold War—brought bases and U.S. military personnel in the islands and enabled the recruitment of young Filipino men into the U.S. military labor force. Throughout the twentieth century, Filipinos migrated along the global currents of militarization, becoming seasoned travelers of U.S. empire, essentially suturing the category "Filipino American" to its U.S. colonial genealogy. In this chapter, I examine how the geographic vastness and the politics of a Filipino American hip hop vernacular are made possible through the United States' century-long pivot to Asia and the consequential installation of Filipino communities in military bases worldwide. Furthermore, I investigate this vernacular's response to these migratory and spatial formations. U.S. bases in the Philippines, the Pacific, and throughout the continental United States have served as cultural conduits to the growth of hip hop within Filipino communities. This chapter, therefore, establishes a material foundation that shapes culture. The overwhelming number of influential Filipino American hip hop artists who have connections to the U.S. military, especially those whose fathers migrated via U.S. recruitment in the Philippines, suggests the extent that militarization has shaped the expressions, movements, and embodiments of recent generations of Filipino Americans who have embraced hip hop culture as their dominant mode of expression and identification since the early 1980s.

The metaphor of currents helps congeal together the symbiotic episte-mological flow between the cultural politics of Filipino American hip hop performance and the structural determinations of militarization. Setsu Shi-gematsu and Keith L. Camacho use the metaphor of currents to "signal how militarization operates across temporal and spatial boundaries."[6] Similarly, in *Filipino Crosscurrents*, Kale Bantigue Fajardo develops a crosscurrent frame-work (in part) to imagine oceanic migratory flows on a global scale. Currents illuminate the ways in which the contours of Filipino American culture are formed by the global flows of U.S. militarization, especially flows via U.S. Navy migrations. Not simply about the "guns and troops," however, this chapter echoes Vernadette Vicuña Gonzalez's concerns in recognizing militarization's process of "ideological, political, and cultural control."[7] Militarization is an essential component to the aesthetics, politics, and embodiments circulating within Filipino American hip hop performance. Hip hop, therefore, offers a crucial counter-discourse to the United States' racialized and colonial his-tory and geographies. In this way, a Filipino American hip hop vernacular is contoured by a colonial legacy—it can be described as postcolonial culture.

Filipino American emcees Geologic and Bambu proficiently testify to the reverberations between U.S. militarized currents and a Filipino American hip hop vernacular. The two artists' biographies provide a critical lesson of the interlocking between Filipino American hip hop performance and military migration. Geo's father migrated along militarized currents as a U.S. Navy serviceman, which brought his family around the world. Mirroring the post-colonial nature of his father's migration, Geo's mother was also a participant of global flows of Filipino labor as an early recruit for domestic work in Italy. She met Geo's father in Italy, where he was stationed at the time. Because of his father's navy career, Geo was born in Long Beach, California, and grew up in Honolulu, Hawai'i, and Bremerton, Washington.[8] Geo's geographic migrations and proletarian sensibilities offer a critical reimagining of Fili-pino American communities, especially as regards to this community's class dynamics and spatial mapping. As a sailor, Bambu's father also migrated to Bremerton. But, Bambu's story differs slightly because the emcee grew up in several districts in Los Angeles, which were not necessarily navy or military communities. Yet, as Bambu shows, these areas were still highly militarized in the sense that young men of color living there have been aggressively sought as recruits. Having served in the U.S. Marines, Bambu's experiences reflect the realities of military presence in poor and racialized urban areas.

I begin by outlining U.S.-Philippine "special relations," which resulted in the long-term military occupation of the former U.S. colony. Understanding this relationship, military bases broadly function as conduits of cultural interactions—as imperial contact zones—among diasporic Filipinos and similarly displaced and vulnerable communities. Second, expanding on the culture of inhabitants of these imperial contact zones, I examine Geo's proletarian narratives. Following what Roderick N. Labrador calls "Asian American hip-hop musical auto/biographies," I read the lyrics emerging from artists' songs as narrations motivated by the synergism between the individual artist and a collective audience.[9] Geo's musical poetics reflect the experiences of a "Filipino American military class," a positionality that shapes the aesthetics and political stakes of a Filipino American hip hop vernacular by offering a critical "bottom-up" perspective of Filipino American culture. Next, I observe how Geo and Bambu's interviews and music narrate the ways in which military communities assemble a larger imperial home that resides within a globally expansive geography. Finally, I analyze the Blue Scholars' antiwar anthem "Back Home," which further elaborates these artists' discursive symbiosis between home and empire. The music video for "Back Home" visualizes the struggles and gendered relations of members of the Filipino American military class.[10] This video bears witness to ongoing U.S. overseas war making that found its footing in military excursions in the Philippines, inviting memory of the United States' "special relations" with the Philippines.

Imperial Contact Zones and "Special Relations"

A Filipino American hip hop vernacular testifies to the development and intimacies of racialized communities emerging out of the militarized violence of the expanding American state. Within militarized spaces, Filipino Americans have been remaking military towns into social landscapes productive for their hip hop cultural expressions by taking advantage of military community centers, gyms, and recreation halls. Given these resources, young Filipino Americans have created rich cultural spaces and shared community among otherwise disparate racial and regional groups. These military bases functioned as imperial contact zones of interaction and collaboration.[11] These imperial contact zones where young Filipino Americans live are spread throughout a variety of geographies, including small port cities in militarized geographies around the world, particularly in locations where colonial interaction and encounter occur in multiple spaces and venues inside and beyond the metropole.[12]

For many Filipino Americans, militarized contact zones have been im-
portant conduits of people and culture, especially in the dissemination and
development of hip hop within a network of Filipino American communities.
For example, DJ Kuya D, a veteran Filipino American DJ from Queens, New
York, and Virginia Beach, explains the eclectic qualities of hip hop among
Filipino Americans in Virginia Beach, a navy community host to a large
Filipino American population: "[Virginia Beach hip hop is influenced by]
the navy or the military. It's a broad mix of where people come from here.
You know navy babies who travel a lot from the West Coast, back and forth,
here and there." Martin Briones, an emcee and music producer from Virginia
Beach, also comments on the mix of styles that came through his city: "So
growing up here, there was always people coming and going. We always had
people from New York coming down, moving here, going to school with me.
But then we also had people from California or from the South that would
also come here. So, it was a wide variety of influences."[13] Growing up across
the country, Geo describes a parallel series of migratory encounters: "In that
the interaction, you're kind of forced to have [that interaction] not only with
other Filipinos who are in the same situation, but with people from other
backgrounds. You were in contact with people—other Americans, you know
Black Americans, white Americans from all over the country. Even in Hawaiʻi
out of all places. I'd meet someone from the South whose family grew up
in New York. Then they were gone like two years later. So, there was always
this movement of people from other backgrounds as well as from Filipinos
from these other areas."[14] Geo describes the multiple meanings of his song
"Motion Movement" (2003), including how the currents of militarization
shaped his family's encounter with imperial contact zones:

> At the time, it was definitely more of motion and movement as far as "social
> movements" and at the same time, b-boy, b-girl, physical dance, cultural
> movement, and using our bodies rhythmically—an idea that both being one
> in the same. But embedded in the lyrics themselves is the story of move-
> ment, "migration movement," both as immigrant diaspora, transnationals
> and what not, and then also even once we made one migration from one
> country to another, the migration within this new country from place to
> place. And being part of a community where that's constantly happening.
> My history specifically being Filipino family from military background,
> pops in the navy, also being in a different elementary school every two-three
> years, having a new set of friends every two-three years.[15]

In his reflection on the meanings associated with "Motion Movement," Geo
expands motion and movement as multipurpose allusions to organized resistance, hip hop performance, and the migration of his family along imperial

contact zones. For the artist, migrating along militarized currents influenced both the text of his music as well as its poetic tenor.

The sheer magnitude of Filipino presence in these militarized spaces brings the former subjects of U.S. empire to the postcolonial center. It is beyond this chapter's scope to catalog even a sliver of Filipino American hip hop performers who are associated with the military. But it is worth mentioning a few notable performers with family connections to the military. Garnering from interviews and observing their music over the years, I have noted these performers' military backgrounds. Anna Sarao's father was in the navy, and she grew up in the navy town of San Diego. Anna is credited for being a crucial leader in organizing Southern California's hip hop competitive dance scene, which has now grown in international relevance. Rocky Rivera, who hails from the Filipino American hip hop artist factory of the Excelsior District in San Francisco, was born on Clark Air Base in Pampanga, Philippines. Her family relocated to the Bay Area, where her father was stationed on Treasure Island. Bay Area–based hip hop photographer Leo Docuyanan was raised in the military community of Southeast San Diego. The Digital Martyrs, who are based in Oakland, California, come also from a navy community in San Diego. Emcees Son of Ran and Pele also hail from San Diego. Hip Hop dance activist and original Kaba Modern member Cheryl Cambay comes from a navy background in Cerritos, California. Jojo and Bobby Gaon, founders of isangmahal arts kollective in Seattle, migrated along a navy base route from Charleston, South Carolina, to San Diego and to Bremerton. Artist and community activist Che has navy roots in Virginia Beach and resides in Jacksonville, Florida. Apl.de.ap, whose African American father was stationed in Clark Air Base, is perhaps the most celebrated Filipino American hip hop artist as a member of the pop group the Black Eyed Peas. Chad Hugo of N.E.R.D., music partner to Pharrell Williams, boasts a lucrative and award-winning musical career as a beat producer. Having a navy background, Hugo is from Virginia Beach.

The development of Filipino-populated contact zones located in disparate militarized cities evidences an imperial mapping resulting from the United States' serial propensity for overseas war. Before George W. Bush's and Barack Obama's wars in Iraq and Afghanistan, there was William McKinley and Teddy Roosevelt's war in the Philippines at the end of the nineteenth century and the beginning of the twentieth century. The Philippines was subjugated as a U.S. colony after the pacification and genocide of people in the Philippines. As a result, Filipinos, legally designated as U.S. nationals until the 1934 Tydings-McDuffie Act, began their migration to the U.S. metropole to labor in agriculture, nursing, and the military.[16] The recruitment of Filipino men

TABLE 1. Racial and ethnic demographics of select cities/counties with a large U.S. Navy base, 2010 (U.S. Census Bureau)

		Jacksonville, FL		Virginia Beach, VA		San Diego County, CA		Bremerton, WA	
Total Population		821,784		436,979		3,095,313		37,933	
White	White %	488,473	59.4%	301,492	69.0%	1,981,442	64.0%	28,615	75.4%
African American	African American %	252,421	30.7%	84,807	19.4%	158,213	5.1%	2,388	6.3%
Asian (total)	Asian (total) %	35,222	4.3%	26,720	6.1%	336,091	10.9%	1,656	4.4%
Filipino	Filipino %	14,458	1.8%	17,003	3.9%	146,618	4.7%	1,053	2.8%
Filipino % of Asian			41.0%		63.6%		43.6%		63.6%
Chinese	Chinese %	2,500	0.3%	2,138	0.5%	49,395	1.6%	50	0.1%
Chinese % of Asian			7.1%		8.0%		14.7%		3.0%

Source: Mark Villegas, "Race and Ethnic Demographics of Select Cities/Counties with a Large U.S. Navy Base," *Empire of Funk: Hip Hop and Representation in Filipina/o America.* Copyright © 2014 by Cognella, Inc. Reprinted with permission.

into the lowest ranks of the navy began during the early 1900s, continued after Philippine independence under the U.S. diplomatic mantra of "special relations" with the former colony, and lasted until 1992.[17]

Jesse Quinsaat documents the extent to which Filipinos became a "brown skinned servant force":[18] nine Filipinos were recorded as navy personnel in 1903, 178 by 1905, 2,000 by 1917, 6,000 by 1919, and dropping to a constant number of 4,000 or 4.5 percent of the navy after World War I. During World War II, the Japanese occupied the archipelago and Filipinos engaged a guerilla campaign against the invaders until U.S. forces returned to conscript Filipinos into its military. After U.S. naval bases were secured from the Japanese, 2,000 enlisted between 1944 and 1946. Between World War II and 1973, over 22,000 enlisted, with an annual quota of 2,000 Filipino enlistees set in 1954.[19] The legal authorization that enabled the significant jump in enlistment in the latter years, even after Filipinos became citizens of their own nation after independence in 1946, was due to the Military Bases Agreement of 1947 between the United States and the new Republic of the Philippines, which heralded the era of euphemistic "special relations" between the two nations.[20] According to the agreement, the U.S. military could lease twenty-three sites in the Philippines for ninety-nine years and continue to recruit Filipinos.[21]

As signatures of U.S. power, military bases in the Philippines significantly transformed Philippine society in what Yen Le Espiritu calls "centers of wealth amid local poverty."[22] The physical proximity of the United States via the military was so palpable for many Filipinos that Roberto, one of Martin Manalansan's informants in his study on gay Filipino migrant men, commented that while growing up he believed "America was just an hour bus ride away."[23] In spaces like Sangley Point, Subic Bay, and Clark Air Base, the real and symbolic aspirations of grasping a real and imagined United States molded everyday social relations. In terms of labor and social mobility, young men's hopes were influenced by enlisted and retired Filipino navy men returning to coach and conduct seminars on joining the navy, this on top of the opulence retired navy men exuded in their hometowns, flaunting their Americanized excess.[24] In terms of sexual relations and work, prostitution became a staple industry for Filipina women and Filipino men in these contact zones.[25] The possibilities of sexual relations and reproduction resulted in a population of mixed-race Filipinos, as shown by the biography of Apl.de.ap, who, after gaining worldwide accolades as a member of the pop group the Black Eyed Peas, has become a Pampangan hometown hero.

U.S. military presence did not just transform the Philippine urban environment, it shaped militarized cities in the continental United States, in Hawai'i, East Asia, Europe, and wherever else U.S. military boots and ships landed. Imagining contact zones as more globally dispersed than the U.S. military towns of Sangley Point, Subic Bay, or Clark Air Base in the Philippines blurs the global boundaries that distinguish where the domestic United States ends and where the foreign begins. These contact zones share an existing as well as constantly flowing population of colonized, racialized (e.g., Filipino and African American servicemen used as feminized labor on ships), and cyclically recruited groups. Throughout the twentieth century, as DJ Kuya D, Briones, and Geo point out above, Filipino men and their families traveled along imperial routes, creating a circuitry of militarized Filipino communities. Within these spaces, Filipinos from this military diaspora have mingled, culturally collaborated, and sexually reproduced with people of varying racial backgrounds who share their environment. U.S. servicemen and their families stationed at bases in the Philippines (and throughout Asia) have played a vital role in socializing hip hop (and African American culture in general) to local inhabitants.[26] Much more, Filipino Americans flowing along the currents of U.S. bases interacted with each other and with non-Filipinos, creating "a new set of friends" as they moved. "Special relations" bred another kind of special relations.

"Plantation Style: Yellow, Brown, Black Majority"

The complex set of power relations associated with these migratory and multiracial contact zones generate a cultural politics particular to Filipino Americans living within these social landscapes. Many Filipino Americans with a parent who migrated via military recruitment tend to inhabit a social and economic stratum in many ways distinct from those occupied by Filipinos who obtained professional degrees prior to migrating to the United States. In his music, Geo brings attention to what I call the "Filipino American military class," opening the discourse of post-1965 Filipino migration that should be appreciated for its diversity educationally, geographically, and socioeconomically. This diversity gives more complexity to post-1965 Filipino cohorts, which is often referred to as the Filipino professional class, or what Dylan Rodriguez calls the "post-1965 Filipino American national bourgeoisie."[27] Conventional post-1965 Asian American and Filipino American narratives tout the emergence of highly skilled, highly educated workers who received training in Asia and, as a result, benefited from U.S. immigration preferences. However, preceding, concurrent, and mixing with these post-1965 migrants (and family-sponsored and undocumented migrants) are less-formally educated Filipino men and their families settling in military towns.[28] Studies detailing the latter demographic, as well as Kale Fajardo's ethnography of Filipino international maritime transportation workers, elucidate the role of Filipino men and masculinities in post-1965 Filipina/o global migration, whose recent scholarly discourse has been in some ways defined by the global migration of Filipina domestic workers and nurses.[29]

To better appreciate the cultural significance of Filipino military men's migration, it is important to bring attention to the structures linking militarization and masculinity. For example, Oliver Wang's glimpse at the social, disciplinary, and even aesthetic significance of Filipino American DJs' participation in Junior Reserve Officers' Training Corps exemplifies the interweaving of militarized life and these predominantly male DJs' hip hop socialization.[30] The functioning of a Filipino American hip hop vernacular, however, is not exclusive to Filipino male practitioners—certainly, Filipina artists, promoters, and fans have proved integral to the fostering of this vernacular.[31] Regardless, militarized masculinity can offer a lens with which to investigate the workings of social relations in Filipino American hip hop performance. Particularly instructive is Suarez's study on Filipino navy men's self-making through intergenerational kinship and peer networks as shaped in imperial spaces. My investigation borrows Suarez's outlining of vertical and horizontal social relations, but extends these forms of Filipino American cultural mediations to the workings of commercialized leisure and popular culture.

The gender, sexual, and class power relationships emanating from the Filipino American military class queries the historical conditions that prompt Filipino migration. The racialized, gendered, and working-class hierarchies produced by military migration offer a bottom-up genealogy of Filipino American culture and class identification. The only foreign nationals allowed enlistment into the service by virtue of the bases agreement, Filipino men performed the menial and dirty work as the "brown-skinned servant force" of what reporter Timothy Ingram of the *Washington Monthly* in 1970 called a "floating plantation."[32] Abundant, low-paid, and racially segregated, Filipino men supplied the labor for the military to grow and function. Filipino men were prohibited from elevating from this labor stratum before restrictions on Filipino rank mobility were relaxed in 1973, a move Quinsaat insinuates was motivated by bad press and a congressional investigation on the use of stewards.[33] When on shore duty, Filipino labor appeared in other sectors of the federal government. With a sense of pride, my father and his navy buddies would tell stories of Filipinos serving "as high up" as servants in the White House for the office of the president of the United States.[34] The irony, of course, is that the pride felt by Filipino men who worked in such esteemed institutions—and their buddies who aspired to these positions—was only made possible for them as racialized, feminized, and menial workers. Through heteronormative family formation and fatherhood, these men reauthorized meanings of Filipino masculinity, manhood, and citizenship as patriotic navy men within these otherwise devalued positions.[35] Yet, their sense of belonging to the United States was always conditioned by their subordinate status; their patriotic subjectivity was conditioned by their segmented labor on the floating plantation.

The symbolic and demographic significance of Filipino American proletarianism underscores the multiplicity of post-1965 Filipino Americans. It is important to emphasize that many Filipino Americans in the military class—including patriotic navy men and their children—do comply with a type of conservative Filipino Americanism that aspires for "civil recognition" and "cultural valorization."[36] Nonetheless, focusing on the colonial and neocolonial particularities of the Filipino American military class attributes more complexity to the culture and demographic characteristics of post-1965 Filipino American communities. Filipino migrants embody what James Clifford describes as "discrepant cosmopolitanisms," or diasporic displacements inseparable from histories of often violent economic, political, and cultural interaction.[37] For Filipino migrants, "discrepant cosmopolitanism" varies according to their avenue of travel. Unlike members of the post-1965 professional class who were educated in the Philippines and may bring with them a sense of civic and national propriety and educational exceptionalism (they were the ones who "made it"), migrants from the Filipino American military class carry much more tenuous and ambivalent educational and civic experiences, with these men historically lacking college degrees due to their being recruited for the purpose of the navy's low-ranked positions. In her interviews, Espiritu gives a glimpse of the educational backgrounds of these men: "As one of the 'early Navy people,' Ricardo Reyes referred to the post-1960s Filipino recruits as 'a different breed': 'During my time [the 1930s], the schooling is very low, like I know one of my shipmates could not write his name. He just put an "X" on his paycheck.'" Although the educational backgrounds of Filipino navy men shifted over time, with more degree holders enlisting around the 1960s, this demographic remained largely without college experience. Much more, regardless of their education, Filipinos were assigned steward positions, members of the "brown-skinned servant force" and inhabiting the status of modern citizen-subjects not as exceptional professionals but as expendable bodies of the neocolonial U.S. state.[38]

In addition to the challenges brought by a limited amount of social and economic resources, many Filipino Americans of the military class have faced disillusionment and instability in the domestic sphere. Having to move around because of their navy parent being stationed at another base, Filipino American youths would be frequently forced to adjust. Geo states that part of being a military brat involves "not knowing where we're going to be next year, who my friends are gonna be, and even living in a community where people are coming in and out. You'd have friends for two years, and then your best friend is gone forever."[39] With the navy father often "on duty" on the navy base and, for months on end, serving overseas, Filipino American youths can testify to the impact of not having a father around at critical moments in their lives. Riz Oades documents these "downsides" of growing up in a military family, which include "periodic travel or relocation, constant struggle to make new friends and leave them behind, and the hardship of not having a father or a father figure during extended periods of absence." On returning, many Filipino navy fathers would attempt to assert their patriarchal authority over their children despite having experienced physical and emotional distance. One of Oades's interviewees describes his navy father as resembling a "barking drill sergeant." "I almost find myself saluting him," Michael Simpao states. After retiring, Filipino navy men, especially those without a skill applicable outside of the navy, can become burdensome to the family, which is not used to his everyday presence in the household. Oades also notes that these men can also have social, economic, and occupational problems due to their unpreparedness in civilian life.[40]

Even if members of the Filipino American military class do have less privilege when it comes to family stability and economic resources, they access federal benefits available exclusively to military families. Through its paternalistic accommodations, the militarized federal sector granted a plethora of resources, such as funding for higher education and additional economic entitlements. Oades notes the financial security and exclusive benefits afforded to military households: "There were three identifiable assets of growing up in military households. First is the financial security. If the father had not joined the military, economic safety would not have existed. The second is the exclusive benefits gained, such as the ability to shop at the discounted and tax-free Navy Exchange and Commissary. The last advantage is the outstanding assistance package that the Navy provides its servicemen in the form of health care, housing subsidy, and paid college tuition."[41] The military put up families in (often infamous) navy housing, where Geo and countless other Filipino Americans spent their childhoods socializing with other navy brats. Through the navy's Morale, Welfare, and Recreation (MWR) program, they had free access to basketball courts, pools, gym, parks, and even party spaces.[42] As crucial venues of socialization, these public spaces fostered a production of hip hop among young Filipino Americans. Where the suburban garage was an important stage for the creation of a Filipino American DJ scene in Daly City, California, the military base provided a stage for hip hop on the sleek floors of community centers, racquetball courts, and officers' clubs.[43]

As described above, the class, educational, and familial dynamics of the Filipino American military class poses distinct, often-overlooked, facets of post-1965 Filipino American communities. Filipino American hip hop performance offers a counter-discourse to narrow narrations of these communities. In his music, Geo narrates his quotidian experiences as a member of the Filipino American military class. In the intro to "Proletariat Blues" on the Blue Scholars' *The Long March EP* (2006), the emcee portrays teenage life as a grocery bagger at the Navy Commissary. Before the first verse, he speaks casually: "Bagging groceries on base for just tips, no salary. Wouldn't even make enough to buy a CD. And next thing you know, moms is picking me up from jail for stealing CDs from Blockbuster." His first verse goes on to describe the low-paid and unhappy work environment, the way hip hop became diversion, and the "plantation style" racial makeup of his fellow baggers, many of whom would be cycled into the military.

Back in the days when I was a teenager
Minimum wage earning, rocking an apron[44]
I was pushing hella carts asking plastic or paper
To bastard ass customers plus most of us had,
Relatives working in the same supermarket
When boss wasn't looking rolled the dice on the carpet
In the lunch room, listening to Biggie and Nas
But not as much as Snoop, Forty Water, and Pac
Me, I rocked the Walkman instead writing rhymes
In my head often bored, I'd recite them out loud
And memorize a song long before I'd write it down
In lunchroom freestyles is where I learned to clown
Plantation style: yellow, brown, black majority
Half the young cats either enlisted in the army
Or the navy or marines, but I was having dreams
And I ain't even halfway there yet.

For generations, the Commissary has served as a central place for Filipino service people to meet other Filipinos and build a network for mutual support.[45] For the children of these men, the grocery store offered a similar function but also gave opportunities for income-making, however petty. In his verse above, Geo paints a picture of his work experience at the Commissary, replete with small moments of resistance outside the scope of the boss and during spells of boredom, such as rolling dice, listening to Biggie Smalls, Nas, Snoop Dogg, E-40, and Tupac, and memorizing self-authored songs.[46] Geo suggests leisure at the Commissary, similar to leisure at MWR venues, were crucial to facilitating hip hop social practices. Employment at the Commissary by countless Filipino American youths (and, as Geo states, these youths' relatives) in navy towns points to a common spatial and work experience that overlaps with military working-class culture. Work at the Commissary functioned as a preliminary and an auxiliary space of military working-class culture. Geo's description of a plantation style racial and class structure in the Commissary composed of young people who will likely end up in the military visualizes the cyclical flow of militarization in these communities.

Having also grown up in navy towns, I can relate to Geo's verse. I pushed carts at the Navy Commissary in Jacksonville. My brother, along with a cadre of blue apron–wearing Filipino American (many, if not most, who were mixed-race) high school students, worked for tips as baggers at the military-operated grocery store. At the end of the day, I would receive a fraction of their tips handed to me as a wad of cash. The high school baggers' coworkers were short, dark-skinned Filipinas who were perhaps relatives of

Filipino American military families or the wives of white or Black American servicemen. When we lived in Long Beach, my eldest brother also worked in this below-minimum-wage industry, wearing the same blue apron, bagging groceries alongside Filipino American and African American teens. This job seemed like a rite of passage my brothers and my friends: it provided quick cash and an opportunity to socialize with peers who provided the latest knowledge about music, dance, slang, and fashion. The Commissary, with its posse of high school-aged navy brat baggers, also functioned as a conduit to cycling in young recruits. With job prospects slim for navy brats, who were familiar with the benefits and security of the navy experienced firsthand, my oldest brother seriously considered joining, along with a number of my friends (both young men and women) who happened to work at the Commissary. Many actually enlisted and are now traveling the global network of navy towns. In the era of the United States–led global war on terrorism, they have made rounds in Afghanistan and Iraq.

The Navy Commissary provides a starting point to imagine the stakes and sensibilities of working-class Filipino American culture. The metaphor of the plantation—the Commissary for Geo and the navy ship for Ingram—is fitting for characterizing the working spaces of Filipino Americans in the military class. The "yellow, brown, black majority" who make up the labor in the Commissary as described by Geo resonates with what Jayna Brown calls the "global reach of plantation economies and the transnational migratory patterns of exploited labor."[47] What is in essence a global U.S. plantation that practiced slavery and indentured servitude economies across the U.S. South, Hawai'i, and the Caribbean was populated (and are still largely populated) by a "yellow, brown, black majority." It is worth noting that these former U.S. plantation economies—Hawai'i, Puerto Rico, and cities in the U.S. South—have a storied history of militarization. Geo's lyrics certainly do not equate plantation labor with Commissary labor, but he draws a poetic connection to the exploitation involved in the labor extracted from racialized and colonized bodies. In this way, Geo connects (Ingram does so more directly) plantation labor to the extraction of colonial and neocolonial labor from racialized bodies in the military. The militarized and working-class experiences of Filipino sailors illuminate the process of racial structuring in what Espiritu calls differential inclusion, "whereby a group of people is deemed integral to the nation's economy, culture, identity, and power—but integral only or precisely because of their designated subordinate standing."[48] The reliance on racialized, migratory labor to guarantee the economic and military dominance of the United States animates the metropole's historical necessity of creating differentially included subordinated classes. Much more, as Geo attests in the lines "Half the young cats either enlisted in the army / Or the navy or marines," the Commissary is coterminous with the floating plantation by functioning as a gateway to the militarization of the children of Filipino recruits who enlisted in the Philippines.

If hip hop's cultural stakes are anchored to underclass angst, then the proletarianism of military-class Filipino Americans plays a key role in shaping the contours of a broader Filipino American hip hop vernacular.[49] The Blue Scholars derives its namesake by punning "blue collar" with "scholar," thus intertwining the group's proletariat identification with its pedagogical imperative. In "Blue School," Geo raps, "I'm a Blue Scholar worker studying the art of labor to create flavor to relate to listeners." A review of Bambu, Rocky Rivera, and Son of Ran's musical catalog would reveal these artists' proletarian sensibilities. U.S. overseas expansionism, racial segregation, and the exploitation of low-wage labor shaped the geographical vastness and social segmentation of the Filipino American military class. Given this, Geo as well as other Filipino American hip hop artists modify the educated, professional narrative of a post-1965 Filipino Americanism. The other side of the story of post-1965 Filipino migrants includes the less-educated, more-proletarian Filipino migrants whose relationship to modernity reflects U.S. racial segregation, differential inclusion, war making, and overseas expansionism. By focusing on the militarized currents circulating within the cultural politics of a Filipino American hip hop vernacular, we can better understand the migration of Filipino bodies and culture flowing with the memory of U.S. empire.

"Every Home that I've Known, Every Block I've Ever Seen": Home in the Violence of Geography

In "Come On Y'All," a song by San Francisco Bay Area Filipina American emcee Ruby Ibarra featuring Geologic, Geo evokes the theme of home in the song's first verse. The emcee narrates his biography in which every "home" and "block" where he has lived is described by its migratory military culture:

> Every home that I've known
> Every block I've ever seen
> Military hoods, everybody eventually leaves
> Relocated to the B [Bremerton]
> Right before I was a teen
> 98 to Seattle, settled down, finally
> If I ever feel the need to retreat

To a place that's familiar
It'll either be Hawai'i or the Bay
Where the people who share
The same shade that I be.

His impression of home or a "place that's familiar" includes "people who share the same shade that I be." For Geo, then, home involves a layering of both its militarized space and his skin's shade, that is, a racial position defined not only by color but also a set of social relationships. This layering, in effect, alludes to militarization's power to order people's spatial and social arrangements. If U.S. imperialism has determined the patterning of Filipino American communities in the continental United States, in Hawai'i, and virtually anywhere in the world the United States installs a base, then home for militarized Filipino Americans spans the expanse of the U.S. empire.

A Filipino American hip hop vernacular testifies to the formation of racialized communities predicated on the violence of the expanding U.S. state. In his examination of African American rapper Nas's album *Illmatic* (1994), Sohail Daulatzai uses the term "violence of geography" to describe the presence of slums in urban areas the world over. In linking New York City with the ghetto conditions in the slums of the Third World, he reveals how the "politics of place" are shaped by military violence and capital flows. He reminds us that "these global realities and the new landscapes of power that have emerged as a result of the global economy are deeply intertwined with hip-hop's own history."[50] The intimacy of the military and racialized urban space is documented in early hip hop lore. In the 1982 hip hop film *Wild Style*, the young Puerto Rican graffiti artist Raymond crawls through the window of his Bronx projects' bedroom to find his brother Hector dressed in an army uniform, pointing a gun at Raymond, mistaking him for an intruder. Hector later tells Raymond, "Stop fucking around and be a man; there's nothing out here for you!" Hector, embodying the respectable U.S. soldier-citizen who escaped the ghetto, is disgusted at the do-rag on Raymond's head and the graffiti culture absorbing Raymond's life. Raymond responds to Hector's pessimism, gesturing to the graffiti art in his room, "Yes there is: this!" Adilifu Nama posits that this scene, whose audio sample introduces Nas's *Illmatic*, represents young Black and brown youths' commitment to transform rather than flee their social space.[51] For Nas to begin his album with this scene indicates the intersections of urban blight, the militarization of poor people of color, class and gender aspirations linked to the military, and practitioners' commitments to hip hop performance despite the constraints of their environment.

The violence of geography informs the multiple and global presences of
U.S. imperialism, which in this case begins with the occupation of the Philippines by the U.S. Army beginning in 1898 and the subsequent installment
of military bases throughout the twentieth century. Just as hip hop history
references the "new landscapes of power" as evidenced in the urban blight
of New York, the phenomenon of Filipino American hip hop performance
references the violence of geography by alluding to U.S. genocide during
the Philippine-American War, military occupation and base installations,
Filipino militarized migration, and the clustering of diasporic Filipinos in
U.S. bases. Although the U.S. ghetto, Third World slum, and U.S. military
base have differing historical origins and structural arrangements, imagining
geographies of violence helps us critically grasp the spread of U.S. hegemony,
material inequalities, and cultural possibilities that result in the subjugated
statuses of inhabitants in these geographies.

Reflecting their integral roles in further advancing imperial frontiers, military bases confuse and confound the boundaries of the U.S. nation-state.
Because of their instrumentation in global conquest, domestic military towns
within the fifty states function as annexes to U.S. militarized zones overseas. This unorthodox geographical confluence of "foreign" and "domestic"
zones upsets popular understandings of the spatial composition of the United
States. Instead of a map that imagines a solid, coherent continental United
States with (distorted) inclusions of Alaska and Hawai'i, a more complete
map of U.S. empire should consider its scattered, overseas territories in the
Pacific and Caribbean and bases worldwide. Even more, in the obverse, a
world map that considers U.S. overseas installations in places like the Philippines, Guam, Puerto Rico, Okinawa, South Korea, Germany, and Italy
should be shaded the same color as military towns in Bremerton, San Diego,
Honolulu, Jacksonville, Pensacola, and Virginia Beach, thus illustrating a
globally scattered and amorphous (not continental) empire with citizens
abroad and members of the colonized diaspora (e.g., Filipinos, Chamorros,
and Puerto Ricans) living "at home."[52] This unorthodox mapping resurfaces
the early twentieth-century legal dramas that attempted to distinguish where
the foreign and the domestic begins and ends as the United States expanded
to the Pacific and Caribbean.[53]

Imagining U.S. domestic militarized zones as coterminous with a global
U.S. imperial apparatus expands the frontier of the U.S. "homeland," forming an omnipresent geography that serves as a reminder to the structural
conditions of militarization that have shaped the possibilities of Filipino
migration. Shigematsu and Camacho write of the United States with this type
of immense reach: "to circumscribe our understanding of 'America' to the

continental United States—as previous paradigms have tended to empha-size—is myopic in terms of the reach of American empire." Further, they cite the structural dispossessions inflicted on militarized populations in Asia and the Pacific, in which U.S. militarization shapes "the historical displacements and migrations of the populations we now refer to as Asian American and Pacific Islander."[54]

Within these militarized spaces, as mentioned earlier, Filipino Americans have been remaking their military town into a landscape productive for their hip hop cultural expressions by taking advantage of Department of Defense–funded resources such as community centers, gyms, and recreation halls. Rather than a space of abject urban blight, military towns offer MWR spaces and access to health care to communities defined by state-operated violence. Given these resources, young Filipino Americans create rich cultural spaces—they create home—within geographies of violence.

Along with resources, these geographies allowed for community building among otherwise disparate racial and regional groups. For Geo, migrat-ing along currents of these geographies meant the possibility of interacting with similarly displaced and racialized people from a military class. He be-lieves Filipino Americans from military communities were the "first wave of people [Filipino Americans] to break out of our bubbles" and become cul-tural vanguards.[55] As Geo suggests, constant movement influenced the ways militarized Filipino Americans experienced hip hop in their communities. Similar to DJ Kuya D and Martin Briones's descriptions of navy migrations within their communities, Leo Esclamado, a hip hop dancer from Jackson-ville, Florida, recounts the untethered and multiregional Filipino American party scene in his hometown: "The Fil-Am party scene was a mecca of dif-ferent regional influences. While Jacksonville was in North Florida, Fil-Ams were right in the center of the Miami Bass/Reggae scene from Orlando and Miami with its Caribbean influences. There were military families who mi-grated to Jacksonville from the West Coast who were "housin' and breakin' in California."[56] Given the constant movement of Filipino Americans in mili-tarized currents, Filipino Americans not only "broke out of their bubbles," but different "bubbles" (regional cultures) shaped and formed the cultural dynamics of young Filipino Americans. This experience lends credence to the notion of militarized Filipino American hip hop performers functioning as cultural vanguards in their craft.

Bambu illuminates the links between the military and the formations of Filipino American culture. Although he did not grow up on a military base, his biography illustrates how the violence of geography pervades beyond the base. In his song "Moms," Bambu recounts his parents' migration from the

Philippines to Bremerton to Los Angeles. The song opens with a description of his father, a sailor stationed in Bremerton. Bambu's mother, who remained in the Philippines after his parents wed, migrated to Bremerton to join her husband, having discovered that navy spouses were not required to pay airfare:

> In the navy he was stationed all the way across the globe
> So, she said, "fuck it," took a trip
> She was tipped, spouses fly free
> Yolanda straight dipped.

The song then narrates Bambu's father's financial troubles, despite being in the navy, disappointing his mother's expectations of America told to her by missionaries in the Philippines. In an itinerant, migratory fashion, the song changes tempo, moods, and cadence in three distinct sequences that transition from funky-jazz, to slow-jam soul, and to Bay Area hip hop–hectic. "Moms" gives an unflinching exposé of his family's hard times in Los Angeles, which featured poverty, alcohol and drug use, and the murder of his cousin, lamenting the violent geography in which he was raised. Bambu's hard upbringing led to a life of crime and gang activity, resulting in him following his father's footsteps in joining the military. After serving six months of jail time for armed robbery, U.S. Marine recruiters literally waited for Bambu at his trial in order to enlist him.[57] Bambu narrates the shared role of violence in both gang and military life. In "Upset the Set Up," a frantic-sounding song featuring Atlanta-based African American rapper Killer Mike, Bambu recounts his transition from gang life to military service:

> I went from a street gang thang
> Then I joined the military fleet marine force thang
> From a little bitty gang in the south of Los Angeles
> To dragging bodies outta they house to help a government.

He points out the irony of gang and military recruits being asked to die to defend their homeland and hood: "Then we find out we gettin killed for a hood / And we don't own a single speck of dirt on that hood." Interpreted broadly, Filipinos' relationship to a "hood" (or home) in "Upset the Set Up" is multiple: is their home in the Philippines, the United States, Long Beach, or Bremerton? The theme of alienation from one's own hood—the violent geography which structures their life and death chances—reverberates in the geography of Filipino American culture. Bambu articulates the geographic displacement for Filipinos in the diaspora, where locations of home and hood are forged by U.S. military violence.

As a young soldier, Bambu became more aware of global racial politics. In an interview, he describes a revelatory experience identifying with the inhabitants of East Timor: "What it did was politicize me, especially when we went to East Timor, which is off the coast of Indonesia. There was a big conflict there and we went to support the Australians and these people [the Timorese] looked just like me. When I was a civilian without uniform, I remembered they'd double check my ID when I come back on base."[58] Here, Bambu may not define East Timor as home, but Bambu's identification with people whose country is a landing ground for U.S. Marines' boots illustrates how the military's global reach resonates with racialized people's otherness in the United States.

The military has had a commanding presence in Filipino American lives, demonstrating an awesome capacity to shape a domestic and global social order. As Shigematsu and Camacho note, "U.S. war waging has become an integral, if not naturalized, part of the grammar of these (im)migration narratives."[59] Geo and Bambu critique militarization's impact on displaced and vulnerable people. Their itinerant biographies as members of a militarized Filipino diaspora signify how currents of militarization situate their positionalities as imperial migrants displaced in their block, hood, or home.

"Back Home" in Empire

Off Blue Scholars' album *Bayani* (2007), which is Filipino for "hero," "Back Home" contributes to the Bush-era antiwar, pro-people musical canon for which the Blue Scholars are known. The Blue Scholars remind listeners in the predominantly white city that conditions are not equal in Seattle and people of color are seldom the beneficiaries of the region's technology boom or supposed cultural liberalism. "Back Home" provides an example of the duo's attempt to show the Emerald City's lesser-known underbelly by highlighting Seattle's racialized and militarized communities who live in spaces of local and global violence.

"Back Home" begins with a slow and steady kick-snare-clap. The song is laced with the croon of a woman's voice, almost weeping, responding to haunting punctuations of piano notes. The crawl of a piano chord interrupts a brief pause in the beat as Geo raps, "And it begins where we left. A brother chased after by death until he catches his breath." These words capture the song's elegiac, anguished sentiments that weave together the business of the U.S. military with the deaths of beloved family members. The music video for "Back Home," perhaps the group's most celebrated antiwar anthem, opens with Geo and the Scholars' beat maker Sabzi standing in a green cemetery, headstones surrounding the duo like a regiment of soldiers. The camera intercuts images of "everyday people," zooming in and out of their stoic faces as they hold up handwritten signs with words such as "Silence Is Defeat," "Struggle with Love," and "Justice." Mostly people of color, they also hold portraits of their absent family members—young men and women—who have fallen as casualties of war.

Accompanying this montage of images, the video follows the steps of a young Filipina American girl who walks through a variety of public spaces, including a school campus, a heap of rubble where a building once stood, and a sidewalk where a young Black man is splayed across a graffiti-painted wall as he is cuffed by a police officer. The girl passes an army recruiter in the school parking lot who counsels a young man, a scene that signals the overlap of educational institutions and the militarization of youths. Harkening to Bambu's upbringing in Los Angeles, Geo acknowledges the ubiquity of recruiters in certain neighborhoods: "So next time you see recruiters in your school or your crib / Tell 'em thank you for the offer but you'd rather you'd live / We got more than just our bodies to offer, so fuck a coffin." The girl acts as a witness to the conditions of her surroundings, which are interwoven with images of policing, neighborhood destruction, and a security state maintained by the recruitment of working-class youths. The camera returns to the girl's home, where at the doorstep she, her sister, and her mother embrace the girls' young father dressed in army fatigues deploying solemnly.

The video comments on the gendered positions among militarized subjects by reproducing the feminized roles of the girl as passive witness and the mother and sisters as inhabitants of the domestic sphere, or "back home." On the other hand, the young father occupies the masculinized role of the militarized yet expendable agent of the state. Geo begins his next verse: "And somewhere a soldier kissed his family goodbye / And he was walking like a warrior with water in his eyes / He left in late September, said he'll be back in July." As the family prays at the dinner table absent the male family member, Geo continues to narrate the fate of the girl's now-broken family: "Now the child is asking, 'Mommy, why did Daddy have to die?' / She says he fought for freedom but knows it's just a lie / Cuz her father was a veteran with benefits denied." Here, Geo references the long-standing scandal in which Filipino veterans who, as colonial subjects of the United States at the time, fought under the U.S. flag during World War II but were stripped of promised military benefits after President Truman signed the 1946 Rescission Act.[60] Many surviving Filipino veterans and younger generations of Filipino Americans continue to hold public protests in demanding a remedy and compensation for this act of injustice.[61] The music video reenacts the theme of "loss" signaled by protestors who grieve their veteran heroes' curtailed military benefits and robbed masculinity.

"Back Home" links the Filipino veterans' controversy, an earlier colonial moment of U.S.-Philippine relations, to current dramas in Filipino American militarization. The recruitment of young Filipino men on Philippine bases in Pampanga, Cavite, and Subic Bay preceded the practice of military recruitment in poor communities of color in the continental United States depicted in the music video. "Back Home," then, not only condemns U.S. militarization in contemporary contexts but also comments on the longer legacy of U.S. militarization in the Philippines. In the chorus, Geo chants,

Bring 'em back home
For my brothers and my sisters who been gone too long
We sing, bring 'em back home
And I don't wanna keep singin' this song.

The video's multiracial, seemingly immigrant cast of military families holding signs and portraits provides a mournful denouncement of the designed military pipeline for immigrants to achieve citizenship, but the Filipino American family grounds the video's critical message to the historical particularities of U.S. militarization's presence in Filipino lives.[62] The song concludes with the woman's singing voice becoming more prominent, trilling in a blues lament, mirrored in the video by the tragic conclusion to the Filipino American family's narrative: a military vehicle arrives to the family's home not bearing the girl's father, but a grave-looking, uniformed stranger approaching stiffly and cradling a letter. Grasping her heart, the young mother, as a helpless, female victim, wails and collapses on the doorstep before the soldier can utter the news of her husband's death.

Sadly, Geo had to "keep singin' this song." The Trump administration inherited President Obama's pivot to Asia, as seen in the mission Operation Pacific Eagle, which called for intensified U.S. antiterrorism efforts in the Philippines, bringing back "home" to the Philippines U.S. troops to U.S. empire's twentieth-century extension in the east.[63] And in June 2019 the USS *Montgomery* docked in Davao City, President Duterte's home city, as a sign of U.S. support against Chinese incursion in the West Philippine Sea.[64] With the signing of the EDCA, the location of home, which in the song represents a return to the continental United States (perhaps Seattle) where young troops won't die in combat in Iraq or Afghanistan, can now ironically refer to a return to Geo's ancestral homeland, where, along with the Caribbean, the United States began its overseas imperial project. The EDCA is a reminder that, for both Americans and Filipinos, "home" is in U.S. empire, spanning from manifest destiny to the endless global war on terrorism. Geo's chants of "back home," therefore, is not only a cry to bring troops safely back to awaiting families, but it also signals a return to an imperial center that continues to commit local and global violence on vulnerable people, a violence made visible by the murder of Jennifer Laude by U.S. Marine Joseph Scott Pemberton in Olongapo City in 2014 and by the integral role of U.S. forces in the botched Oplan Exodus assault on a rebel Muslim group in Mamasapano, Mindanao, in 2015.[65]

As "Back Home" visualizes, "special relations" occurring in America's overseas contact zones echo among militarized people on the continental United States who are vulnerable to military recruitment and state violence. Geo articulates cultural currents that are never static but constantly migrating in global imperial currents. The creation, circulation, and sustaining of a Filipino American hip hop vernacular owe much to the mapping of these contact zones, which produce culture not simply by virtue of these zones' localness, but also due to their locations in a global network found in Olongapo City, Subic Bay, Honolulu, Virginia Beach, Bremerton, and multiple homes elsewhere.

The next chapter begins where we leave off: Islam in the Philippines as a political symbol of resistance against U.S. military occupation. For many, Muslim Filipinos represent a kindred spirit of defiance against the encroaching violence of geography. Bringing attention to Islam in the Philippines recalls a history of geopolitics aimed at subduing Muslims' sovereignty and way of life in the region. As colonial subjects forcibly included into the U.S. colonial state, whereas the Spanish colonial administration allowed them a level of political sovereignty, Muslim Filipinos wreaked havoc against U.S. occupiers during the Philippine-American War, seeming almost bulletproof against U.S. weaponry. For many Filipino American hip hop artists, these Muslim warriors offer an alternative Filipino history in artists' efforts to recuperate and elevate anticolonial culture.

CHAPTER 2

"Civilize the Savage"

Toward Islam, Filipino Origin, and the Golden Age

Prologue: Sovereign Clash

On January 25, 2015, Philippine police commandos and six U.S. nationals conducted a botched raid dubbed Oplan Exodus in Mamasapano, a municipality in the Autonomous Region in Muslim Mindanao located in the Southern Philippines. The operation ended with the killings of at least forty-four commandos, four civilians, and eighteen rebels, including Zulkifli bin Hir, a bomb maker wanted on a $5 million U.S. bounty. The Mamasapano incident and a subsequent series of bloody encounters have displaced over eighty thousand people and jeopardized a landmark 2014 cease-fire between the Moro Islamic Liberation Front and the Philippine government seeking to end fifty years of regional hostility. According to bilateral defense treaties, U.S. military forces in the Philippines cannot engage in combat, except in self-defense. The U.S. embassy denied that U.S. forces participated in the operation except in helping to retrieve the dead. This denial contradicted reports of U.S. forces' "substantial" involvement, which included the funding and training of the operation, sightings of U.S. drones in the area prior to and during the clash, the presence of a U.S. Army helicopter after the incident, and the relinquishing of Zulkifli bin Hir's dismembered index finger to the FBI.[1]

U.S. special forces provided support two years later in Marawi as Philippine forces struggled to retake the city from Islamic State militants in a deadly battle lasting five months. Despite threats made by Philippine president Rodrigo Duterte to dissolve the U.S. alliance in favor of a possible Chinese military partnership, U.S. troops were on the ground during the siege to provide surveillance and technical assistance.[2] In Marawi, the largest Muslim city in the Philippines prior to the siege, the infrastructure was decimated and mass numbers of civilians were displaced. Two years after, recovery remained painstakingly slow as Duterte vacillated his public allegiance between the emerging regional power China and the former colonial power the United States, which, as we've already seen, maintained "special relations" with the Philippines throughout the second half of the twentieth century.

The Mamasapano and Marawi clashes offer a grisly reminder of U.S. military re-garrisoning of the islands. Despite the removal of U.S. bases from the Philippines in 1992, the United States steadily increased and sustained its military presence in its former colony.[3] The 1998 Visiting Forces Agreement, the 2014 Enhanced Defense Cooperation Agreement, and U.S. command in counterterrorism missions in Muslim Mindanao indicate an invited curbing of Philippine sovereignty and the Republic's acquiescence to foreign occupation. U.S. military support of operations in Mindanao represents the unresolved nature of sovereignty in the archipelago and the intricate and often violent negotiation of territory among competing power brokers. The Catholic-majority Republic of the Philippines, Islamic State militants, marginalized residents in Mindanao, and the militarized U.S. state have laid out the stakes of national self-determination in the region. This series of events, therefore, have put into relief the contested terms of national space in the Philippines. Much more, the historical and continuing presence of Muslims channels several centuries of Philippine cultural unease, with colonial orchestration (Spanish and U.S.) perpetually arranging who is and who is not welcomed in Philippine society. These events signify geopolitical antagonisms that continue to segment the Philippines.

My earlier analysis of military bases as contact zones laid the structural and material foundation of a Filipino American hip hop vernacular by observing the impact of militarization in the lives of Filipino American hip hop participants. U.S. military bases were important in facilitating the circulation of Filipino communities around the world, thus shaping the dynamics of Filipino American politics. In outlining hip hop culture's role in facilitating Filipino Americans' encounter with Islam and Muslims, this chapter keeps in mind U.S. militarization in the Philippines. Mindanao counterterrorism efforts reveal a return of the United States' century-long geopolitical interest in Muslim Philippines, with U.S. bases in the Philippines having provided the material conditions to make possible the clash between Moros and the U.S.-sponsored Philippine state. With media attention channeled toward U.S. affairs in the so-called Near and Middle East, the general public has remained largely unaware of the bloody encounters perpetrated by U.S. forces in the Philippines.[4] Through their spiritual, political, and artistic expressions,

Filipino American hip hop artists, however, have been steadfast in narrating the intricate and unresolved status of Muslims in the Philippines—from the era of Spanish conquest to Muslims' modern struggles for autonomy. In "The Rundown," Filipina American emcee Rocky Rivera forges a militant comradeship between Palestinians and Muslims in Mindanao: "Lick a shot for my people's up in Palestine, especially up in Mindanao, fightin for they way of life." Artists like Rivera are making known the presence of Islam in Southeast Asia, a recognition that yields expressions of political solidarity with displaced and marginalized Muslims worldwide. These artists offer a reminder: the past is never really past, and U.S. presence in the Philippines in recent times reiterates centuries-long colonial strife.

Filipino Emergent

In the 2007 flyer for the Mighty 4 hip hop competition held in San Francisco, a portrait of the late Filipino American graffiti artist Mike "Dream" Francisco is drawn next to the portrait of the late "Godfather of Soul" James Brown. The opposite end of the flyer shows Malcolm X. Malcolm's face is featured twice, looking up to the sky and peering down at the b-boy cipher happening in the center, where a circle of hip hop fans and dancers surround a single dancer. The flyer artist, Pres One, a Filipino American from San Diego, inserts the emblem of the Universal Zulu Nation, a pioneering hip hop cultural organization started in the South Bronx, New York. Above the cipher, and above an image of the Bay Bridge, Pres One depicts a crescent moon, a symbol of Islam. The Philippine flag is embedded in the Mighty 4 logo, which is positioned next to the words "carry on tradition" paired with a Black fist.[5] The Mighty 4 is an event started in 1998 by Paulskee, a Filipino American b-boy from Union City, California. The array of signs featured in Pres One's 2007 flyer assembles a hip hop cultural imaginary invoked at events like those organized by Paulskee.

Pres One's flyer illustrates how a Filipino American hip hop vernacular is shaped by a hip hop imaginary and spiritual areas of racial belonging. In particular, Islam in a Filipino American hip hop vernacular equips performers with a set of politics and embodiments responding to the violence of war in the Philippines and centuries of colonial degradation in the archipelago, offering Filipino Americans empowering and fulfilling modes of belonging. As postcolonial subjects with historically subordinate positionalities relative to Spain and the United States, Filipino Americans' longing for a different reality suggests a response to unacceptable subjugation. When Odessa Kane asks, "What's in a name?" in his song "The Pen and the Gun," the Muslim Filipino American/Chicano winner of the 2013 San Diego Music Award's

best hip hop album references the significance of naming/renaming in decolonial practices:[6]

> If we ain't met yet
> Let me introduce myself
> They call me Kane
> Father, husband, Muslim
> What's in a name?

Hip hop offers generous opportunities for fun and community building while
simultaneously inspiring cultural decolonization through self-creation. Hip
hop's cultural lexicons and political embodiments, therefore, empower Filipino Americans to reevaluate their very names and the category "Filipino."

Ironically, however, Muslims in the Philippines historically represent the
limits of Philippine national identity. In fact, the storied mistreatment of
Muslims in the Philippines suggests the failure of the modern Philippine
nation-state, which under earlier Spanish and U.S. governance operated on
the principle of pushing out or eliminating undesirable subjects.[7] At the tail
end of Spanish colonial rule, the Catholic Tagalog-speaking elite, including
Philippine national hero José Rizal, extended Spanish practices of othering
Muslim groups; this nation-aspiring elite cohort privileged Christianized
"Malays" as the authentic Filipino race and regarded Muslims as uncivilized.[8]
The Philippine elite's preference for a Christianized Filipino culture reflects
the linear Philippine national mythology of Europeanized progress, whereby
Spanish and eventually white U.S. contact inaugurated stages of Philippine
modern development. Despite predating the arrival of Europeans, for Rizal
and his peers, Muslims were deemed unfit for national representation.

For Odessa Kane and Pres One, Muslims stand in for a more redeeming
way of inhabiting history and the world. Filipino American hip hop performers' encounter with Islam and Muslims illustrates a longer authoring of the
terms of Filipino belonging that seeks a greater sense of dignity, sovereignty,
and civilization. In this way, Filipino American hip hop performances are
a sequel to the unfinished process of defining the "Filipino race," a project
undertaken by Rizal and his contemporaries. However, unlike the *ilustrados*
(the educated and nationalistic Filipino elite) of the late nineteenth century
who reinforced a form of European racial hierarchy by actively disavowing
Muslims, Filipino American hip hop participants offer a critical counter-
modernity that valorizes Muslims by utilizing hip hop's empowering racial
and spiritual language.

To demonstrate the ways in which Filipino Americans recuperate and reclaim these abjected members of the archipelago, I observe Filipino American

hip hop artists' both externally and internally directed politics, appreciating the fluid flow and mutual constitutions between these political directions. In terms of their externally directed politics, I focus on Filipino American hip hop performers' strident Third World, anticolonial identification with Islam. The nexus of anticolonialism and Islam is particularly inspired by the racial solidarity projects led by African American Muslims, the Muslim International's global anticolonial struggle, and Muslim resistance against the United States and the Philippine state. Next, in order to examine Filipino American hip hop artists' more internal explorations of Islam (their cosmological and spiritual considerations), I investigate the various usages of the term "golden age." Nostalgic golden ages represent a more desirable time and place, such as a precolonial Muslim Philippine past as well as an era in the late 1980s and mid-1990s, when Black radical politics were flourishing in hip hop. Because of its flexible and resonant utility, the golden age is a useful metaphor to illustrate a Filipino American hip hop vernacular's convoluted pathway to a revered Muslim community, whereby performers mainly encounter Islam not via Muslim Filipinos but through U.S. hip hop culture. Unlike their counterparts in the Philippines who "revert" (or return) to Islam because of their more proximate identification with Muslims in Southeast Asia, Filipino Americans' version of Islam is routed through U.S. Blackness.[9]

Filipino Americans are participating in what Su'ad Abdul Khabeer calls "Muslim Cool," which outlines the cultural and epistemological intersections of Islam, Blackness, and hip hop.[10] In very explicit ways, articulations of Islam in a Filipino American hip hop vernacular are largely indebted to a longer tradition of Black spirituality promoted by African American Islam and the Black Arts Movement. Through hip hop culture, Filipino Americans take up representations of Blackness to de-authorize the hegemonic codes of white life. Filipino Americans and African Americans' cultural pursuit of reclaiming spiritual dignity reveals these groups' shared "special fascination with history and its recovery by those who have been expelled from the official dramas of civilization."[11]

"For the Last 500 Years Been in a War": The Muslim International and Anticolonial Struggle

Bambu's opening song, "Make Change," on his 2008 album . . . *Exact Change* . . . features an excerpt of a speech made by Malcolm X. Malcolm as hip hop's "prophet of rage" epitomizes the album's message of consciousness manifested into action: "Once you change your philosophy, you change your thought pattern. Once you change your thought pattern, you change your attitude. Once you change your attitude, it changes your behavior pattern. And then you go on and do some action."[12] In the album, Malcolm, who appears again in the song "Spare Change," represents a militant voice on the eve of the election of President Barack Obama. In resurrecting the spirit of the slain Black Muslim visionary of the mid-twentieth century, Bambu calls for a more meaningful form of social activism rooted in Black radical protest, rather than found in the triumphant, multicultural liberalism sweeping the nation as the first Black president was ushered into the White House. For Bambu, Malcolm—not Barack—becomes the spokesperson for genuine social change. In evoking the metaphor of a knife stabbed into Black people's back, Malcolm's voice appears again on the opening track "Bronze Watch" on Bambu's 2012 album . . . *One Rifle per Family*, released at the dawn of President Obama's first term, proposing a provocative vision of national reconciliation. Malcolm suggests that progress can be achieved when the knife is first pulled out and we begin to "heal the wound that the blow made." He continues: "And they haven't even begun to pull the knife out, much less try to heal the wound. They won't even admit the knife is there." Even after four years of a Black president, Bambu suggests, the knife is still pierced inside the bodies of Black people, and perhaps in the bodies of other aggrieved groups. As a prophet himself forecasting the minimal impact made by the promises of candidate Obama in 2008, Bambu has been consistent in promoting a change in listeners' "philosophy." Like many other Filipino American hip hop artists, he in his own way implores his peers to change their "thought patterns" so as to "go on and do some action."

Islam in the African American Imaginary

Malcolm X's rebellious lyricism illustrates that alongside the protest found in Black radicalism has come the process of spiritual transformation among African Americans, with Islam as a cornerstone of Black affirmation and empowerment. The mid-twentieth century saw African Americans' defiant upending of their subordinate status in the United States, identifying with Black people and liberation struggles around the world, and, as Malcolm demonstrated in his global travels, connecting with a Muslim Third World.[13] Sohail Daulatzai writes, "Malcolm's role as iconic figure was a testament to the enduring political vision that he had crafted, for Black Islam in hip-hop culture reclaimed the interpretive authority over Black destiny in the United States and imagined a different community of belonging with very different possibilities for freedom, in which Black peoples would be seen not as national minorities but as global majorities." Daulatzai pioneers the task of situating Muslim emcees—such as Ice Cube, Gang Starr, Rakim, and Black Star—within a political context of Reaganism, the first Gulf War, and the war on terrorism. Hip hop, Daulatzai shows, connected to a global network of Muslims: "With the presence of Islam and Malcolm X, hip-hop culture became a powerful way to explore how its poetry, aesthetics, and political imagination not only forged a redemptive vision of Blackness in the face of the remixed racism of the post–Civil Rights era, but also a radical alchemy of art and politics that shaped and contributed to the nuances and textures of the Muslim International."[14]

Hip hop has been crucial in mediating earlier Black freedom cultural strategies into the contemporary period. Melani McAlister describes the construction of a new Black culture during the mid-twentieth century that included a search for "not only Islam but also renewed interest in the signs and symbols of pre-Islamic and traditional African religions (such as the Yoruba religion) as well as the study of ancient Egypt."[15] African Americans' exploration for a spiritual belonging precedes the cultural and political milieu of the mid-twentieth century, with the rise of the Moorish Science Temple in what Richard Brent Turner calls "the first mass religious movement in the history of Islam in America" in the early 1900s.[16] With distinctly African American racial language, such as the Asiatic Black man narrative, the Moorish Science Temple and its successor the Nation of Islam (NOI) wove together a fabric of a resistant Black worldview that continues to shape Black cultural ideology. African Americans' counter-spirituality and cultural projects of self-affirmation that turns to an abstracted and mythic "Asia" contributes to the counter-discursive politics of what Bill V. Mullen terms "Afro-Orientalism," which, among a number of features, is grounded in "the attempt by black Americans, from the origins of the Republic, to link with larger radical and revolutionary projects originating outside the shores of the American empire."[17]

African American cultural history also exhibits the ways in which counter-modernities often present convoluted imaginaries of spiritual home. Focusing on the practice of Islam among African Americans yields a counterintuitive historiography regarding African American Muslims' indexing of a genealogical, geographical, and spiritual home. In a 1970 NOI publication, the influential African American Muslim organization suggested that Blacks must relocate out of "uncivilized" places: "ignorance and savagery here [in the United States] and there in Africa must be removed and replaced with the modern civilization of Islam."[18] Instead of Africa, Asia became the root of

Black racial origin according NOI teaching. Preceding the NOI, the Moorish Science Temple of America and its mysterious leader Noble Drew Ali claimed even more grandiose racial origins for modern Blacks in the United States, who he believed were descendants of ancient Moroccans.[19] Felicia M. Miyakawa writes that the leader's teachings professed a more geographically spread Black origin: "According to Noble Drew Ali, the Moorish civilization at its height (around 1500 B.C.E.) extended from the area today known as Morocco to North, South, and Central America, encompassing even the mythical Atlantis."[20]

Islam became a transformative route of belonging outside of and against white imperial Christianity. Given that they can trace their Muslim heritage to some of the earliest of their ancestors who were forcibly brought to the Americas, African Americans claim Islam as their own, as "the Black man's religion."[21] African Americans became skeptical of Christianity, especially during a time of social upheaval in which the mantra of Christian brotherhood did not seem to work against violent, state-sanctioned white political revanchism.[22] More and more, Christianity was linked to Eurocentrism and global power domination and Islam became associated with a dark, anticolonial Third World. In 1962, James Baldwin wrote, "God, going north, and rising on the wings of power, had become white, and Allah, out of power, and on the dark side of Heaven, had become—for all practical purposes, anyway—Black."[23] The externalized political demands of what became Black Power in the late 1960s after Malcolm's death functioned together with the internal conversions of an empowered Black people.

Simultaneous to African Americans' political and spiritual reclamations of the mid-twentieth century existed the artistic imperative created in the Black Arts Movement. In this movement, cultural producers explored aesthetics of Blackness and at the same time attempted to find a radical break from whiteness and the west. Much more, the movement attempted to foment political action.[24]

While the smoke from the social upheaval smoldered in New York, hip hop was incubating in the ruins. Branching from the Black Arts Movement, hip hop took cues from Black Power, inaugurating a generation of post–civil rights sensibilities and politics. In 1973, Afrika Bambaataa formed the Universal Zulu Nation, borrowing language from the Nation of Islam and conforming it to the tastes of African American and Puerto Rican youth in the Bronx, which included gang culture, partying, and having fun. Daulatzai writes that "to many, hip-hop came to be seen as the torchbearer for the Black Arts Movement." Throughout hip hop's forty-plus-year history, especially during hip hop's golden age roughly between 1986 and 1994 when hip hop "emerged as an aesthetic, lyrical, and also thematic force," African Americans continued their cosmological explorations seen in the hip hop's bourgeoning cultural canvas.[25] Contributing to the "loop of Muslim Cool," an epistemological circuit of cultural reciprocity described by Su'ad Abdul Khabeer, Islam returned to drive the political tenor for a post–civil rights generation, becoming what would be called hip hop's official religion.[26]

For the most part, Islam's legibility in hip hop has been invisible yet present, with a documented sharp decline of Muslim rap parlance beginning in the late 1990s.[27] Hip hop hardly announces itself as Muslim music, perhaps partly because of some interpretations of Islam consider music haram or forbidden.[28] Another possible reason for Islam's hidden presence in hip hop is the esoteric nature of Black Muslim parlance as an appealing aesthetic. Islam has historically formed the cultural foundation of hip hop, but it also shapes hip hop's sensibilities through its mystique and supposed unknowability. The sparks of language on Islam in hip hop music, though, has been just enough for listeners to explore the faith on their own. As hip hop musician Usama Canon says, "that little spark was enough for me to take interest, and go study it."[29] On Islam's foundational yet somehow obscure role in hip hop, Daulatzai writes, "But if you peel back the layers (or barely scratch beneath the surface), that initial look of surprise will soon turn to awe. Because not only is Islam part of hip-hop culture, it's central to its very foundation."[30]

Syncretic Radicalism in Filipino Americanized Islam

As active participants in a Black cultural tradition inherited from Black struggle decades before, Filipino Americans in hip hop have also become participants in a political project of decolonial solidarity. Filipino Americans' identification with the radical politics of the Muslim International, such as Bambu's invoking of Malcolm X, points to the particularities of a Filipino American postcolonial quest for cultural and historical redemption. Filipino American poet, educator, and political activist Freedom Self-Born Allah Siyam credits the influence on his cultural and political consciousness of the album *Blowout Comb* (1994) by the hip hop group Digable Planets: "There is no other album that was comparable to the impact of *Blowout Comb* on my decolonization process. These thirteen tracks would be the soundscape that would accentuate my own journey from an *eighty-fiver* to one with knowledge of self through the lessons of the Five Percent and later anchoring my worldview in dialectical and historical materialism, the philosophical cornerstone of Marxism."[31] Similarly, in the song "Olmec Mask," whose title

references the African-like faces of ancient Mesoamerican monoliths, Odessa
Kane weaves Muslim internationalism together with revolutionary Marxism:

> I've sensed evil since preschool . . .
> You got me fucked up
> I don't play that, fool.
> Plus I'm Muslim
> I chill with them Arabs, too.
> I'm on some worldwide
> You sniffin pearl white
> What you ain't learn right?
> Went the wrong way at the turnpike.
> I turn spite into love
> I turn right to show up
> To turn the club into a revolutionary's gatherin.

At the same time that they seek belonging outside the boundaries of the
modern nation-state via Malcolm X's internationalism, Filipino American hip
hop performers like Siyam and Kane articulate an aspiration for a Marxist-
oriented revolutionary Philippine nation-state, thus upholding the primacy
and urgency of a Philippine national project. In this aspiration, their expressions expand Filipinoness to include otherwise disavowed Muslims in the
Philippines, thus collapsing Muslim Third Worldism, Muslim regionalism,
and Philippine nationalism in syncretic radicalisms that would otherwise
compete. For these artists, Muslims in the Philippines symbolize radical
people who contribute to "a reconfiguration of the 'Filipino' category as part
of struggles for national liberation in the Philippines."[32]

Siyam and Kane's introspective, spiritual examination and outward, radical manifestations of their Filipinoness find a peculiar precedence in the
anticolonialism of elite Filipino ilustrados of the late 1800s. Where Siyam
and Kane's processes of anticolonial self-making are spiritually and politically reinvigorated by Islam, the ilustrados' practice of corralling and in-
venting Filipino racial—and national—belonging was premised on religious
exclusion. As we've already seen, since the inception of the Philippines as a
Spanish colony, Muslims in the Philippines have represented an archetypal
Other; ilustrados took their cue and reproduced this Othering in their nation-
building project. Like their Spanish and ilustrado forebears, early U.S. Army
administrators treated Muslims as uncivilized savages. However, unlike their
forebears, after a series of violent and genocidal projects of "pacification"
in the Moro Province, the United States adopted a policy of forced inclusion of Muslim territory into their colonial statecraft. Where Spain granted

the Muslim Mindanao region generous autonomy throughout the Spanish colonial period and where ilustrados espoused an ideology of racial science that pushed Muslims and other non-Christian "wild tribes" outside of an aspirational Filipino modernity, U.S. colonizers regarded these groups as "special wards" of the state.[33] Deprived of a voice in Philippine national representation—whether through Spanish governance, through ilustrado nationalism, or under U.S. Army rule—Muslims' Otherness was attributed to their "uncivilized" nature.[34]

In the later phases of U.S. colonization, rather than overtly treating Muslims as subordinate wards, U.S. administrators and Filipino politicians feebly attempted to integrate Muslims and even "Filipinize" them into the Philippine colonial body politic by offering token representation in the National Assembly.[35] By 1930, after a process of "civilian-izing" members of the Moro Province, the defiant region formally became a part of the Commonwealth of the Philippines.[36] Muslim political affiliation, particularly in regard to the Muslim political elite, would continue to sway between cooperating with Manila-based Filipinos and the Americans during the U.S. colonial period. On top of post–World War II government policies that promoted Catholic Filipino settlement in Mindanao, the 1968 Jabidah Massacre, in which the Philippine Army executed Muslim recruits, sparked existing militant Moro groups to rise up and demand separatism and more autonomy. Soon after, Muslim ethnic groups would consolidate under the identity of Bangsa Moro, or Muslim nation.[37] However, continuing a strategy of cooperation, which secured the Muslim elites' social position, since the 1990s, Muslim leaders in Mindanao are content to receive millions in U.S. aid.[38]

Despite Muslim's fluid political affiliations, for radical Philippine-based non-Muslim nationalists during the 1970s, Muslim rebellion against foreign intervention "epitomized nationalism."[39] For these radicals, a recuperation of the Philippine nation via Muslims' refusal mythologized an anticolonial Philippine nationalist identity. If civilization for ilustrados and U.S. colonial administrators denoted the capacity for representation in modern nation building, then the extolling of Muslims by these 1970s Filipino nationalists overhauls the paired logics of civilization and modernity. The Philippine nation and the Filipino subject, then, are reiterated but resignified to fit nationalists' needs despite actual cases of Muslims' collaboration with U.S. administrators or Muslims' resistance to the Philippine state.[40] In Vicente Rafael's words, the Muslim-turned-Filipino "simultaneously acknowledge[s] and erase[s] the historicity of the term. [This] and other anachronistic usages of Filipino indicate the term's ironic origins, even as that irony is set aside."[41]

Filipino American hip hop artists, particularly those formally associated with Philippine left organizations, revitalize the Muslim-turned-Filipino discourse of their 1970s counterparts. The Philippine Other becomes the model for an alternative national subjectivity, one that, to repeat James Baldwin's words, symbolizes a non-European other who arrives "out of power" to offer an alternative future. For some artists, Muslims in the Southern Philippines embody a heroic, masculine, and martial nationalism, even if Philippine society represents a complex and pluralized battleground of national, linguistic, religious, and regional memberships, with Muslims inhabiting fluctuating positions between autonomy and state cooperation. Muslims in the Philippines have historically situated themselves within a Southeast Asian maritime network—a more localized and ancient Muslim International preceding Spanish conquest—constituted by a series of sultanates and *datus* governing regional trade.[42] The cultural legacy of this Southeast Asian worldview, with kinships exceeding and preceding the boundaries of the nation-state, continues to hold importance for Muslims in the region.[43] So, in a sense, when Rocky Rivera in her song "The Rundown" "licks a shot" (fire a bullet in the air) for her people in Muslim Mindanao "fighting for they way of life," she is right, but they just may be fighting for a *non*-Filipino way of life.

To be fair, some Filipino American hip hop artists may actually be in political alignment with Muslim autonomy or separatism in Mindanao, thus belying the Marxist-oriented, mass solidarity doctrine of the Philippine left. The vagueness or untroubled syncretism of their positions gives these artists poetic latitude in navigating and articulating the complex political landscape of the Philippines. Whatever the case—whether artists' expressions advocate for Muslim autonomy or Muslim-Filipino solidarity—the aggrieved but aggressive Muslim Filipino symbolizes a lauded anticolonial figure. The popular mythology of Lapulapu, who is credited with killing the Portuguese explorer Magellan and is thus considered the first Filipino national hero, perhaps best exemplifies the masculine and martial Muslim who rejects European religion and occupation. Rocky Rivera takes on a gangster, headhunting persona in her "Married to the Hustle" (performed under her former name, EyeASage), recalling the image of Lapulapu as nationalist-warrior:

> We invented guerilla
> A conquistador killa
> Ask that [expletive bleeped on recording] Magellan
> Got his head in my village.

Thanks in part to the discursive considerations of Moro anticolonialism, "Filipino" is given generous deliberation and critical exploration among hip hop artists. These artists critically evaluate the meaning of "Filipino"—in all of its contradictions—and in turn contribute to its epistemology. "Filipino," in essence, stands as a categorical fiction used for various purposes, as demonstrated by Rizal's Malay Filipino universality or by Filipino radicals in the 1970s. The unresolved contradictions and constant rewriting of "Filipino" opens rich opportunities for Filipino Americans to participate in their own self-authoring. As Filemino Aguilar observes, "the 'Filipino race' is an ambiguous, unstable, and even empty signifier."[44] In an effort to emphasize the modern construction of "Filipino" as attached to the emergence of Philippine nationhood, Rafael reminds us that "las islas Filipinas . . . existed for more than three centuries before there were any Filipinos. . . . A clear and undisputed fit between the Philippines and Filipinos is far from complete, and in fact, may never be realized."[45]

Interpellating bodies in the Philippines has always been anchored to the anticolonial meaning-making of national subjects. The practice of naming and renaming, then, is a significant and meaningful act for Filipino American hip hop performers who seek a postcolonial subjectivity, with Islam helping to generate the possibilities for an alternative cultural and political universe. Freedom Self-Born Allah Siyam, who officially changed his name, astutely illustrates:

I was given the name Arthur Gatcho Cupp at my physical birth. I took the name Freedom Self-Born Allah Siyam to represent my liberation or at the very least a lengthy process of unchaining the brain.

Freedom because I had learned that no one is free while others are oppressed, and through my discipline as an educator I intended on mastering the science of pedagogy to free the dumb, deaf, and blind. *Self-Born Allah* to indicate what year I got Knowledge of Self and the year I discovered that Allah was closer to me than my jugular vein, as stated in the Quran's Surah 50:16, and Psalms 82:6, and John 10:34. And *Siyam*, for Siyam is a Tagalog and Ilocano word for the number nine, and traces its origins to the Arabic word referring the third pillar of Islam, the practice of abstaining from iniquities, particularly during the ninth month of the lunar calendar, the holy month of Ramadan.[46]

Embedded in his new name, Siyam elucidates a linkage of Filipino languages and Arabic, a linkage that signifies his "looking back" as he refashions his spiritual future. In his interview with Yasiin Bey (also known by his former stage name, Mos Def), Daulatzai rightly recognizes the relationship between Muslim spiritual conversion and the act of renaming: "The act of conversion that you're [Bey] talking about holds such powerful meaning. Malcolm talked about it and the importance of the name change and the embrace of the 'X'—the unknown—and the refashioning of a new kind of self, particularly for Black people in the context of the United States."[47]

For Malcolm X (formerly Malcolm Little, and later El-Hajj Malik El-Sha-bazz), Freedom Self-Born Allah Siyam, and Yasiin Bey, their names reflect a defiant and empowering inhabitation of the world. Just as "Filipino" remains a sensitive and purposeful designation among various constituents, hip hop artists and religious converts respect greatly the weight of a name: the "what" of a person is inexorably sutured to the "who." When Odessa Kane introduces himself in "The Pen and the Gun," he is introspective in posing the meaning of his name and identity: "They call me Kane / Father, husband, Muslim / What's in a name?" In the song, Kane keeps the question open-ended and doesn't seek a resolved answer, allowing the categories to float. Of Frankie Quiñones's pseudonyms, journalist Quan Vu writes, "Originally, Quiñones created the name Odessa Kane by playing on the words *odyssey* and *cocaine*, presenting himself simply as 'a cat exploring the dope.' Now, with the help of his wife, he's transformed that into an acronym for 'ODE to Strength, Solidarity and Action.'"[48] Vu describes Kane's music as cultural weapons of political protest, especially given that his EP (extended play) is titled *Cuetes & Balisongs* (*cuete* is Spanish for "pistol" and *balisong* is Tagalog for "but-terfly knife"). As a cultural worker devoting his craft to political protest and liberation of the Philippines from foreign occupation, the article notes, Kane was organized into leftist Philippine political activity. In the article, Kane states, "we're still suffering as a result of foreign occupation in the Philip-pines."[49] For the emcee, identity and radical political action are paramount in his work. For Kane, militant Muslim autonomy and Philippine national radicalism converge, as it does in the works of his Filipino American peers. For example, according to the article, the cover image of *Cuetes & Balisongs* features a vintage photograph of Bangsamoro Muslim Fighters brandishing heavy weaponry. "Bangsamoro" refers to the region of the Southern Philip-pines that since the 1968 Jabidah Massacre has struggled for separation from the Philippines. If Kane intends to represent these Bangsamoro fighters as waging war against the Philippine nation, then the visual messaging of his EP would be discordant with a Philippine nationalist political agenda.

The "who" of Muslims in the Philippines, Kane reminds us, is not mono-lithic. In "The Pen and the Gun," Kane exposes the treachery of dynastic Muslim power brokers in Mindanao as he mourns slain journalists massacred by a leading Muslim political clan during an election held on November 23, 2009.[50] As "one of the deadliest single events for the press in memory" in

FIGURE 7. Cover of Odessa Kane's *Cuetes & Balisongs* (EP CD, Red Lotus Klan, 2014). Courtesy of Odessa Kane.

the Philippines, in which fifty-seven people were slaughtered, Kane demonstrates that those inhabiting a Muslim identity can still replicate and uphold structures of feudalism and disrupt goals for democracy in the Philippines. Sharing Kane's sentiments, Bambu vividly re-narrates this brutal episode in his song "Massacre." Kane, as well as Bambu, understand that structural change is in the hands of poor people—the masses—regardless of religion.

The anticolonialism embodied by Muslims in the Philippines, and more specifically those who are locked out of political power, symbolizes a radical hope for Filipino American hip hop artists. Moro resistance to initial U.S. colonialism, which by some accounts lasted until 1914—well past the official end of the Philippine-American War in 1902—emboldens nationalistic Filipino

Americans' charge of a protracted war against neocolonialism existing in the Philippines today. Through the syncretic radicalisms of Filipino American hip hop artists, Moros become Muslim Filipinos, patriotic warriors engaged in ongoing anticolonial struggle against past and present U.S. occupation in the archipelago. On the cover of Bambu's 2012 album . . . *One Rifle per Family.*, Los Angeles–based Filipino American graphic artist Manila Ryce visualizes the stakes involved in Moro struggle alongside the Philippine left. The picture centers a Moro family portrait, but with the gender roles reversed: the mother stands holding a gun, and the father sits holding the child. Ryce further explains: "in highlighting the underrepresented Moro struggle for liberation, the definition of what it is to be Filipino is broadened beyond Manila-centered conceptions to include more than just the paternally racist perception of the 'little brown brother' we too often embrace ourselves."[51]

For Manila Ryce, the Moro family invites a critical consideration of a larger Filipino national identity and resists U.S. racism in its redeeming of a more self-determining and masculinized Filipino subjectivity. With its reversal of traditional gender relations and communist inspirations, Ryce's portrait illustrates the power and militancy Moros encompass in a Filipino radical imagination that spans a long history of anticolonialism in the archipelago. Manila Ryce's Moro family is also reminiscent of W. E. B. Du Bois's African American portraitures in the 1900 Paris Exhibition, in which Du Bois attempted to depict post–Reconstruction era Blacks with confident dignity, challenging white revanchist stereotypes of Blacks as poor, uneducated, and inherently inferior.[52] The blankness behind the family stands out, which at once draws attention to the family but also alerts us to the starkness of the white canvas, as if the family is decontextualized and displaced. My second reading emphasizes the Moro family's anonymity, giving no evidence of Moro political space or identity, and making it difficult to conclude that the family is even Muslim. They could be seen as non-Muslim leftist rebels. But, the album's first song, "Bronze Watch," gestures toward the family's Moro link. "Bronze Watch" begins with an instrumental introduction featuring kulintang gong music, a musical tradition in Southeast Asia that precedes Spanish arrival and is associated with non-Christian communities in the Philippines, including several Muslim communities. The kulintang enters rapidly then melts into a 4/4 hip hop beat, at which point Bambu enters with a staccato rap style mimicking the gongs. The emcee recalls the recent killings of African American boys, exemplifying the political alliances forged by many Filipino American hip hop artists. Importantly, "Bronze Watch" concludes with the voice of Malcolm X commenting on our failures in social progress.

FIGURE 8. Cover of Bambu's album . . . *One Rifle per Family* (Beatrock Music, 2012). Artwork by and courtesy of Manila Ryce.

Moros recuperate erased colonial memory, animating a spirit of anti-im-perialism. In "Lookin' Up" by Bambu and Prometheus Brown (together as the group the Bar), Bambu delivers a tragic opus to a colonized Philippine condition. He opens his verse: "I'm from a place where the system's still feudal, and the masses still colonized." Countering this gloomy structural reality,

Bambu recalls historical Filipino heroics, alluding to the Visayan warrior
Lapulapu:

> It's the blood of the Visaya
> Where we never said "sire"
> Where the Spanish fought hard
> But the fighter never tired.

Bambu continues with a history lesson of Muslims' precarious sovereignty at
the dawn of U.S. colonial state-building in the Philippines. With the signing
of the Treaty of Paris in 1898, the United States annexed the Philippines from
Spain, including the Muslim South. However, under the Bates Agreement of
1899, the United States temporarily avoided war with Muslims. The agreement
promised a certain amount of autonomy in the region, including noninterfer-
ence with some Muslim traditions and local governance.[53] But soon enough,
the United States unilaterally abrogated this agreement and began bloody
military campaigns in the Moro Province. For Filipino American emcees,
Muslim martial resistance, such as Lapulapu's refusal to submit to Magellan
and Moro's sovereign intransigence, represents courageous anti-imperialism
in the Philippines.

Bulletproof Familia

For some Filipino American hip hop artists, the Philippine-American War
represents a permanent wound that, despite alluding to death, helps uplift
Filipinos' capacity to survive. War becomes a stitched into the Filipino condition. For example, in the Blue Scholars' song "Talk Story," Geo chants in
call-and-response, mimicking the litany-meditation of a Catholic novena:

> For my children's well-being, I declare war
> Hacienda Luisita, I declare war
> For the last 500 years, been in a war
> To make sure we don't have to see five hundred more.

In "Wounded Eyes," Geo uses "wounded eyes" to symbolize a condition
of permanent loss to reference war's requisite violence. This loss, though,
becomes a gift for the seer, who adopts a critical vision as a witness to the
truth in his trauma: "My wounded eyes seen through the lies / Many soon
to die. Who am I? / A student. I study to survive." Geo articulates the self-
reflective motivations of a postcolonial subject whose source of sustenance
is knowledge of historical trauma—war—and the seeking for a better future.
Slightly modifying his refrain, he later signals to a collective Filipino fate in

the face of trauma: "Many brutalize. So *we* rise / and fight for the future we strive." Geo ties together a shared Filipino condition both in the Philippines and in the United States by keeping the location (time or place) of trauma ambiguous, acting as a space and time traveler, a survivor with wounded eyes who witnesses multiple atrocities across generations and space. In the same song, he references the killing of up to one million Filipino civilians during the during the United States' invasion of the Philippines:

> They kicked in the door waving the four-five cal
> One million died, I survive, I reside
> Where the struggle and the hustle coincide
> At this moment in time, a shift in the tide
> Get the blindfold lifted from your eyes
> And see what we see and stop pretending it's alright, man.

Geo cannot "pretend it's alright" when American modern weaponry symbolized by the notorious Colt .45-caliber ("four-five cal.") helped commit Filipino mass death and perpetuate permanent war.

Given the memory of genocidal injury and militant resistance depicted in "Talk Story" and "Wounded Eyes," Geo and other artists imagine Moros as almost invincible Filipinos, whose bodies were able to withstand the onslaught of modern weaponry. The U.S. Army's use of the Colt .45-caliber is a recurring metaphor used by many Filipino American hip hop artists. The powerful weapon was issued for the U.S. Army for its campaign against Muslims who famously refused to die when shot by smaller bullets. As James R. Arnold writes, "An officer who had served in the Indian Wars remarked, 'Even the veteran Indian fighters . . . had to learn that a Moro *juramentado* ["running amuck" in a suicidal attack] was more dangerous than a renegade Apache and twice as hard to kill.' Stories abounded about incidents such as the one in which a juramentado fought for five minutes, struggling and slashing the whole time, in spite of his fourteen bullet wounds, including three to the skull. Such incidents led to a reevaluation of the standard American handgun, the .38-caliber revolver."[54] For Filipino nationalists, the need for the U.S. Army to upgrade has come to represent a warrior-like Filipino resilience. Tellingly, in Seattle the newsletter of the Filipino leftist group Anakbayan is named 45 Kaliber Proof. The weapon is a staple metaphor for many nationalist Filipino American hip hop artists. For example, in "Married to the Hustle," immediately after Rocky Rivera alludes to Magellan's beheading, she raps, "They invented a bullet, couldn't take us down." Furthermore, in Blue Scholars' "Commencement Day," a cautionary tale to students who graduate from school without knowledge of their history or social conditions, Geo drops the name of Anakbayan's newsletter: "Ay yo we made it / 45-caliber proof / And your teachers don't believe that you can handle the truth." Here, the Colt .45 carries two possible meanings: "We" are bulletproof Filipinos who defiantly "made it" despite the United States' technologically upgraded genocide. Or, in another interpretation, "we" are "proof"—living evidence—of such an atrocity. Whatever the case, Filipinos—here including Moros—"made it" through an episode of death and are present now to testify the "truth" of their survival. For Geo, the condition of Filipino death and survival is substantiated by Muslim pacification. The concept of the "modern" Filipino, then, is constituted by the death of savage Muslim bodies and the necessary technological upgrade in the application of the U.S. Army's gratuitous violence.

Bambu's "So Many" also names Muslims as Filipinos in revolutionary struggle and comments about Philippine wars resulting in the spreading of the Filipino diaspora. The song begins with a "white girl voice" repulsed by the overwhelming amount of Filipinos "here." Despite (white) abhorrence to a stifling Filipino presence, Bambu proudly includes himself in a larger community of Filipino belonging: "The whole Philippines, mi familia, so I fight, *we* fight / Had to come up with a bigger gun to kill us." The bigger gun used to "kill us"—the Colt .45—points to an originary crisis that initiated a series of transformations to a larger Filipino *familia*, such as the migration of Filipinos set in motion by a U.S. colonial infrastructure promoting warm body exports of "so many" Filipinos. For Bambu, U.S. genocide against "us" enables a legacy of Filipino struggle: "From a country where the revolution still fightin . . . I'm Filipino than a muthfucka." In "So Many," Bambu visualizes an abundance of Filipino life—however repulsive to some—that at its origin was determined by a moment of death.

Return to the Golden Age:
Gods, Devils, and Filipino Origin

While some Filipino American hip hop artists express a militant, outwardly politicized reverence of Muslims in the Philippines, as shown earlier in this chapter, other artists have sought Philippine Islam as an internal spiritual resource in their process of Filipino self-authoring. In the Mustafa Davis–directed documentary *Deen Tight*, DJ Raichous, a Filipina American DJ from San Diego who converted to Orthodox Islam, explains her parallel journey as a DJ who digs for records and found her "original" religion in Islam: "The search for the record is the digging experience. And it's that whole journey that you went through to look for it, which is what is the essence of a digger.

And parallel to that was my journey to Islam because I learned about digging for your heritage. And I also learned that the original religion in the Philippines was Islam." *Deen Tight* presents a traditional interview-based documentary exposé and features Muslim American hip hop artists, revealing the hidden history of Islam among the descendants of African Americans and Filipino Americans and Islam's importance for self-reclamation in the here and now. For the interviewees, hip hop is essential to exploring their spiritual belonging. DJ Raichous's appearance is unique: she is only one of two women interviewed in the film, the only woman who is visibly Asian, and the only one to wear a hijab that covers her head, neck, and shoulders. Raichous's scenes expose her multiple layers of alienation and disassociation: although Islam is seen as an Arab domain, she is Filipina. She practices hip hop, a form of U.S popular culture, but Islam, in its more modest versions, seems distant from the spectacle and sonics of hip hop. She discloses: "It's difficult when they associate Islam so much with Arab culture when you're in American culture. And you're just trying to get the skeletons of the religion and apply it to a different body." As if visualizing to the alienation of her "different body" as a non-Arab and as a Filipina living in the United States, the film juxtaposes Raichous, peering downward, together with the U.S. flag, suggesting their inherent discrepancies. Scenes where she wears both the hijab and DJ headphones visualizes another possibility, as the seeming visual disassociations melt away while Raichous defiantly asserts agency in being hip hop, Filipina, Muslim, *and* the controller of the dance floor. As the documentary explains, according to some versions of Islam, playing music and many kinds of dancing are considered *haram* (forbidden), yet Raichous fully embraces and enjoys the sounds and spaces of hip hop and plays the role of party controller. Raichous exemplifies the negotiation of Filipino Americans' self-narration, iterating Khabeer's "loop of Muslim Cool," with hip hop operating as a key cultural resource to exploring a more preferred Filipino sense of history and spirituality.

The spiritual conversions (or what is sometimes called "reversion") to Islam by Raichous and her mentor, DJ Kidragon, who is Filipino American and also featured in *Deen Tight*, challenge the cultural and spiritual supremacy of white imperial Christianity. This "looking back" is a defiant and self-affirming reorientation of one's soul, which, as elaborated earlier, was a cultural strategy enacted by Black Americans throughout the twentieth century. Similar to Black Americans' embrace of a reimagined genealogy to the Tribe of Shabazz, Egypt, or Atlantis, Raichous's traces her ancestral belonging to a nostalgized pre-Hispanic Philippines. Pre-Hispanic Philippines did host a strong Muslim presence as part of a Southeast Asian Muslim maritime network, and

Raichous's claim of Islam as the Philippines' "original" religion points to a desire to connect with a Philippine civilization preceding several centuries of western cultural and material genocide. However, homogenizing Islam as the "original" religion casually disregards the complex and multitudinous spiritual practices abundant in pre-Hispanic Philippines.

Furthermore, in interpellating otherwise contested bodies in the Philippines as Filipino, Raichous, along with her nationalist Filipino American counterparts already mentioned, reinforces the sentiment that "Filipino" can be delimited according to geopolitical boundaries. The Philippines as a geography—be it colony or nation—has only become intelligible after Spanish and U.S. colonialism constructed its geographical borders. The Philippines is a modern construction, with the Americans establishing its boundaries more rigidly than the Spanish.[55] Therefore, DJ Raichous's "originality" contradicts the genesis of "Filipino" contingent on its colonial context. Vicente Rafael writes: "The Filipino nation did not emerge as the return of a glorious past that had been repressed by an alien invasion. Instead, it was precisely the coming of outside forces that allowed for its genesis."[56] In her search for Filipino authenticity, Raichous, then, disregards the constructed history of the Philippine nation. Ironically, José Rizal and his ilustrado peers invented a Philippine nation that categorically excluded Muslims.

Raichous's parallel journey—digging for records as a hip hop DJ and digging for her Filipino heritage—proves instructive. Instead of a "looking back," I propose it is more useful to think of Filipino American hip hop artists' reclamation of Islam's supposed historical and spiritual authenticity as a "looking around," or, to use Theodore S. Gonzalves's term, a looking "laterally" instead of literal historical reclamation.[57] Or, as in Raichous's wording, their glancing toward Islam involves a *parallelism*. Filipino American hip hop performers' lateral or parallel looking around situates hip hop as a crucial cultural conduit to exploring postcolonial spiritual and cultural possibilities.

A Preferred Golden Age

To help unpack Filipino American hip hop performers' intricate glances toward Islam, I evoke the concept of the golden age to refer to a temporal and spatial preference that provides a sense of nostalgia and redemption, like Raichous's admiration for a precolonial Muslim Philippines, Latinos' embrace of Muslim Andalusia, or African American Islam's turning to Asia as a spiritual homeland. The golden age also recalls a moment in hip hop history between the late 1980s and mid-1990s when the genre supplied listeners with an abundance of racial empowerment and politically radical knowledge.[58] For example, a song that nostalgizes a more desirable era in hip hop is "I Used to Love H.E.R." by the popular hip hop artist Common, who is Muslim. Released in 1994, the song sexualizes hip hop as a woman who loses her pure, authentic, Afrocentric ways as she is corrupted by the commercial hype of West Coast gangsta rap. The Filipino American hip hop group the Native Guns also nostalgizes this same hip hop era. In their cheery retrospective "1995," the Native Guns mark the year 1995 as a formative moment for their Los Angeles–textured hip hop golden age. In the song, the duo recite a litany of hip hop artists who influenced their styles and political consciousness. Starting his verse with a nod to Biggie Smalls's signature hit "Juicy" (also a retrospective song), Kiwi raps,

> It was all dream, I used to read URB Magazine
> When it was made of newsprint and it was still free.
> I would turn it to page three
> Table of contents, interview with KRS and Chuck D.

Excavating a golden age discourse clarifies the ways in which a Filipino American hip hop vernacular operates in a non-linear, networked trajectory in its routing Filipino American self-narrations through African American counter-narratives. African Americans and Filipino Americans are diasporic people displaced by the mechanisms set forth by white imperial plunder, forcefully suspending their links to spiritual or civilizational home, throwing their spiritual belonging in flux. Richard Wright elucidates a similar dynamic in his concept of being "split" as a Black person "of the West": "This double vision of mine stems from my being a product of Western civilization and from my racial identity, long and deeply conditioned, which is organically born of my being a product of that civilization. Being a negro living in a white Western Christian society, I've never been allowed to blend, in a natural and healthy manner, with the culture and civilization of the West."[59] So too, then, have African Americans followed a nonlinear path to spiritual belonging. Wright's contention that he cannot "blend, in a natural and healthy manner" to white civilization directly summons the host of spiritual, political, and artistic cultural strategies employed by African Americans to imagine themselves as members of a larger global and cosmic community, as inheritors of a glorious golden age prior to or outside of white imperial plunder. As people of "double vision" being *of* western civilization only because of their disavowal *from* it, African Americans have been actively pursuing counter-narratives that bring dignity and futurity to their bodies with a particular glance toward Islam and the "East."

Filipino Americans also signify a counter-modernity that defies the cultural authority of white civilization, with Islam helping to reorder the status quo of global and cosmic power relations. Yasiin Bey refers to Muslim
conversion as "reversion" given that Islam teaches the concept of *fitrah*, or
the "a state of oneness that Muslims believe all humans are born into." He
explains: "[We] are coming back and reacquainting ourselves with ourselves.
And so I think, in that essence, 'revert' is a proper term. And it is also a conversion, a transformation. But it's not a departure from yourself. It's really
a full integration of your highest self. And actually, even beyond the self,
you know?"[60] Like Bey, Filipinos in the Philippines have been undertaking
a reversion process. Unlike Bey, for Filipinos in the Philippines, the roles of
African American spiritual figures like Malcolm X and Islam in a hip hop
cultural imaginary in their reversion process is less evident. These are key
differences between Philippine-based reverts to Islam and that of Filipino
Americans. Called the Balik Islam movement in the Philippines, Filipinos
from the archipelago who share a nation space with Muslims and become
familiar with Islam as overseas contract workers in the Middle East "return"
to what they see as the Philippines' dominant religion prior to arrival of
Spaniards. Vivienne S. M. Angeles elaborates: "Balik means 'return', and
'Balik Islam' means 'return to Islam'. This notion of return stems first from
the belief that Islam, which means submission, is the first religion of man
and second, from the fact that Islam was already a dominant religion in
the Philippines before the coming of the Spanish colonizers in 1521. . . . The
converts had been taught and are very well aware of this historical information. They understood therefore that being Balik Islam Muslims means
taking part in this return to their original religion."[61] Instead of Philippine
precolonial religion, for Filipino Americans, hip hop culture typically directs
their pathway to Islam. In this way, their reversion resonates with Yasiin Bey's
spiritual journey, in which hip hop culture, and Black vernacular culture
in general, inaugurates a self-transformation and a connection to a larger
Muslim community. The "balik" or "return" for some Filipino Americans
may eventually involve a spiritual return to Islam in the Philippines, as with
Raichous, but for the most part, the "balik" for Filipino American reverts is
a loop through Black spiritual redemption.

The Digital Martyrs, originally composed of brothers Scotty and Darnell,
are also reverts to Orthodox Islam who locate themselves in Islam's expansive
spiritual and cultural world. The Oakland-based hip hop artists are part of
a transnational network of Muslims and are anchored to a community of
African American Muslims in the East Bay Area of Northern California.
The Digital Martyrs seek to act as catalysts of greater Filipino American

FIGURE 9. The Digital Martyrs' *Ballad of the Bullet* poster. Courtesy of Darnell Mirador.

representation while promoting Islam in their lyrics and art.[62] Filipino American graphic artist Jeffrey Miciano designed the promotional poster for their mixtape *The Ballad of the Bullet*, a title that evokes Malcolm X's famous speech "The Ballot or the Bullet." The spired and arched architecture of the building depicted on the poster suggests traditional Muslim architecture, which in the context of Philippine colonial history can offer a substitute to the Spanish Catholic churches that dominate the architectural terrain of the Philippines.[63] The edifice on the poster, then, can be an ode to the mosques in the southern region of the archipelago, standing in to reclaim a Philippine civilization from Spanish spiritual and material hegemony. The moon logo at the top, designed by Darnell, mimics the iconic Muslim crescent (as seen in the Mighty 4 flyer), but is stylized to resemble the Philippine national flag's eight-point sun. Embedded in the moon is the Muslim shahada in Arabic, "There is no god but God, Muhammad is the messenger of God."

Golden Ages from Al-Andalus to Southeast Asia

The spiritual revivals of Raichous, Kidragon, and the Digital Martyrs trouble the long arc of Philippine national identity, the archipelago serving as a battleground of European anxieties of a Moorish takeover. Cultural productions in Spanish colonial Philippines narrate the necessity of Muslim death in order to promote Catholic Philippine life. Spanish theatrical *comedia* in the Philippines, which has shaped the aesthetics and ideology of Philippine film, was built around themes of conflict between Christians and Muslims in Iberia.[64] Manila, colonial Philippines' spiritual and commercial center, was established as a Catholic stronghold, with Santiago Matamoros (Saint James the Moor-Slayer) adored as the city's patron saint. To this day, Santiago Matamoros's heroic slaughtering of Moors in Iberia is immortalized in stone above Fort Santiago in Manila's Intramuros district. Santiago Matamoros as a symbol of Christian reconquest of Al-Andalus (Muslim Spain), which flourished as a political entity in Europe between the eighth and fifteenth centuries, exemplifies an ideological battle for the spiritual reputation of Spain (and by extension, the west). This anti-Muslim sentiment passed from the Spanish to elite, nationalistic Filipinos. As we've already seen, ilustrados deemed Muslims as essentially not Filipino. The ilustrados decided that the *indios* who were endowed with modern capacity were from culturally Hispanicized linguistic groups, such as Tagalogs and Ilocanos.[65] U.S. authorities during early U.S. colonial occupation designated Muslims in the archipelago as wards of the state and later as collaborators of convenience.[66] More recently, exemplified by the Oplan Exodus fiasco, the contentious relationship effectively continues between the U.S. military–abetted Philippine state and the marginalized Muslim regions. Raichous and the Digital Martyrs' modes of Muslim reclamation of the Philippines subvert this deep-seated anti-Muslim sentiment in the islands. These artists help symbolize a revival of a golden age of Islam in the Philippines, and concomitantly in Spain (Al-Andalus). For them, the Muslim villains vanquished underneath the hooves of Santiago Matamoros's horse are no longer the evil Philippine or Spanish Other.

Filipino Americans' strategic identification for something more "golden" than their present and past Filipino historiography cites a more antagonism fomented by the consolidation of fifteenth-century European identity through the conquest of the dark Other. Daulatzai poignantly notes: "For it was through the Muslim that the modern concept of race and its structuring of national identity was born. As Europe and the idea of 'the West' began to cohere around concepts of whiteness and Christianity, race and religion deeply informed each other."[67] It makes sense, then, that Filipino American hip hop artists resituating their relationship to the Philippine nation coincides with a community of Latin Americans and U.S. Latinos who are also reconfiguring their position in the world and revising the terms of their Hispanicization. The mythical golden age of Islam in the Philippines that thrived prior to and without the dominance of the west is echoed in discourses that extol the period of Muslim rule in Spain. Al-Andalus has become a symbol of a more desirable past for some Latin Americans and Latinos in the United States.[68] Cuban nationalist José Martí's declaration "Let us be Moors!" in 1893 is just one of a series of calls for Latin Americans to revere and revalue their Spanish Moorish past.[69] Cultural globalization scholar Hisham Aidi states that "Moorish Spain was a place where Islam was in and of the West, and inhabited a Golden Age before the rise of the genocidal, imperial West."[70] Latino reverts' (including Latino hip hop practitioners') spiritual anchoring to Al-Andalus defies the historical authority of Spain and the west.[71] The trope of the golden age is thus a meaningful signifier for formerly colonized Spanish subjects, where a spiritual home is rooted to a non-Hispanic past.

In addition to its impact among Latin Americans and U.S. Latinos, a revised Iberian genealogy has significance in the retelling of Philippine colonial mythology. Notably, Isaac Donoso Jiménez opens the possibility of Muslim Iberian migration to the Philippine archipelago after their expulsion from the Iberian Peninsula in 1609. He writes, "in the end it is probable that the first European who reached the Philippine archipelago was not an Iberian Christian, but an Iberian Muslim." Hence, in order to legitimize their colonization, the "discovery" of the existence of Muslims in the archipelago for Spanish conquerors shifted the war with the "enemy" from the Mediterranean to Southeast Asia by linking Muslims in the Philippines to those in Iberia.[72] It seems, then, that along with bodies, war migrated from Europe to the Southeast Asian archipelago. Thus, a consideration of Al-Andalus not only provides a reimagining of a more "golden" Iberian past, it also probes questions regarding an epistemology of Philippine settlement and the beginnings of Spanish antagonism against Muslims in the archipelago. Whatever the case, Raichous and the Digital Martyrs imagine an alternative possibility of a Philippine past, which concomitantly reconsiders the imperial role of Europe in the subjugation of Hispanicized colonial subjects.

Hip hop remains a dominant mode of exploring a more desirable golden age of Filipino belonging, but a romanticized Philippine Muslim past appears in other Filipino American cultural forms. In the extravagant Pilipino Culture Nights along the West Coast and their variants throughout the nation, Muslim-designated Philippine dances—often grouped in what is called the Moro suite—are usually the choice dances among Filipino American college and high school performers. Barbara Gaerlan argues that this preference for the Moro-themed dances stems from students' desire to embody the myth of Moros as regal, proud, civilized, and unconquered by the Spanish. She notes that for these dancers, the Moro suite represents a "kind of 'Golden Age' of Philippine independence on which Filipinos everywhere can look back with pride."[73] Islam as metonym for culture supplants the "impurity" of colonial heterogeneity found in the vague designation "Filipino culture." Overall, from Spain to Latin America to the Philippines, Islam represents a more desirable inhabitation of history and the world that was permanently shaped by the primal antagonism fomented by European racism against the dark, Muslim Other.

The Asiatic Black Man Meets the Truer Asiatic

This unsettling of imperial Europeans' temporal and geographical determination of colonized people's lives is indebted to African Americans' much longer tradition of spiritual and cultural redemption through Islam. For African American Muslims, the golden age trope also venerates a more glorious culture than what is offered by Europeans but is more capacious in its geographical imagination than in the Iberian and Philippine contexts. For example, as already mentioned, Noble Drew Ali's mythology of Moorish civilization took in lands on both sides of the Atlantic and even encompassed the mythical Atlantis. Asia occupied an increasingly central valence in claims to Black civilization for African American Muslims, who expanded a Black spiritual home beyond Africa and embraced a global geography that connects with the Muslim Third World.[74] During the early twentieth century, the biologically inferiorizing term "negro" lost credence in African American self-identification. Richard Brent Turner notes the founder of the NOI's disowning of "negro" in exchange for Black's "original" identity: "[W. D. Fard] preached that the word 'negro' was a misnomer for the people of the Black African diaspora; this name was created by the white race to separate African Americans from their original Asiatic roots."[75] Helping create a racial-spiritual combination of "Asiatic-Blackness," Fard preached that African Americans were "lost members" of the "original Black nation of Asia, the Tribe of Shabazz." Similarly, the boxer Muhammad Ali once stated on a radio show: "I am not a Negro. . . . I am Muhammad Ali. . . . And I am an Asiatic Black man."[76]

The trope of the Asiatic Black man pervades in hip hop music. The hip hop soundscape, especially during hip hop's golden age of the late 1980s and early 1990s, was textured by the lessons of the Five Percent Nation of Gods and Earths, which practices an esoteric numerology and teaches that Black men are the embodiment of God. Some scholars trace the Five Percent Nation's cosmology to the Moorish Science Temple of America and the Nation of Islam; Five Percent Nation founder Clarence 13X was an NOI follower.[77] Rap became an essential medium to spread Five Percenter knowledge, especially given the simultaneous rise of hip hop and the Five Percent Nation in New York City during the 1970s.[78] Commenting on the NOI's influence on the Asiatic Black trope, Daulatzai writes: "The NOI redefined and expanded Black identity beyond the United States and in relation to the Third World, using terms such as the *Asiatic, Asian black nation, Afro-Asiatic Black Man*, and the *Asiatic Black Man*, all of which echoed [early NOI leader] Elijah Muhammad's claim in his seminal text that 'we are descendants of the Asiatic black nation . . . the rich Nile Valley of Egypt and the present seat of the Holy City, Mecca, Arabia.' As a result, the Nation of Islam 'provided an alternative to—and in some sense a fundamental critique of—the nation-state.'" Asia in Black Islam was popularized by golden age–era hip hop artists such as Big Daddy Kane, Gang Starr, Brand Nubian, the Wu-Tang Clan, and Rakim who referred to themselves as "original Asiatic Black men."[79] "This is Asia, where I came," raps Rakim in his song "Casualties of War," which criticizes Operation Desert Storm in the Persian Gulf. Golden age hip hop artists promoted older golden age mythologies.

Given the widespread usage of the Asiatic Black trope beginning in the early twentieth century and continuing with hip hop music today, the role of Asian people becomes curious in the racial-spiritual world of Black diasporic Islam. During World War II, the former leader of the NOI, Elijah Muhammad, advocated the side of the Japanese imperial army: "The Asiatic race is made up of all dark-skinned people, including the Japanese and the Asiatic Black man. Therefore, members of the Asiatic race must stick together. The Japanese will win the war because the white man cannot successfully oppose the Asiatics."[80] As has been demonstrated, Black identification with Asia intertwines with claims to civilization with a rising imperial Japan operating as an embodiment of Asian power that rivaled white global hegemony. Recalling Bill V. Mullen's Afro-Orientalist discourse of racial solidarity, African Americans' political and spiritual remapping of Asia thus often privileged an orientalized and re-masculinized vision of an abstracted and mysterious Asia, of which more powerful Asian hegemonies inhabit the Asiatic paradigm.[81] Asians, representing an "oriental decadence" threatening the west mentally and corporeally, provided a more desirable embodiment for a rivaling Black sense of being, whose ascribed primitiveness only offered physical peril.[82]

For Filipinos, membership within a threatening Asiatic civilization has always been scrupulous, especially given the archipelago's long and intimate legacy with the west. Under Spanish and U.S. governance, Filipinos have rarely been categorized as embodying "oriental decadence" but were rather marked as a deficient race in need of white salvation and tutelage. However, in the beginning of the twentieth century after large-scale Chinese and Japanese migrations to the United States, Filipinos were deemed members of a "third Asiatic invasion." During this period, they became associated with, even if only tangentially, to the racial markings of Asiatic, Oriental, and Mongolian, especially when it came to the their legal and extralegal rights and limitations as U.S. nationals in the context of labor and sexual competition with white men.[83] Even during this period, Filipinos' racial mixture and ambiguity tended to relegate them in special racial categories including Malay, brown, and a combination of Negro and Mongolian, all of which posed legal ramifications for citizenship, naturalization, and rights to sexual access.[84] Hence, given Filipinos' proximate racial distance from "Asiatic civilization" in a broad sense, the cognitive convolution becomes entangled as the "Asiatic" in Black Islam meets the savage "Filipino." Filipino American hip hop performers arrive at Islam via Black Muslim counter-narrative, which in turn exalts Asia—specifically the Arabian peninsula—as the origin of Black civilization. Some versions of Filipino Americanized Islam, then, requires a compartmentalized disregard for the Orientalism of Black Islam with which Filipino Americans may not identify: the original Asiatic Black man emerged not from Southeast Asia but from the Near and/or East Asia. At the same time, Filipino Americanized Islam, with its foundation in hip hop, is indebted to Black spiritual redemption. As we've already seen, for some Filipino American Muslims this intricate cultural pathway has led to a cultural solidarity with Philippine Islam and a veneration of a precolonial golden age in the Philippines. "Asiatic civilization" for Filipino Americanized Islam in this case *is* located in Southeast Asia.

As Elijah Muhammad held an expansive and flexible view of who is to be considered "Asiatic" in his racial pairing of the Japanese and the Asiatic Black man, some Filipino American hip hop artists issue syncretic interpretations of Black Islam's spiritual and political subjects. The group MastaPlann playfully re-signifies Elijah Muhammad's Asiatic Black discourse by assuming True Asiatik Tribe personae.[85] MastaPlann is composed of Filipino Ameri-

cans from California who gained fame in the Philippines after emigrating
there in 1992. As golden age–influenced artists, they identified with Five
Percent hip hop, especially Rakim Allah, whose famous lyrics in the anthem
"Paid in Full" begin with "Thinkin of a masta plan." As Filipino Americans,
MastaPlann recirculate the tropes of the "Asiatic" both to reaffirm Asiatic's
vernacular validity and also to elaborate on its invented currency. As such,
the Filipino "Asiatic" moves beyond Filipino racial categorization as Asian
by fusing with NOI and Five Percent racial worldviews. The True Asiatik
Tribe illustrates the circuitous identificatory practices of a larger "tribe" in the
Filipino diaspora. As supposedly "truer Asiatic" people, Filipino Americans
arrive at the intersection of the vectors that make up a history of U.S. racial
anxiety: the "East" and U.S. Blackness.

Original People from the East

As Asiatic can carry meanings of Blackness, Asianness, and racially insurgent
embodiments, being "original" can also register a multiple set of racial possibilities in hip hop. For example, in recounting his journey of political and
spiritual consciousness, Siyam explains his study of "original people" in the
consciousness-raising group "360 Nation":

> I loved these folks from the jump, for they were humble and thoughtful
> people, dedicated to improving their spiritual lives through the study of
> original cultures and pre-colonial spiritual traditions. Through brother
> G-Hod Amen in the Central District, I learned a lot about Kemet, what
> black Africa's Egypt once was called, and was introduced to a number of
> influential writers of black history and or spiritual traditions of black people.
> . . . We also studied Santeria, Voudoun and their African roots in Ifa . . .
>
>   In 360 we studied and shared what we learned through thoughtful ob-
> servation and diligent study. We built, we meditated, we improved our
> ways and actions. We studied pre-colonial Africa, pre-colonial North and
> South America, and I tried to get my hands on anything about pre-Spanish
> Philippines.[86]

Here, Siyam demonstrates the ways in which "original" can include a range
of colonized people, such as those of the Philippines. "Original," then, in the
contexts of both Elijah Muhammad and Siyam's epistemology, as well as in
Raichous's Muslim reversion, symbolizes a buried but rediscovered sense
of being.

Correspondingly, for Geo, the "knowledge of self" pedagogical principle
of the NOI, Universal Zulu Nation, and the Five Percent Nation reverberates
soundly. Reiterating the words of Nation of Islam founder W. D. Fard, Geo

writes: "Filipinos are also [of] a 'lost-found' nation—robbed of our nation-hood and livelihood by the same people who robbed the Africans and the rest of the world. . . . With no knowledge of who we are and how we came to become an oppressed, nationless diaspora, we have no hope of fighting imperialism."[87] In his twinned call to knowledge of self and anti-imperial political action, Geo designates the Philippines as a nation-yet-realized, thus readopting an Afro-Orientalist "lost-found" nation in Arabia/Near/ Middle East to the Philippines—perhaps more poetically than spiritually. In "No Rest for the Weary," Geo's rhymes excavate—and write—a Filipino "knowledge of self":

> Igniting the cipher sessions I'm deciphering life,
> Blending both theory into practice.
> I write vernacular and actual fact
> God, no posturing.

Geo suggests that intertwined with divine reflection is a project of knowing. "Actual fact" in Five Percent vernacular stresses that God and knowledge is not mysterious but can be found and claimed "right here" on earth. "Actual fact" informs Geo's critical pedagogy of Filipinos' "true" history amid the lies of the colonizer.

Geo, who is not a Muslim revert but takes artistic liberties in his poetics, crafts much of his lyricism utilizing the rhetoric of the Five Percent. In Five Percent "actual fact" philosophy, Black men are referred to as Gods and women as Earths. In poetically embodying God in his lyrics, Geo inscribes onto his Filipino body the African American inversion of a savage status to a masculine divinity. In the song "Opening Salvo," Geo again evokes this God-savage inversion, accompanying his re-divinity with a critique of colonialism: "Right now I want to thank God for being me. My soul won't rest until the colony is free." And in "No Rest for the Weary" he says, "But this song ain't a psalm waiting for God to answer / Brothers call me dog, they got the letters backwards. I'm back with a plan of attack to repossess my name, face, and history." Continuing in "Opening Salvo," Geo articulates the link between his artistic motivation and the liberation of the Philippines:

> 1896 revolution incomplete
> Silence is defeat, my solution is to speak
> Resurrect the legacy of martyrs I beseech
> Time to choose a side: It's the mighty verse the meek
> My big brother Free brought the word from the East.
> We're the bullet in the middle of the belly of the beast.

In the verse above, Geo alludes to the group Sentinario ng Bayan and its mobilization of Filipino Americans in the mid-1990s through the remembrance of the 1896 Philippine Revolution against Spain. Extending the revolution to a contemporary moment in the Filipino diaspora, he references Freedom Self-Born Allah Siyam, who traveled to the Philippines (the "East") and returned with the message that Filipino Americans must be militant elements ("bullets") in the center of U.S. empire (the "beast"). In evoking the Philippines as the "East," Geo craftily borrows from Black Islam's reconfiguration of Asia—the "East"—as spiritual home.

For Siyam and Geo, the NOI and the Five Percent Nation provide essential resources for signifying a Filipino decolonial political imaginary. Starting off as poets in the Seattle-based group the isangmahal arts kollective, whose motto proclaimed "subverting cultural genocide," Geo and Siyam sharpened their craft within a Filipino American space that embraced heterodox and experimental imaginings of Filipinoness. Reminiscent of the renegade aesthetics associated with the Black Arts Movement of the late 1960s, isangmahal and a number of other Filipino American poetic spaces nurtured during the late 1990s such as the Balagtasan Collective and L.A. Enkanto in Los Angeles and 8th Wonder in the San Francisco Bay Area would form cultural and political foundations for many Filipino American hip hop artists.[88]

Seattle's Filipino American poetry scene would breed one of the city's most recognized emcees in Geo. The *Blue Scholars* album—a sonic document composed of antiwar Bush-era anger, hip hop golden age boom-bap nostalgia, indigenous Filipino soul meditation, Third World rage, and Seattle street soliloquy—has anchored Geo's poetics throughout his career. *Blue Scholars*, compared to Geo's subsequent albums, articulates a more internal and urgent reflection of spiritual orientation.[89] Grounded in a strident critique of the intersections of Christianity and white colonialism, Geo, like many other popular Filipino American emcees such as Bambu, Kiwi, Rocky Rivera, and Bwan, envision a position in the universe that goes against the white racial values often found in the imagery of Christianity.

Filipino Americans' formation of artistic spaces such as isangmahal demonstrates how Filipino Americans' are direct beneficiaries of the Black Arts Movement and inheritors of a longer lineage of African American spiritual and political consciousness. Echoing the poetics of the Black Arts Movement, hip hop's poetic canon brings into relief earthly and divine values assigned to racialized people. The poles designating "savage" versus "civilized" and "devil" versus "god" that reverberate in hip hop's poetics, especially abundant in Five Percent rap where certain white people are described as "the devil" and Black men are uplifted as God, illustrate the stakes involved in an imagined cosmic encounter. Much as Islam has represented for African Americans a self-affirming counter-civilization that rivals the claims of white modernity, Islam serves as a resource for many Filipino American emcees and poets in their critique of white colonial religion. In the anticolonial and Five Percenter–tinged song "No Rest for the Weary," Geo condemns the hypocrisy he finds in the civilizing mission of white colonizers in the Philippines and perhaps beyond: "They claim civilized with they animal ways."

Filipino American hip hop performers' internal meditations that "redefine what is meant to be divine," to use Geo's words from his song "Burnt Offering," follow a larger tradition of African American counter-modernities that form the spirit of hip hop culture. In "No Rest for the Weary," Geo traces the migratory pattern of an itinerant Filipino American spiritual vernacular: "From the East, my brotha, we came / The lessons might change, but the essence / Of the message is the same." As Asia has offered a more expansive spiritual and geographic home to a redemptive African American universe, hip hop has provided the resources with which Filipino Americans use to reevaluate their sense of belonging—moving from savage children of empire to dignified, original people.

Conclusion: Racial Consciousness in a White Wilderness

In "Talk Story," Geo identifies the antagonists responsible for his colonized and displaced position:

> Who got the guns and the gold?
> Who left us out in the cold?
> White wilderness I travel while in search of my own
> That's why I'm flippin a poem like it was written in stone
> It's for the children seekin answers to the question of home.

The knowledge of self directive he espouses by "flippin a poem" is motivated by the erasure of home perpetrated by plunderers with the guns and the gold. In the white wilderness of the imperial metropole, Geo searches for his *own* sense of belonging. Earlier on, at the brink of Philippine nationhood in the late nineteenth century, José Rizal and his ilustrado contemporaries attempted to answer the question of home and their "own." Desiring membership in civilization by using European modernity's racial logic, the ilustrados claimed a venerable noncolonized Filipino origin and embodiment. A century later, as children in empire, Filipino Americans have been reimagining their natal membership. However, unlike their ilustrado counterparts, they are embracing alternative modernities that perform a critique of a world ordering that mark them as uncivilized in the first place. Filipino American hip hop performances present aesthetics and affinities for new Filipino American subject making, which hold the possibilities for otherwise hidden or perhaps unimaginable alliances among aggrieved, marginalized, and targeted groups.

For over forty years, hip hop in general has been a principal venue for asserting a politics of historical refusal, with Islam as a primary cosmological language for several generations of African American hip hop artists, such as Public Enemy, A Tribe Called Quest, De La Soul, the Wu-Tang Clan, Erykah Badu, Jay Electronica, and Queen Latifa, just to name a few. Filipino American hip hop performers are active participants in contributing to the meaning making of Filipino national and diasporic identity and are redefining the terms of national belonging by critically glancing backward as they move forward. Just as important, they make public the largely overlooked history of Muslims in Southeast Asia and the entrenched presence of the U.S. military in the Southern Philippines. Filipino Americans' representations of Islam and Moros remind us of the plight of Muslim people around the world and the unfinished quest for national sovereignty in the Philippines, a precarious quest seen in the grisly Mamasapano clash.

With the technology to erase bodies, culture, and nationality, U.S. colonizers wielding big guns subjugated people in the Philippines. In light of this death and violence, Filipino Americans travel the white wilderness, continuing a legacy of embracing a language that provides "proof" of white hegemony, that forces us to "even admit the knife is there," to recite Malcolm X. Filipino American hip hop artists are revising the hegemonic terms of Filipinoness, redeeming their savage bodies as civilized and divine and recuperating otherwise disavowed Muslims as historical agents.

The next chapter examines Filipino Americans' participation in and contributions to Afrofuturism, a genre that foregrounds Black people in science fiction imaginaries. Like Islam, Afrofuturism is a prominent aesthetic and epistemological feature in hip hop. Unsurprisingly, both Islam and Afrofuturism were vital intertwining elements in early hip hop culture. The themes of creating counter-modernities and reclaiming lost histories reverberate into my next discussion, which observes what I term Afro-Filipino futurism, a cultural practice that playfully restores Filipino American bodies as alien, robot, and divine.

CHAPTER 3

Nation in the Universe

The Cosmic Vision of Afro-Filipino Futurism

It's for the kids who parents' workin overtime
And for the Filipino kids who gone travel time.
—The Bar, "Barkada"

Comrades of the Future

In Bambu's music video "Comrades," the Filipino American emcee from Los Angeles plays the role of a lone itinerant in a postapocalyptic forest.[1] On a dangerous quest to deliver a sacred book, Bambu must contend with a deadly assassin (played by Filipino American b-boy RJ "KoolRaul" Navalta) and a weaponized drone. Produced, directed, and edited by Ra, "Comrades" offers a healthy mix of the martial arts vagrancy of Morgan from the AMC zombie series *The Walking Dead*, the drone patrols from the 2013 dystopian film *Elysium*, and the stealth of a futuristic Harriet Tubman, altogether overlaid with lyrical messages of service-worker proletarian woes and Third World border crossing. The music video exhibits aesthetic practices in what I call Afro-Filipino futurism, a genre inspired by the cultural tools and artistic inertia established in African American speculative imaginaries prevalent in hip hop culture. Filipino American performances in hip hop, such as Bambu's video, provide themes of alienation and displacement associated with centuries of colonialism in the Philippines. Afro-Filipino futurism can help imagine expansive aesthetics that envision a redeemable or preferable Filipino position in the world and universe.

The video for "Comrades" exemplifies a version of Afro-Filipino futurism that promotes political action through social movement. At first listen, the lyrics of "Comrades," which describe a range of topics such as the triumph of the Arab Spring and labor issues, do not seem to relate to Ra's visuals. Bambu's verses narrate his solidarity with an exploited Filipino worker who copes with drugs and a displaced Mexicana migrant who invites Bambu to an activist meeting. The last seconds of the song loop the chant "hands up, don't shoot" from the rallies in 2014 that called national attention to the killing of African American teen Michael Brown at the hands of a white police officer in Ferguson, Missouri. For Bambu, this collage of social actors come together in collective comradeship. In the "Comrades" chorus, he says, "I am down to rally, I, I will call you family / Cuz I will take a bullet for my comrade, gladly." What threads "Comrades" vignettes together with Ra's video is a theme of brooding neoliberal state power over vulnerable residents—Filipino, Mexicana, African American, and Arab—who resort to various strategies of resistance and survival. Drones, which figure in both the video and the song, reference a hellish mechanized and militarized future that has been unfolding recently as seen in deadly U.S. drone attacks in the global war on terrorism in the Middle East and in lesser-known campaigns in the Southern Philippines.[2] Drones, then, link Bambu and his comrades through their shared condition of surveillance and disciplining, whether conducted by multinational corporations, the military, or the police. At the conclusion of the "Comrades" music video, Bambu surrenders with his hands up as the drone finally corners him. As Bambu turns in surrender, he slings a weapon hidden along his wrist, destroying the hovering machine. Looking through the eye of the damaged drone, the camera falls to the forest floor, helplessly witnessing Bambu's escape. Through quick thinking, martial skill, and patient determination, Bambu delivers the book—filled with pictures of comrades and perhaps tales of hope and plans of victory—to a woman, who shares a prayer with the emcee and looks up to the sky, embracing the treasure.

"Comrades" highlights hip hop's capacity to creatively unhinge practitioners and viewers from the burdens associated with a colonized past. Yet, the song's incitement of action in ongoing social movements is not a strict requirement for Afro-Filipino futurism, much in the same way that hip hop (as a musical or dance genre) has never been expected to follow "proper" principles in social justice campaigns. Just as hip hop culture can be unruly, Afro-Filipino futurism can break the codes of political propriety in its embrace of the funky and otherworldly. For instance, drones also appear in two Filipino American music videos I analyze in this chapter; in these videos, the drones appear to be less associated with the imperatives of a political movement. In the music video for Hopie's "Space Case," tiny clay animated UFO drones hover around and abduct Hopie. The quirky UFOs are not mali-

FIGURE 10. Bambu attacks a weaponized drone. Screenshot from Bambu's "Comrades" music video (Ra, 2015).

cious; instead, they endow the emcee with superhuman abilities and fugitive knowledge. In *Wave Twisters*, a "nerd-boy," comic book–themed animated film based on DJ Qbert's album by the same name, massive drone squids are operated by Filipino American DJs; here, Filipino Americans are insidious, scratching records to activate the squids' flame-throwing attacks, destroying an entire city and imperiling the heroes. The varied representations of these drones—as instruments of the police state, friendly gift givers, or monstrous cephalopods—demonstrate the multiple ways in which Filipino American hip hop artists exhibit and embody their politics.

I begin by showing the multiple political valences in Afrofuturism that illuminate alienation and speculative modes of belonging. In doing so, I offer a historically grounded interpretation of Afro-Filipino futurism as an aesthetic inspired by centuries of white domination that could otherwise be dismissed as merely whimsical. Next, I examine Filipino American leadership in the Universal Zulu Nation (UZN), a hip hop culture organization that has shaped key hip hop aesthetics and praxes over the past forty years. Echoing themes present in my study on Filipino Americans' historical reclamation through Islam, I make the case that the cultural recovery signature to the principles of UZN motivates Filipino American hip hop artists' decolonial and place-making practices. Next, I observe DJ Qbert and the

Invisibl Skratch Piklz's (ISP's) record scratches, communicative practices, and visual worlds as contributing to a larger African American decolonial cultural repertoire. Finally, I interpret Hopie's music videos "Space Case" and "Solar Systems," which I argue introduces a more sophisticated version of ISP's Afro-Filipino futurism. I show how Hopie's exhibition of superhuman and intergalactic consciousness comfortably coexists with feminism and Filipinoness. Bambu, UZN, ISP, and Hopie articulate the multiplicity of cultural politics within Afro-Filipino futurism—a playful and strategic symbiosis of ethnic memorialization and its abstraction into outer space.

Alienated Races

In the VH1 documentary *Finding the Funk* (2013), director Nelson George acknowledges the contributions of Larry Legaspi, who popularized the space-age costumes worn by African American funk artists: "The thing about funk is it embraced freakiness, outsiderness. . . . So you have a gay Filipino man, unheralded in a sense, but is essentially a part of creating the look of funk in the 70s."[3] The universe of funk music and style exemplifies a continuation of a longer lineage of Black aesthetics and philosophy in Islam and jazz that has always explored alternative and counter-routes of Black origin and destiny. The legacies of jazz and funk musicians Sun Ra, Miles Davis, John Coltrane, Parliament Funkadelic, and Earth, Wind, and Fire travel in the universe of more contemporary Black musical forms, such as techno, R&B, and hip hop. The designs of Legaspi anticipated the "freakiness" and "outsiderness" espoused by African American hip hop artists less than a decade later. Funk's costuming, fashion, record sleeve art, drum patterns, and musical samplings would continue in the diverse expressions of Afrika Bambaataa and the Soul Sonic Force, Queen Latifa, X-Clan, Public Enemy, the Digable Planets, Outkast, Kool Keith, Missy Elliot, 702, Janelle Monáe, Flying Lotus, Ras G., and countless other hip hop and R&B artists.[4] Beginning in the 1990s, young Filipino Americans would become prominent participants to these "freaky" and "outsider" aesthetics in what would be called Afrofuturism. Many Filipino American hip hop performers have been inspired by Afrofuturist aesthetics and, like Legaspi, are contributors to Afrofuturism as a genre. Filipino American beatmaker Mndsgn's 2016 psychedelic music video "Cosmic Perspective" epitomizes this deep engagement. A remixing together of Sun Ra's musical teleportation and the ecstasy of an African American church service, the music video depicts a preacher calling forth a congregation of worshippers (including Ras G., Mndsgn, and other musicians) toward a miniature glowing pyramid.[5] The followers, robed in dazzling Afrofuturistic attire, boogie down the aisle toward the pyramid to be transported to another dimension. Mndsgn's ethereal, distorted voice sings,

> You need to find a new direction
> Still navigating through
> To find the right way
> You might need a cosmic perspective.

Filipino American hip hop artists, along with their African American counterparts, have been shifting their musical aesthetic directions to a "cosmic perspective." Mndsgn's music underscores Filipino American hip hop performance's indebtedness to the aesthetics and politics of a Black American cultural imagination. In focusing on Afrofuturism, I build on my examination of Filipino American hip hop performers' creation of counter-modernities through Islam. Ytasha L. Womack describes the genre as "an intersection of imagination, technology, the future, and liberation," which in some cases "offers a total reenvisioning of the past and speculation about the future rife with cultural critiques." In 1994, Mark Dery first used the term "Afrofuturism," ushering in "the serious study of cyberculture and gave a name to the technoculture trends in Black America."[6] The 2018 Marvel film *Black Panther* perhaps best exemplifies Afrofuturism in its most spectacular, financially lucrative, and mainstream form.[7] Since the 1990s, Afrofuturism has been celebrated as a beloved cultural domain for "Black geeks" drawn to science fiction, outer space, and alternative historiographies of Black people expressed in literature, film, music, and other forms of popular culture. For Black geeks and Black cultural producers, these fantastical worlds open important avenues to examine historical traumas, critique current social conditions, and imagine solutions for a more just tomorrow. Kodwo Eshun notes: "Ongoing disputes over reparation indicate that these traumas continue to shape the contemporary era. It is never a matter of forgetting what it took so long to remember. Rather, the vigilance that is necessary to indict imperial modernity must be extended into the field of the future." Alienation echoing from the past into the future is a recurring theme in Afrofuturism that aims to "indict imperial modernity." Specifically, the alien stands in for very real social positions that can be traced back to the trans-Atlantic slave trade. Eshun credits W. E. B. Du Bois's concept of double-consciousness for providing an early model for understanding the trope of alienation: "Afrofuturism uses extraterrestriality as a hyperbolic trope to explore the historical terms, the everyday implications of forcibly imposed dislocation, and the constitution of Black Atlantic subjectivities: from slave to negro to coloured to evolué to black to African to African American."[8]

Inspired by Afrofuturism, I use the term "Afro-Filipino futurism" to help us understand alternative worlds as they relate to a Filipino American racial imagination. Afro-Filipino futurism seeks to give proper respects to Black imaginative culture while illuminating a Filipino historical condition shaped by Filipinos' exclusion or suspension from modernity. Filipino American hip hop artists are instrumental in excavating Filipino subalternity and futurity. Infantilized for centuries by the Spanish and then categorized as savage and primitive during the early years of U.S. colonial administration (illustrated in the chapter 2 discussion on the redemptive power of Islam), the colonized Filipino body has been persistently disparaged as devoid of history and culture.[9] By proposing worlds beyond this world, Afro-Filipino futurism "indicts imperial modernity," to repeat Eshun's words, with imperial modernity represented by four centuries of Spanish and U.S. colonial subordination of Filipino bodies. This proposal thus opens the opportunity to consider an Afro-Filipino resonant historical location in empire and, in turn, shared decolonial imaginaries. Furthermore, in its funkiness, Afro-Filipino futurism muddies "proper" Filipino political subjectivities, such as subjectivities that only valorize leftist radicalism or nationalism. Afro-Filipino futurism, therefore, invites more expansive and collaborative vantages of Filipino subalternity.

The outlandish, alien, and creative community formations of Filipino American hip hop cultural performances respond not only to the civic politics of U.S. racial exclusion but to elusiveness of a popular and durable mythology venerating a precolonial Filipino civilization. These performances, as such, propose alternative genealogies, modernities, and futurities that help outline a process of ongoing Filipino cultural decolonization. These responses contrast the visionary but problematic mythologies of elite Filipino intellectual culture of the late nineteenth century. As illustrated in chapter 2, inspired by European racial taxonomies, Hispanicized Filipino ilustrados embraced Europeanized versions of Filipino civilization for racial self-validation, expelling non-Christianized and darker-skinned Filipino ethnic groups from an aspired Philippine nation. Afro-Filipino futurism, on the other hand, seeks unorthodox routes of identification by detouring away from conventional (and colonial) categories of humanity. The figure of the extraterrestrial alien becomes an alternative and redemptive embodiment in Afro-Filipino futurism, thus rerouting the nationalistic ilustrados' proclivity to approximate Filipinoness to Europeanness and Christianity. Afro-Filipino futurism allegorizes a narrative of decolonization not inspired by historical allegiances to modernity or nationalism. It proposes outer space and the universe as "home" rather than the Philippine nation, whose sovereignty (although briefly palpable after the Spanish period) had been curtailed by a half century of U.S. colonialism and ongoing U.S. neocolonialism evident in the perpetuity of U.S. military presence in the archipelago. Afro-Filipino futurism reroutes Filipinoness from the Philippine nation, from which Filipino Americans are geographically dislocated (being American) and about which they are nationalistically ambivalent (as postcolonial subjects). If national identity affords diasporic people a sense of cultural and racial origin, serial colonialisms in the Philippines compromise a coherent diasporic subject making; this compromise in subject making, of course, is on top of the "wild heterogeneity" of the Philippines as an archipelago home to various religions, languages, and ethnic groups.[10]

A genealogy of Filipino presence in the United States needs to recall its origins in U.S. racial conquest, legalized apartheid, and sexualized violence against Black and brown men. As this book's introduction discusses, for the first half of the twentieth century, both African Americans (as second-class citizens) and Filipinos (as colonial subjects) juggled paradoxical positions in U.S. society as receivers of white racial uplift and sexualized violence.[11] Agricultural interests competing with imported Philippine products combined with the flow of Filipino migration led to the successful passing of the 1934 Tydings-McDuffie Act, which curtailed Filipino migration and changed the status of Filipinos from nationals to aliens. The act was largely motivated by white revanchist political organizations committed to combatting the threat of Filipino males who entered the United States relatively freely as colonial subjects and who dared mix with white women.[12] With the Tydings-McDuffie Act as legal precursor for separation, the Philippines was granted independence in 1946. Yet, in its postcolonial period, the two independent nations continued a neocolonial relationship that ironically increased the number of Filipino migrants to the former colonial metropole. Filipino American hip hop performers of the late 1980s to the early 2000s were largely children of Filipino navy men and professionals migrating to the United States during the 1960s and '70s, a period not even a generation removed from official U.S. colonialism in the Philippines. Afro-Filipino futurism's unconventional decolonial aesthetics enact important cultural labor in exploring the memory of colonialism experienced by Filipino Americans' recent ancestors. In Afro-Filipino futurism, strange worlds and extraordinary modes of intelligence flow from a history of racial domination.

Reading the alien and cosmic themes of Filipino American hip hop performances as part of an Afro-Filipino futuristic aesthetic practice places these performances within hip hop's Afrofuturistic imaginary. But, Afro-Filipino futurism can be considered distant kin to genres of Philippine and Filipino American speculative fiction and science fiction in the visual arts and performance. "Filipino futurism," though, is not a popular descriptor for the latter genres.[13] Oliver Wang coined the term "Filipino-futurism" to describe Filipino American DJs' fascination with "spaceships, eight-armed extraterrestrials, and other figments of science fiction" serving as an "alternative discourse that compensates for the absence of race."[14] Referring to the ISP, Elizabeth H. Pisares nuances Wang's proposition by pointing to the Filipino American cultural infrastructure available for these DJs amid "racial isolation and hierarchy" and ISP's articulation of their Filipino heritage. Harboring a social condition of racial erasure and misrecognition among Filipino Americans generally, as Pisares shows, these DJs function as imaginative bricoleurs in patching together a creative language of racial belonging. She writes that Filipino Americans "must become as agile with the existing racial discourses as their DJs are with recordings from different musical genres to create a language for themselves."[15] So, instead of simply being regarded as an "absence of race," the fantastical worlds created by artists like ISP should be appreciated for their versatile capacity to signify race.

Antonio T. Tiongson Jr.'s study on the deracialization of hip hop among Filipino American DJs, including that of ISP and other Filipino American DJs from the San Francisco Bay Area, provides an important intervention in understanding the problems of liberal racial discourses in the post–civil rights era. His criticism of some hip hop performers' perpetuation of the problems of color blindness rightly illustrates that one's participation in hip hop does not necessarily mean one values hip hop's Blackness or Black people. Filipino American DJs' self-narration, Tiongson contends, "are generally oriented toward the future and outer space in contrast to that of African Americans."[16] My analysis reconsiders such a "contrast" by offering a reminder of African American cultural producers' fixation on the future and outer space and by appreciating Filipino American hip hop performance's versatile capacity to signify race, including outer space. DJ Qbert, for example, designs his interviews to be overtly facetious and even sarcastic. In an interview with Roderick N. Labrador, Qbert compares his role as a DJ to theater:

> Well, it's theater. . . . If you want to be a character that is a Filipina/o character, that's fine. But make it the best you can be. If you want to be a clown up there, if you want to be a gay rapper, do whatever you want. If you want to be the naked rapper, that's fine but there needs to be some skills. It's all theater. People don't see it as that they're up there as an actor. We're up there performing a character. But if you're an actor, you need some skills, too. You can be whoever you want to be. It's your stage.[17]

For Qbert, being Filipino, naked, or gay is theatrical—they are flattened as
equal categories of identity performed on stage. His interview underscores
both his defiant evasion of identity and his awareness of performance as a
practice, an unruly but illuminating understanding of racial identity (or
nonidentity) that betrays the signifiers of identity observable in his sonics
and visuals.

Bambu's postapocalyptic comradeship, Filipino American leadership in
the UZN, the freaky sonics of ISP, and the extraterrestrial communion of
Filipina American emcee Hopie exemplify the ways in which Afro-Filipino
futurism reconstitutes race as a key cultural politic. Afro-Filipino futurism at-
tends to the dynamic and capacious orientations of Black vernacular culture,
actuating the future and outer space as vital imaginaries. The historical fact
of colonialism in the Philippines may have forged a geography of subordination and domination in the archipelago for four centuries. But since the
end of the twentieth century, Filipino American hip hop performers have
been articulating alternative claims to belonging by situating themselves as
members of an intergalactic universe whose presences exceed the strictures
of imperial geographies and consciousness. Afro-Filipino futurism provides
a stage to enact a sense of cosmic justice, or the reparation of cosmic injuries.
According to U.S. Secretary of State John Hay in 1904, the march of U.S. imperialism into the Pacific and the Caribbean represented a "cosmic tendency."[18]
By embracing a cosmos that is full of affirmation and life, a different kind
of "cosmic perspective," Filipino Americans' creative representations revise
the violence and death associated with Hay's idea of colonial inevitability.

Interplanetary Rock from the Boogie Down

In a party flyer from the early 1990s, the artist DJ Rhettmatic of the world-
renowned turntablist group the Beat Junkies portrays three Cerritos-based
Filipino American hip hop luminaries—graffiti artist Rich One, graphic artist
Eric Sanford, and DJ Rhettmatic—in an Afro-humanist style reminiscent
of De La Soul or A Tribe Called Quest. While Sanford sports a peace sign
pendant, Rich One and Rhett display their UZN emblems. Surrounding
the trio are shout-outs to a compilation of popular hip hop acts who share
a pro-Black, Afro-humanist message. As West Coast youths, the trio's tight
identification with the mainly New York–based hip hop artists exemplifies
the dominance of New York–based hip hop at the time (particularly a UZN
Bronx River hip hop origin mythology), a dominance that many diehard
hip hop enthusiasts would embrace even after the mainstream rise of West
Coast rap in the early 1990s and southern rap in the late 1990s. This flyer

FIGURE 11. United Kingdom DJ crew party flyer with shout-outs to many New York–based artists. Artwork by Rhettmatic. Courtesy of Mark Pulido.

demonstrates how the cultural iconography of UZN's brand of hip hop survives throughout the years and has become a mainstay around the world. In a FuseTV interview, DJ Qbert points out the New York–style artwork on his crew's record sleeve: "Because of all that East Coast influence, we were trying to be like East Coast on the West Coast. So all the people were claiming 'West Coast,' we were claiming 'East Coast.'"[19] UZN has functioned as cultural glue to prioritize hip hop's Bronx origin myth and New York centricity across several UZN chapters around the world.

As Rhettmatic's flyer shows, Filipino Americans have long been invested in taking up UZN's cultural mission to preserve and expand what is deemed as authentic hip hop. In many cases, they were pioneering leaders in the organization. Alex Aquino, founder of the premier DJ competition the International Turntablist Federation, established UZN in San Francisco in 1992. UZN's hip hop universe has long reverberated for many Filipino American hip hop heads. Eric Sanford's introduction to UZN provides an instructive example of Filipino Americans' early encounter with the organization. As a young b-boy in the late 1980s and early 1990s, Sanford performed in downtown Los Angeles hip hop clubs. Dancing with a particular breaking style in the face of b-boy culture's decline (and even ridicule) in Los Angeles, his talent attracted the attention of Zulu Gremlin, a member of UZN and the Rock Steady Crew. Sanford was recruited into Rock Steady Crew, a renowned New York–originated b-boy organization that expanded membership across the United States at the time. He soon joined UZN, a decision his fellow Cerritos-based Filipino American friends Rhettmatic and DJ Curse had already made. Sanford says: "We were drawn to the Zulu Nation because the birth of Hip Hop and the Zulu Nation go hand in hand. You don't have one without the other. The coast was irrelevant because true Zulus don't seek division. And we recognized and appreciated the principles Zulu Nation stood for."[20] Even in the Philippines, hip hop performers will credit the UZN for appearing early on in the archipelago to export their brand of hip hop. In an interview, legendary b-boy Jmasta from Manila reiterates UZN's mantra of peace and unity while trying to solidify UZN's authority as containing *the* original hip hop history: "We are one nation, take care of our planet, we are all brothers and sisters in this. Visit www.zulunation.com. Read the history."[21]

I attended the annual "Meeting of the Minds" UZN conference hosted by the All Tribes San Francisco chapter in 2014. The packed event in the Mission Cultural Center for Latino Arts featured some of the Bay Area's most influential hip hop artists, radio personalities, and community organizers. As UZN members entered the space, they greeted each other with the Zulu handshake and embrace. The mostly African American and Latino audience and panelists mixed with a sizable Filipino American presence. Even the food vendor was a Filipino American caterer. Richard "Patience" Olayvar, a Filipino American emcee from San Francisco's Mission District, was the host and helped introduce guests who spoke on the topics of gentrification in the Mission District, police brutality, the current state of the hip hop music industry, and hip hop's involvement in political movements. Rudy Corpuz, founder of the antigang nonprofit organization United Playaz, spoke on stage with local middle school youth about being born into gang life in the South of Market District, the importance of seeking peace, and the importance of staying away from drugs. Corpuz wore a baseball cap adorned with the Philippine three stars and sun and rocked a Philippine flag UZN-styled emblem around his neck. After appearing as a guest on a panel, Gabriel "Ahki Zulu Delrokz" Delacruz, former UZN All Tribes Chapter president and a DJ, concluded the conference by asking the audience to join him in the "Isang Baksak" (Filipino for "one fall") clap, a ritual of solidarity performed by early Filipino and Mexican farmworkers in California and rehearsed by several generations of Filipino American college students to honor Filipino farmworkers' role in the labor struggle.

FIGURE 12. Universal Zulu Nation All Tribes chapter "Meeting of the Minds" event in San Francisco in 2014. Photo by the author.

Founded in 1973, UZN organized the artistic energies of youths in the Bronx and named itself the "first family of Hip Hop Culture," representing as the originator, protector, and messenger of authentic hip hop culture.[22] UZN formed as an extension of the Black Arts Movement imperative of social uplift, intertwining themes of African American radical imagination arising during the mid-twentieth century. Energized by a newly defiant African American spiritual movement, an assemblage of counter-spiritual elements influenced UZN worldviews. Islam, Ancient Egyptian (Kemetic) symbols, biblical citations, UFO-ology, and cyborg technology adorn the esoteric and seemingly improvised resources that circulate in UZN imagery.[23] This temporally fused aesthetic illustrates fictional writer Ishmael Reed's concept of "synchronicity," or "putting disparate elements into the same time, making them run in the same time, together."[24] The late Ras G., renowned Los Angeles beat producer, describes this eclecticism in his music as "ancient timelessness."[25]

Afrika Bambaataa, the cofounder of UZN, personifies the organization's bricolaged "ancient timelessness."[26] Jeff Chang writes that "[Bambaataa] began imposing his own order on the chaos of representations" surrounding the young UZN founder in the late 1960s.[27] A highly aestheticized iconography surrounds Bambaataa. For example, on the cover of the All Tribes chapter (San Francisco) informational pamphlet, with the ambience of the celestial universe around him, Bambaataa pumps his fist forward (not upward in the militant Black Power gesture) and wears a medallion in the shape of the continent of Africa, a "Zulu" button, and a medallion representing the ancient Egyptian ankh. The music video to his famous "Planet Rock" (1982) with the Soul Sonic Force features a swirl of George Clinton futurism, a combination of Mad Max, Egyptian high priest, Native American, and pimpage chic together with a heavy dose of b-boy toughness and teenage party energy. Emerging out of the psychedelic soul and cosmic funk of Sly and the Family Stone, Parliament Funkadelic, and other 1970s Black musical acts, Bambaataa embodied a new era of post-radical cool. Jeff Chang writes that "so many of the archetypes of the hip-hop generation seem to rise from the body of facts and myths that represent Bambaataa Aasim's life—godfather, yes, but also original gangster, post–civil rights peacemaker, Black riot rocker, breakbeat archaeologist, interplanetary mystic, conspiracy theorist, Afrofuturist, hip-hop activist, twenty-first-century griot."[28]

Tellingly, Bambaataa's imagery and philosophies are grounded in strident anticolonial politics. Bambaataa derived the name "Zulu Nation" from his fascination with Michael Caine's 1964 film *Zulu*, which recounts British colonial defense against fierce Zulu resistance in 1879.[29] Bambaataa remembers the impact of the movie: "To see these Black people fight for their freedom and their land just stuck in my mind. I said when I get older I'm gonna have me a group called the Zulu Nation."[30] According to the UZN "Infinity Lesson 2," the original Bambaataa became bulletproof against British forces in South Africa. Part of a set of principles to the UZN "way of life," this lesson narrates the earlier Bambaataa beseeching his people to "abandon the signs and objects of European culture—except for their guns."[31] In addition to Zulu anticolonialism, Bambaataa inherits mid-twentieth-century new Black cultural politics that reclaims ancient Egypt as evidence of the flourishing of a precolonial Black African civilization.[32] Even more to the point, Bambaataa's Kemeticism follows the political imagination of jazz, soul, and funk artists, which sees the science and cosmology of ancient Egypt as providing a portal to a post-Earth community.[33]

Without a doubt, Bambaataa's UZN is securely wedded to the anticolonial politics of Black consciousness. Unlike the performances of racial evasion DJ Qbert and ISP, who are also associated with UZN, Bambaataa's cosmic vision is one of self-reclamation by exploring one's "true" Black identity. However, similar to Qbert and ISP, as a "universal" cultural organization, racial legibility—for example, memorializing Blackness as an identifiable category—is often aesthetically abstracted. Seemingly contradictory flows between self-reclamation and "universal" abstraction, UZN's prerogative of "self-transformation," influenced by the NOI and the Five Percent Nation

FIGURE 13. Pamphlet for Universal Zulu Nation All Tribes chapter event.

of Gods and Earths, evidences the organization's valuing of the sacredness of redeemed Black lives. UZN takes up a cultural politics of cosmic justice, reaching from the pyramids to the stars above. The "universal" in the Universal Zulu Nation, then, is not the "universal" of the French Enlightenment that abstracts identity, power, and history but a "universal" abundant with *space*—as in the universe. Of hip hop's transnational success, partly due to UZN's outreach and education efforts beginning before rap's crossover appeal, Bambaataa believes the culture should achieve the next step of literally reaching outside the planet Earth. Harkening to the theories of early jazz musician Sun Ra, Bambaataa seeks to connect with other planets via music: "But now our big vision is as we become galactic humans, that we start taking hip hop when we start traveling to other planets."[34] An excerpt from *The Green Book* of UZN's "Infinity Lessons" reinforces Bambaataa's interplanetary ambitions: "We, the Universal Zulu Nation are an organization and a universal nation, for all people on this planet so called Earth, as well for alien life form of people in the universe, whether you're from Mars, Venus, Jupiter, Saturn, Pluto, Earth, etc. We the Zulu's are not foolish people to believe that we are the only life in the universe and that the creator, (Allah, Jehovah, Jah, Yahweh, God or whichever name you wish to call the Almighty One) is only limited to producing LIFE only on the planet so called Earth." Clearly, Bambaataa's philosophy of "life" deauthorizes the earthly "person" as an exceptional category of life. The excerpt continues, "We as Zulu's who are from many different races, colors, and creeds should not be afraid to hear different views coming from humans or aliens from other planets."[35] This philosophy disturbs human racial categories by extending "universal" value to nonhuman interplanetary beings. Anchored in ancient Egypt and South African anticolonialism and enriched by the prospects of a post-Earth community, racial difference for Bambaataa is a paradox: there is no difference among people because we are all galactic beings, but we are galactic beings according to the political and aesthetic terms of Afrofuturistic Black redemption.

But before hip hop is transmitted to other planets, as Bambaataa and UZN exemplify, it must first reach earthly saturation. As "Planet Rock" prophesied, UZN's mission of peace, unity, and having fun would soon reach around the world, with UZN chapters in the Philippines, Japan, France, and Germany. Vague on political goals and maintaining an esoteric recruitment process, the UZN has attracted an array of mostly male members, including talented DJs and dancers, Afrocentric purists, and celebrities. In the early 1990s, when UZN attempted to build membership in the West Coast, it met an already thriving Filipino American hip hop cultural infrastructure.[36] Filipino American practitioners were drawn to UZN's reclamation of the street, dance floor, and their own bodies for the purpose of pleasure, competition, and expression. They also absorbed UZN's pedagogical imperative to learn about obscured histories and civilizations. Largely thanks to the active fostering of West Coast breaking and DJ crews in the early 1990s by the New York–based Rock Steady Crew, whose formation of the Rock Steady DJs enhanced the presence of South Bronx–born "purist" hip hop culture, as well as the educational efforts by West Coast UZN chapters, Filipino Americans from San Diego to Seattle became cultural vanguards of UZN's empowering and fun-centered brand of hip hop, serving at times as international ambassadors for the organization, traveling to teach hip hop classes around the world.[37] Filipino Americans have been active members in UZN chapters; some join by completing an initiation process consisting of mastering "lessons," and others are inducted into the group by virtue of their exceptional contributions to hip hop culture. Filipino Americans in the Bay Area are key leaders and artistic visionaries in UZN and have become woven into the region's rich African American music and dance community.

Early in UZN's creation, Bambaataa crafted the intentional interplay between aesthetics and transformative pedagogy. UZN espouses the saying "knowledge of self," a mantra issued earlier by the Nation of Islam's Elijah Mohammed.[38] In his "Message to the Youth and Young Adults of the World" on the UZN website, Bambaataa declares: "You must seek knowledge: Knowledge is to know and is the foundation of all things in existence. Knowledge is infinite. Knowledge is to know thyself and to know others. Knowledge is to know your surroundings, environment, the nature of life and death, animals, the solar system, the universe, the past, present, and the future. Knowledge is to know The Supreme One."[39] As already mentioned, Bambaataa inherited the legacies of Black Power, funk music, and African American Islam. "Knowledge of self" for the organization, therefore, is strongly linked to a larger legacy of Afrocentric spiritual redemption. As Chang notes, "rather than rebelling against an unjust society by accomplishing externalized movements against systems and institutions, seeking one's own truth, 'having a true reckoning with one's god within,' and 'overstanding' injustice in the world has always been the UZN's method of 'politics.'"[40] Within UZN's pedagogical discourse, alongside the mix of South African and Bronx River hip hop history, and NOI-inspired guidelines on appropriate hygiene and dietary consumption, are indigenous, Latino, and Filipino historiographies. In some Bay Area UZN chapters, I am told, new members were required to study "Infinity Lessons" on Philippine revolutionary and nationalist heroes, U.S. colonization of the Philippines, precolonial Philippine history, and the contributions of Filipino Americans in hip hop.

Somehow confounding binaries and essentialism, Filipino Americans navigate the UZN's bricolaged Afrocentric, post-Earth universe while at the same time exploring their own Filipinoness. But these negotiations don't represent a tension or a contradiction. Applying UZN as a cultural resource, Filipino Americans are applying strategies of belonging that imagines another world—a new "universal nation"—where they can manifest their humanity. UZN's pedagogical imperative is a critical catalyst to mobilizing cultural codes of Filipino American racialization. Absent a Filipino subjectivity not molded by European and white American domination, Filipino Americans are inscribing their own visions of nationality and belonging. For Filipinos who are "robbed of our nationhood" because of centuries of colonization, to use the words of Filipino American emcee Geologic, UZN and hip hop in general become cultural proxies for a colonized Philippines.[41]

Chapter 2 outlines the powerful role of Islam in shaping African Americans' redemptive racial position in the world in forming dynamic and syncretic spaces of home and origin. For example, NOI founder Wallace Fard Muhammad preached that African Americans descended from the "original Black nation of Asia, the Tribe of Shabazz."[42] Filipinos in the Philippines and Filipino Americans have been seeking kinship and redefining national space through their representations of Islam. For colonized and racialized people, the concept of nation is paramount in the process of self-making, whether it be expressed by the Nation of Islam, Five Percent Nation of Gods and Earths, UZN, or by radicals fighting for a decolonized Philippine nation. Of course, as we know, the nation in these cases are shaped by visionary glances outward in connections to Third Worldism and international solidarities. For colonized people, the nation represents land reclamation, cultural and political sovereignty, and geographic boundary making for a freedom yet to arrive. For example, Nuyorican DJ Tony Touch reimagines the nation by splicing together Puerto Rican liberation, Taíno neo-indigeneity, and UZN party-rocking in his 2000 album *The Piece Maker*. Touch begins his song "Toca's Intro" with Bonz Malone's playful remixing of the U.S. pledge of allegiance: "I pledge allegiance and have to brag about the united weights in America. And to this republic for which we dance, the Zulu Nation, in the yard, is the invincible, with ability to touch this for yall."

The nation according to the poetics of Bambaataa and other hip hop cultural authorities is much more capacious than modern nation-state formations.[43] Even if the term "nation" is appropriated by Bambaataa and his Black nationalist forebears (e.g., the NOI and Amiri Baraka), because of their border-crossing and mobile relationships to geographic space, these versions of the nation are incongruous to the defining features of the modern nation. Instead of an instrument of military competition, resource accumulation, and geographic delimitation, UZN has redefined the nation as an *outer* space of belonging. Cosmic abstraction flows together with anticolonial or precolonial worlds in UZN's universal nation, giving breath to an expansive politics that seeks a redemptive Black universe. In hip hop, the concept of nation is flexible, neither strictly subscribing to the autonomous, self-determination of Garveyism nor the integrated national brotherhood of Martin Luther King Jr. Tiongson summarizes the multipurpose usage of "nation" in hip hop cultural historiography. Beginning with the example of the language of nationalism in the documentary film *Planet B-Boy*, Tiongson identifies the problems of practitioners' professed allegiances to the so-called hip hop nation and the subsequent iterations of this hip hop nation by cultural critics and scholars. For Tiongson, of particular criticism is the use of hip hop nationalism's inheritance of "the masculinist logic of black nationalism, which serves to sanction the objectification of women."[44] It is true that the many hip hop practitioners adhere to strict legitimizing exercises (some could say hazing) to determine membership status in the proclaimed hip hop nation. Tiongson demonstrates the authenticating strategies of Filipino American DJs who claim space in the hip hop nation, which he shows is largely premised on rhetorical color blindness that benefits non-Black practitioners. Also evident in b-boy culture, determining who is "real" in hip hop has been an obsession for many practitioners.

Instead of interpreting the usages of nation to develop an analysis of practitioners' claims to belonging to a hip hop nation, I seek to unpack it as a critical cultural imaginary, however flawed, restrictive, or contradictory. I read the abstraction of race in hip hop's iterations of the nation as rich with alternative embodiments and racial epistemologies. There is political value in being funky. For some Filipino Americans, the temporally and geographically defiant version of hip hop's funky nation—or funky universe—becomes a space for channeling modes of being Filipino. In the "Reel Hood Heroes" interview with Delrokz, the then-UZN All Tribes president holds up a book titled *Philippine History and Government throughout the Years*. "Knowledge is infinite and you gotta go out there and get it for yourself. School only teaches you so much," he proclaims, mirroring the Five Percenter requisite of pursuing an otherwise obscured self-knowledge. Delrokz's incitement to learn about history not taught in schools not only gestures to the erasure of Filipino history in textbooks, but it also credits recuperative projects that address the irretrievability of a Filipino national subjectivity. In the next scene of the online interview, Delrokz shows off a DJ Qbert collectible toy and pays homage to Qbert and ISP for putting "Filipinos on the map as far as DJs and really representing Daly City." Daly City and San Francisco in general are home to one of the largest concentrations of Filipino Americans in the United States and have come to be representative of a West Coast, Filipino American hip hop origin story, given the renowned Filipino American DJs and dancers who hail from the region. Discussing the pedagogical mandate of the UZN, Delrokz reiterates his transcendental quest for truth: "I want to know every side of the story, so I can know my own truth, what I believe to be true."[45] Delrokz's interview illustrates the overlapping of a supposedly attainable Filipino national history and the creation of Filipino subjectivity through Filipino American representation in hip hop. The aspiring for Filipino knowledge of self in this scene alludes to the routing of Filipinos on the map of hip hop and Daly City as much as it is a roots Filipinos to the "natal" of a Philippine nation.[46] For Delrokz, the relative absence of a

Filipino historical narrative motivates knowledge of self while prompting opportunities for collaboration and community building through hip hop. In this case, the funky hip hop nation generates Filipino racial consciousness: the infinite nature of knowledge-attainment yields precious memorialization. The gaps—synapses—of Filipino historical legibility inspires powerful truth-telling practices.

Since the public revelation of sexual abuse allegations against Bambaataa, it is unclear how Filipino Americans—and members in general—currently situate themselves within the UZN organization. As I've already noted, many high-profile members have publicly resigned. Not surprising, UZN leadership has come under strict scrutiny because of its casual discrediting of the people accusing Bambaataa. Author and former UZN member Adisa "The Bishop" Banjoko removed Bambaataa's picture and name from the cover of his book *Bobby, Bruce, and the Bronx: The Secrets of Hip-Hop Chess*. Banjoko's blog states that "the Universal Zulu Nation has a potentially corrupt founder and a sinister set of top tier leadership that enabled him in a Vatican style scenario."[47]

Filipino Americans' practices of self-determination and social change in the UZN have proven that the organization cannot be reduced to the legacy of one man. It has operated as a transformational "school" for Filipino Americans recovering knowledge, thus helping to fulfill a desire to make visible a Filipino epistemology. As Delrokz shows, a search for Filipino knowledge of self is given resources that flow within the aesthetics and imaginaries of Afrofuturistic hip hop. As the next section demonstrates, Filipino racial legibility through historical memorialization is not the only route of decolonial processes for Filipino American hip hop performers. The synapses of Filipino knowledge formation can produce quirky and inventive expressions of Filipinoness. Aliens, extraterrestriality, and interplanetary motifs can operate as spaces of belonging and modes of defiance, reflecting Afrofuturisms' propensity to elude the legibility of racial memorialization and instead embrace more abstract categories of identity.

Alien Intelligence

The song "Crosshairs" begins with the sizzle of a teleportation beam, a zap of a laser ray, and pings from a satellite, all kept in time by a snare drum. "Crosshairs," from Filipino American emcee Bambu's album *Sun of a Gun* (2013), evokes the ways DJ Qbert, the song's producer, seems to constantly speak to extraterrestrial life forms with his music. On top of Qbert's deep tumbling of bass drums, Bambu levels a witty and adversarial critique of

U.S. surveillance, U.S. gun culture, and the hypocrisies of U.S. overseas war policies. At the end of his first verse, Bambu summons the DJ, "Q, talk," to which Qbert "breaks it down" by conducting a clinic of turntable wizardry with virtuoso cuts of the vocal sample "I could break it down." While Bambu sends clear and confrontational vocal vibrations, Qbert's electronic vibrations are cryptic and strange. As Bambu's urgent messages transmit to politicized listeners, the quirky beeps, rumbles, and scratches in "Crosshairs" exemplify a trademark "Q, talk" that seems to transmit to outer space.

Qbert's abstract approach to music finds affinities with (and contributes to) a larger hip hop artistic repertoire that utilizes science fiction aesthetics and motifs. Christine Balance writes about Qbert and his turntablist crew, ISP: "These new phonographers insist listening ears travel through the inner spaces of music with out-of-this-world sounds created by encounters between humans and machines. This is the stuff of science fiction, as well as the postcolonial and postmodern, where and when shifting temporalities create spaces to flip the beat and reimagine the future."[48] Relaying the notion of Filipino American cyborg connectivity, Kodwo Eshun quotes DJ Mix Master Mike of ISP: "We think as instruments."[49] If Filipino American DJs are sentient cyborg musical instruments, then their desire to communicate must involve a superhuman level of cognizance that cannot be described as merely human and surely exceeds the so-called primitive. Terming "skratchadelia" as the chaotic yet rhythmic sounds of turntablism, Eshun gestures to the extraterrestrial communicative noises blaring from the DJ's instruments: "skratchadelia encrypts its tones, demanding alien listeners tuned into the open secret hidden in static, receivers who can hear a new world in its garbled frequencies."[50] ISP's eccentric skratchadelia were most prominent in the late 1990s and early 2000s in the form of mixtapes, DJ battles, and radio skits. In the 2001 documentary *Scratch* by Doug Pray, Mix Master Mike professes that "scratching to me is another kind of intelligence." In another scene, Qbert reflects on his musical communion with aliens: "Since earth is kind of like a primitive planet, what about the more advanced civilizations? How does their music sound? So, I would imagine whatever they're doing, and I guess that's how I come up with my ideas."

Also released in 2001, the South by Southwest film festival award-winning animated film *Wave Twisters* relishes in DJ Qbert's psychedelic communications.[51] "In *Wave Twisters*," Balance writes, "as with ISP's musical recordings, the adolescent (nerd-boy culture) and the avant-garde (sound and film technologies) comfortably co-exist."[52] The sonically and visually collaged and frenetic Star Wars parody utilizes "nerd-boy" comic book superhero and supervillain tropes popular in hip hop visuals exemplified in the record art of the Soul Sonic Force in the 1980s and continuing with artists such as the Wu-Tang Clan, Outkast, and MF Doom. The glorious absurdities, however, are obvious as the film's breakdancing, blue-skinned protagonist Julio Azul, aka the Dental Commander, wears a head mirror and green medical scrubs, conducts bloody surgery on robots and alien beings, and travels to outer space to overcome the diabolic schemes of Lord Ook, the crime boss voodoo doll, and his henchman, the Red Worm, who lives inside the belly button of a luchador-masked baby. The Dental Commander and his crew must preserve the "Lost Arts," aka the hip hop cultural elements (established by the UZN) from erasure by dispatching turntable scratches as deadly weapons. Conceivably, the dentist hero could represent a sarcastic jab at the stereotypical medical career aspirations of the Filipino American petite bourgeoisie; the Dental Commander is heroic not because he happens to be a good dentist, but because he is an intergalactic traveling, cybertechnology-savvy, and skilled b-boy–turntablist–alien fighter. If Qbert's sonic imagination attempts to encounter the frequency waves of "more advanced civilizations," *Wave Twisters* conjures an extraterrestrial narrative that bewilders markers of race and humanness. Yet, importantly, at the same time that the film satirizes racial and human categories, it still upholds gender and sexuality roles—in true nerd-boy fashion—with Dental Commander's climactic saving of the helpless and scantily clad token female crewmember Honey Drips from imminent death on a giant spinning laser turntable.[53] *Wave Twisters* aspires to radically upend earthly categories but at moments fails to do so. In the spirit of UZN's hip hop aesthetics, the film juggles themes of memorialization versus abstraction. The conclusion of the film encodes UZN's four hip hop elements (breaking, DJing, graffiti, and emceeing) as sacred objects rescued by the protagonists. The film calcifies the four hip hop elements, gender roles, and superhero/supervillain archetypes while confounding other categories in amalgamating human, animal, alien, and robot beings.

 Wave Twisters is an epic ode to UZN hip hop culture more in the vein of post-Earth, post-human communion rather than a glancing back toward precolonial Africa. The film's evacuation of Blackness encapsulates the diverging racial relationship Filipino Americans have with UZN's multifaceted racial coding. The racial ambiguity in *Wave Twisters* reflects Qbert's persistent evasion of the possible roles of Filipinoness in his artistic experiences. As mentioned earlier, Qbert's take on racial identity in his music decidedly prioritizes skills and art without focusing too much on being Filipino. On top of ISP's flair for bizarre otherworldliness and abstraction, their disengagement with race, ethnicity, and other identities from their performances (e.g., Qbert uniformly categorizing Filipino, gay, and naked) is often seen as a dangerous act of racial evasion betraying the politics of Filipino visibility. Yet, even if ISP members problematically evade racial legibility, the group's "labors of alienation" is in itself a political practice.[54] Echoing Balance's analysis on ISP and Qbert's defiance and disaffection as being part of a longer history of Filipino insubordination, these DJs' performances in both their interviews and creative productions offer alternative, counterintuitive politics of Filipino representation.

Through their sonic abstractions and extraterrestrial motifs, ISP participate in an existing legacy of Black politics and aesthetics as well as in a larger hip hop community that also prioritize these practices. D-Styles, a member of ISP, likens their cerebral turntablist sounds to bebop, which defied the more easily digestible and dance-able jazz music: "Some music we make is just listening music, very similar to the jazz movement in the 1940s when bebop moved away from the traditional jazz dance band."[55] D-Styles's cataloging of ISP's sounds within the longer archive of creative Black music indicates ISP's sophisticated aesthetic awareness. As mentioned earlier, Afrofuturism in jazz, funk, R&B, and hip hop stylize a redemptive belonging in otherworldliness. For many Afrofuturist artists, America and planet earth represent a confining home, and outer space promises a belonging that is friendly to their Blackness. As Sun Ra says in the 1972 film he cowrote, *Space Is the Place*: "We set up a colony for black people here. See what they can do on a planet all their own, without any white people there. They can drink in the beauty of this planet. It will affect their vibrations, for the better of course."[56]

Sun Ra's utopic "vibrations" share a very real musical soundscape in the world of turntablism; Filipino American avant-garde turntablists literally vibe with the soundwaves of an Afrofuturist repertoire. In this way, ISP's Afro-Filipino futurism is not only a method of understanding Filipino history and proposing new modes of political possibilities, nor is it only an accidental alliance of Filipino American and African American creative minds. Their skratchadelia should also be appreciated as contributions to a decolonial cultural project set forth in African American jazz, film, literature, and hip hop. As with Black decolonial cultural practices, ISP's Afro-Filipino futurism yields the knowledge of a cultural project that envisions colonized bodies flourishing outside the authority of the imperial state and its built racial hierarchies. ISP's "weirdest sounds" can be heard as communications signaling for an intimate connectivity with a more expansive and liberating universe.

As we've seen, Afrofuturism employs tropes of the alien and alienation to address Du Bois's concept of double-consciousness and the trauma of dislocation and enslavement. Eshun writes about "the idea of slavery as an alien abduction which means that we've all been living in an alien-nation since the

18th century." With their fictional tale of mutant descendants of overboarded Africans in the Atlantic, the Detroit electro group Drexciya epitomizes an Afrofuturistic penchant for alien mythologizing. Eshun describes Drexciyans as "'water breathing, aquatically mutated descendants,' webbed mutants of the Black Atlantic, amphibians adapted for the ocean's abyssal plains, a phylum disconnected from the aliens who adapted to land." Drexciya's electronic sound replays "the alien abduction of slavery" and the supposed migration of these advanced beings to the continental United States. "They have been here all along and they are you. You are the alien you are looking for."[57]

But for Filipino Americans, critical references to Blackness and alienation meet an obvious cognitive impasse; aliens and alienation inhabit a different racial valence. Double-consciousness is not located in the original trauma of the Atlantic slave trade, but it can allude to the fracturing and curtailing of Philippine diasporic nationhood, the estrangement from a precolonial world, and the violence involved in consolidating diverse groups into a Philippine national identity. Since the docking of Spanish ships in Samar and the U.S. Navy in Manila Bay, Filipino alienation from modernity is at once geographic, civic, and civilizational. The desire to connect with more "advanced civilizations" exemplifies a yearning to exist outside human hierarchies and representations. In a 1998 *URB* magazine interview, for example, ISP members theorize alien contact with their hometown of San Francisco.[58] Of this interview, Balance writes, "the conversation [in the interview] quickly devolves into theories of aliens designing The City as their 'trading base' and the pyramid-shaped Transamerica building as their telephone [aka 'alien's AT&T']."[59]

African Americans' reclamation of ancient civilization and their capacity to engineer enduring monumental structures counters earlier European colonial beliefs that Black Africans were incapable of enlightened self-governance and achieving epic feats.[60] Ancient Egypt and its pyramids hold great symbolic importance for jazz, funk, and the UZN. It is possible that these Filipino American DJs have glanced countless times at the ubiquitous pyramids gracing the record covers of Earth, Wind, and Fire, Herbie Hancock, or the Hieroglyphics, thus making a cognitive connection between popular Kemetic iconography with that of their beloved skyline.

ISP's revisualizing the iconic Transamerica building in San Francisco as a conduit for alien communication, then, reverberates with Black music and hip hop's already-rich mythologies of extraterrestrial-honing Egyptian pyramids. However, instead of ancient Egypt, a structure symbolizing San Francisco's financial district becomes a sacred site, a more immediate point

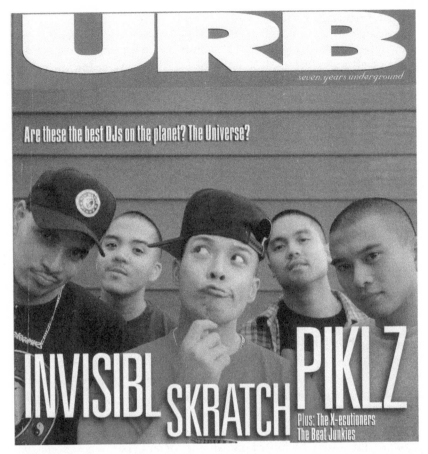

FIGURE 14. Of the Invisibl Skratch Piklz, *URB* magazine cover asks, "Are these the best DJs on the planet? The Universe?" *URB* magazine cover, February 1998.

of recognition for members of ISP. In this instance, for members of the ISP, the idea of a reclaimed homeland, nation, or civilization doesn't venerate a place "over there" in the Philippines, Asia, or elsewhere. For these Filipino Americans, "over there" is strange, alien; San Francisco instead is situated as a proper and preferred homeland. Where modern-day Kemetics seek to reclaim ancient Egyptian monuments for Black Africans and their extraterrestrial kindred, ISP members' transformation of their city to an alien conduit signifies their desire to develop an otherworldly community absent of their own venerable nation or civilization. ISP's San Francisco becomes a modern version of Kemet, a site to invite contact with more "advanced civilizations."

Space Goddess

Inheriting the Afro-Filipino futuristic sensibilities of her San Francisco–based peers Qbert and ISP, Hopie is another notable Filipino American hip hop artist who consults hip hop's otherworldly aesthetics. Beginning her recording career a decade after the height of ISP's fame, she is among the most prolific Filipino American hip hop artists who channels these extraterrestrial affinities in recent years. As a Filipina American emcee from a male-dominated hip hop scene in San Francisco, her lyrics are textured with battle-rap braggadocio that confronts men's low expectations of her skills.[61] Hopie's rapping ability excels not only due to her being a talented Filipina but because she is also a special conduit of cosmic intelligence. She is, in essence, advanced; she is superhuman. In her music videos "Space Case" and "Solar Systems," Hopie suggests that her emcee skills are honed due to an elevated form of consciousness.

"Space Case" is a nonlinear (or synchronistic, to use Ishmael Reed's term) unfolding of a series of abductions.[62] After being taken by alien beings, Hopie is abducted a second time by agents dressed in hazmat outfits on a mission to erase the memory of Hopie's alien encounter, similar to the *Men in Black* movies. True to its nonlinear form, the video begins with Hopie having just woken up from a bizarre dream. Before the beat drops, we hear a cyclical repetition of satellite pings accompanied by intermittent laser beam buzzes. Things don't seem normal as she gazes at the San Francisco skyline from the rooftop of her apartment building. She poses, arms crossed, facing the Transamerica building—the San Francisco "pyramid." Hopie glimpses a UFO in the sky. In a raspy, elongated voice, we hear Hopie sing, "Spaced-out in another dimension. I fell hard into another dream." In the next scene, objects float about her apartment. As she spots a mark on her hand, the prior evening's outing with her girlfriends flash into her mind, with one of her friends drawing a caricature of an alien on Hopie's palm, as if to mark the emcee as the one to be abducted. We see Hopie wandering away from her group of friends in the streets and a beam of light suddenly transports her to a spaceship. Inside the spaceship, Hopie sits on a satellite-shaped throne, having morphed into an alien-like character. Rapping to the camera, she boasts about her emcee skills to an audience of clay animated aliens and mini drone-like flying saucers wobbling around her. "Wait a second, I'm secondary to none," the queen raps before her new fans. Like the disconnect between the song and video in "Comrades," Hopie's battle rap lyricism seems adjacent to the sci-fi psychedelics of the song's sonics and imagery.

After the first chorus, Del the Funky Homosapien recites a guest verse. Del, who is a member of the ancient Egyptian–loving Oakland hip hop crew the

Hieroglyphics, is a real-life artistic mentor to Hopie.[63] As it did Hopie, the space ship teleports the Oakland emcee, and the aliens also enthrone him and treat him to an audience. As soon as Hopie is teleported back to earth, agents swoop down to abduct and surround the artist with microphones. Like the aliens, several agents catch a groove and begin dancing to her lyrics. The agents' abduction, however, is intrusive and clinical: Instead of sitting on a throne, Hopie wears a medical gown and sits on an examining table. Here, "Space Case" depicts a cosmos in direct contrast to U.S. Secretary of State John Hay's "cosmic tendency" rife with imperialism's inevitable march of destruction. The same year that Hay pronounced U.S. colonization of the Philippines as cosmically ordained, the federal government funded the Philippine Reservation at the Louisiana Purchase Exposition in Saint Louis in 1904.[64] The main objective of this constructed ethnological village was to provide public witness of Filipinos' racial inferiority, affirming the colonial justification of white American colonial preparation of Filipinos' for their eventual self-governance.

"Space Case" allegorizes a different outcome of the forced abduction of Filipinos. The agents examine Hopie with clinical curiosity, reminiscent of the scientific examination of Filipino "specimens" at the Philippine Reservation in the St. Louis World's Fair in 1904. Unlike the newly acquired subjects at the beginning of U.S. colonialization in the Philippines, Hopie, as the object of exhibition, boldly speaks back, with the agents marveling at her lyrical virtuosity. Hopie's superhuman powers and appearance, although still marking her as Other, contrast the markings of subhumanness placed on the bodies of abducted Filipinos in 1904. When the agents scan Hopie's memory, flashes of the evening's festivities appear on the monitor: a pleasurable, women-centered space that juxtaposes the anonymous, sterile, and menacing inspection room where the agents have detained her. The words "aliens detected" gleam on the monitor, and the agents inject a needle into Hopie's neck. The event is "terminated." In a nonlinear fashion, the video ends with Hopie earlier wandering the forest prior to her abduction by the agents. She is invited to listen to music produced by her beatmaker, Six Fingers, who summons UFOs in the sky through his beat machine. To the agents, the emcee's communing with aliens is dangerous: Hopie is a witness and participant to a forbidden event. However, the agents' termination of her memory seems incomplete; endowed with telekinetic powers, permanent residue of the evening remains. "Space Case" allegorizes the U.S. program of so-called benevolent assimilation that erased the knowledge U.S. war and occupation in the Philippines through an elaborate system of colonial tutelage. The termination of Hopie's memory, as well, recalls the termination of Philippine state sovereignty at the moment of U.S. "abduction" of the Philippines and literal abduction of Filipino people for anthropological study and exhibition at the St. Louis World's Fair. "Space Case" reimagines an alternative outcome of colonial erasure, one in which a contraband counter-memory filled with communing and otherworldly expression persist in waking life despite the conspiratorial machinations of repressive and obliterating agents.

The music video "Solar Systems" continues Hopie's theme of otherworldly consciousness.[65] This time, the emcee is a deity possessing cosmic intelligence radiating from her mind or her "third eye." "Solar Systems," like the party scene in "Space Case," values woman-centered spaces, complete with graceful and haunting dances by an all-woman cast. The pleasure of inhabiting the expressions of their own female bodies points to Hopie's politics of feminine empowerment, contrasting the boyhood comic book fantasies of Qbert's *Wave Twisters*. In "Solar Systems," Hopie personifies "hope," the driving metaphor throughout the song's lyrics and visual presentation. She suspends binary morality and implies that hope sustains our survival despite its (her) flaws, disappointments, and contradictions. The song opens with these lines:

> Call me a goddess, a devil
> I'm modern and I'm modest
> I'm evil but I'm honest
> At whatever you been sayin'
> I been that
> Even a couple times or more
> I've been war and I've been peace
> And I bit a piece of a man's heart before
> And broken hearts too fell apart too
> Been smart when I done some dumb shit
> Went dumb and deaf and blind side
> Lost vision in my mind's eye
> Envisioned shit that fell through
> Built castles that have held jewels
> But heaven gave them hell too
> I feel you when I tell you.

She implies that the universe has intentions beyond human understanding, so hope is what we grasp in the chaos of a larger, sublime, cosmic system. Hope is both visionary and blind. Surrounded by the stars, Hopie represents an advanced knowledge beyond traditional senses. In parts of the video she dons a veil over her eyes to embody her human persona, which remains naive to the solar system's order. Even her dancers perform graceful movements with their eyes veiled, demonstrating a kinetic brilliance despite their lack of sight.

FIGURE 15. Hopie is an omniscient goddess in space. Screenshot from the "Solar Systems" music video (Dutton, 2014).

At the same time Hopie connects with an infinite universe (or is perhaps a goddess who helps orchestrate the universe), she decides to adjoin "Solar Systems" to her ethnic roots by punctuating the rhythmic climax of the song (the tempo is enhanced) with lyrics in the Filipino language:

> Lahat sa loob ang ating bala (the bullets are in us)
> Sa mga kanta ako ay nakatira (I live with music)
> Tayo talaga totoong hope (We are true hope)
> And hope is the message
> I'm sharing with yall.

Hurling her Filipino language or "roots" into the cosmos, Hopie suggests that her Filipinaness has much more expansive frontiers than the multicultural compartmentalization of her ethnicity. For her, being Filipina accentuates her borderless universe. Instead of a defiant evasiveness of her race and ethnicity assumed by her ISP predecessors, "Solar Systems" shows how Hopie exudes her Filipinaness comfortably without memorializing it. The video assembles Hopie's roots onto an intergalactic scale in a similar vein that the UZN syncretizes Africa, Islam, Egypt, and the cosmos in its iconography to suggest an intergalactic ethnicity. Perhaps her desired audience is fluent in Filipino and her message of hope seeks to reach Filipinos who have yet to manifest their own infinite and sacred potential.

Conclusion: Postcolonial Space

In this chapter, I contrast Bambu's militancy in "Comrades" with the more abstract, strange, and quirky worlds imagined by ISP and Hopie. I also explore Filipino Americans' leadership and belonging in the UZN. Although varied in their political legibility, these performances and embodiments share the aesthetics and thematic characteristics of Afro-Filipino futurism. Not just whimsical, Afro-Filipino futurism allegorizes key moments of obscured or erased Filipino racial history. Furthermore, Afro-Filipino futurist performers inherit and contribute to the aesthetic practices of a larger Black decolonial project.

These Filipino American hip hop performers exhibit the strangeness of white conquest by reminding us that the original aliens to the precolonial Filipino world were white people. In 1905, Philippine governor-general William Howard Taft wrote: "[The Filipinos] are merely in a state of Christian pupilage. They are imitative. They are glad to be educated, glad to study some languages other than their own, glad to follow European and American ideals."[66] A century later, Filipino Americans are revising the terms of European and white U.S. superiority by restoring their bodies as defiant, intelligent, and superhuman; they are mobilizing selfhoods that embrace fantastical and more fulfilling mythologies. Bambu's postapocalyptic comradeship, Delrokz's truth seeking, Mix Master Mike's turntable intelligence, Qbert's intergalactic transmissions, and Hopie's alien communion narrate an ongoing project of Filipino self-creation. For these Filipino Americans, the search for truth, dignity, and civilization is abundant throughout a vast, funky universe. Filipino Americans' creative worlds offer instructive gateways to understanding Filipinos' historical encounter with very real ships carrying aliens from Europe and America. In turn, as colonial subjects, Filipinos would become the aliens of Spanish and U.S. empire. The outsiderness of funk fashion designer Larry Legaspi remains a social status echoing throughout Filipino America's cultural imagination. Outsiderness, though, can inspire a form of fugitive knowledge targeted for erasure by colonizing agents, as suggested in Hopie's video. Filipino American hip hop performance is shaped by and tethered to a history of erased and unreconciled trauma, which brilliantly emanates from performers' funky expressions. To borrow from Hopie: "Instead of letting it destroy me, I let it create me."[67] And, much more, Hopie and her fellow artists have been actively creating vibrant cultural possibilities and comradeships that help inspire alternative worlds.

My next objects of analysis also defy expectations of political propriety. Embracing unruly and messy politics, I observe Filipino American hip hop dancers' embodiments of modernity. Like the imaginative worlds that Afro-Filipino futurist artists manifest, I show how the world-making strategies of Filipino American hip hop dancers enact a cultural genealogy well-rehearsed on the stages of colonial encounter. In Filipino American hip hop dance scenes, the body of the dancer is imprinted with deep memory. Through motion and movement, the body of the Filipino American hip hop dancer performs profound ways of being and belonging.

CHAPTER 4

Postcolonial Bodies, Modern Postures

Erasure and Community Formation in Filipino American Hip Hop Dance Culture

Modern Legacy

The Irvine Barclay Theatre at the University of California, Irvine (UCI), teemed with high school– and college-aged students sporting fashionable, bright-colored hats, athletic clothes, and wild hair. It was hard to distinguish between those who were dancers dressed for the stage and those who were spectators dressed to impress. Parents, many of whom were former Kaba Modern dancers, herded young children to their seats in the opulent auditorium filled with a racially diverse but predominantly Filipino American crowd. The Kaba Modern dedication show, "Legacy: Celebrating 20 Years of Kaba Modern Family and Innovative Artistry" (KM 20), in August 2012 honored the group's two-decade reign and, given the creative labor of the night's performers and the enthusiasm of the multigenerational audience, projected its continued local and international relevance. The program featured performances by Kaba Kids, traditional dancers of the Pilipino-American Culture Night (formerly Pilipino Culture Night, or PCN), various professional dance companies, and a grand assemblage of former Kaba Modern choreographers in the "KM 20 Directors' Tribute." True to the event's name, KM 20 gathered under one roof an extended and tight-knit family of artists and artists in the making.

FIGURE 16. Kaba Modern "Legacy" event flyer in 2012. Screenshot from Kaba Modern Facebook Page.

In 2008, as the programming director of the Festival of Philippine Arts and Culture (FPAC) in Los Angeles, I organized a hip hop dance battle called "Show and Prove."[1] Kaba Modern, PAC Modern, and other college- and high school–based teams from around Southern California participated, attracting perhaps the biggest audience of the festival. The next year, FPAC (which again featured Kaba Modern and PAC Modern) invited Supreme Soul, a predominantly Filipino American crew that (like Kaba Modern) made it to the final rounds of the MTV reality competition show *America's Best Dance Crew* (*ABDC*). Sheroes, which auditioned for *ABDC* and whose members, including Filipina dancers, eventually succeeded in the show as dancers representing different crews, also performed at FPAC that year. In a way, FPAC became like an *ABDC* reunion. The festival featured a bevy of heavy hitters in the Southern California Filipino American hip hop dance circuit. Like the KM 20 anniversary show at UCI and the many other dance competitions I've attended, FPAC provided a space where Filipino American hip hop dancers and their multiracial peers gathered to "show and prove" their embodied ingenuity and fashion sense while building a community, indeed an industry, of dancers. They did this, of course, while inhabiting an explicitly Filipino American cultural space.

In observing the cultural discourses about and by Filipino American hip hop dancers, I scrutinize these dancers' posturing of "modern." Both the mainstream and vernacular qualities of Filipino American hip hop dance culture enact a memory-rich repertoire that exemplifies Filipino Americans' multifaceted "modern" encounters with U.S. culture. I suggest that understanding their performances as a continuation of an intimate engagement with American dance culture re-narrates the terms of Filipino American modern belonging. Hip hop dance is integral to the cultural circulations of a Filipino American hip hop vernacular, exposing the friction between a subaltern counter-discourse and mainstream representational legibility. Taking stock of these apparent tensions, I appreciate practitioners' mobilization of "modern" as wordplay—as an act of punning. Modernity, from its allusions to a colonial era of civilizing the savage to its more recent vernacular usage connoting emergent acceptability, is subverted when it adopts new meanings. Sarita See observes that "puns travel across borders in ways that deterritorialize meaning." Focusing on Filipino American comedy, See situates punning as a linguistic act of survival and resistance for Filipinos, who "emerged from the [Philippine-American War] as theatrical, performative subjects, using wordplay and the ambivalence of language as a matter of survival."[2] For me, the shifting meanings of modern is not so much about deploying insider humor nor about deliberate acts of cultural resistance; rather, the punning of modern performs clever, however unintentional, historical suturing.

The signaling of modern by practitioners achieves a set of syncretic discursive goals that at once asserts an arrival of these dancers as acceptable members of a liberal multicultural society while also alluding to a much longer Filipino colonial encounter with modernity. Filipino American hip hop dancers' discursive maneuvers in their uses of modern is evident in the racial representations of Filipino American hip hop dance culture on *ABDC*. I show that the mainstreaming of Filipino American hip hop dance culture into a narrative of a linearly progressive Asian American "arrival" renders obscure Filipino American bodies and hip hop cultural contributions. Ultimately, I read against the casual tendency to privilege the story of neoliberal meritocracy in hip hop dance. Filipino American hip hop dancers' embodied history and methods of communion with fellow dancers manifest a legacy that cannot be expressed by hegemonic language on race and representation in hip hop dance.

Resonating with my prior focus on Afro-Filipino futurism and its funky subjectivity, queer is useful in describing Filipino American hip hop dancers' vernacular cultural strategies because, for one, many influential Filipino American hip hop dancers are out queer people. Moreover, queer is useful in describing flexible modes of belonging that exceed orderly categories of race, ethnicity, sexuality, nation, and affiliation. Therefore, I read the wholesomeness in the family theme branding the KM20 "Legacy" event as cleverly gesturing toward a more expansive technique of belonging; here, family is code for a more liberating queer community formation. Filipino American hip hop dancers' association with complex layers of racial identification, tradition, sexuality, and family is inspired by what Fiona I. B. Ngô calls "queer modernities."[3] The politics expressed in dancers' queer modernities offer a poignant response to the "proper" politics sanctioned by some observers of Filipino American hip hop performance, as described earlier in this book. In short, rather than promoting a legible politics rooted in the radicalism of mid-twentieth-century U.S. movements for racial and gender justice, these performers offer unruly, messy, and popular strategies to resist power. In this way, by embodying the defiant pleasures and agency garnered in the production and consumption of popular culture, the cultural strategies emanating from these performers point to redemptive forms of queer politics.

Appearing on hit shows like *ABDC*, in anniversary celebrations like KM 20, at Filipino events like FPAC or PCN, or in virtual worlds like YouTube, Filipino Americans inhabit a variety of roles for multiple audiences who gaze on their racialized and sexualized bodies. As trendsetters and industry leaders, Filipino American hip hop dancers represent broader U.S. cultural idealizations rooted in and routed through their dancing bodies. With their fluency in American dance gestures and leadership roles in hip hop dance, Filipino American dancers in this new millennium demonstrate their embodied knowledge of U.S. culture; they give evidence of a cultural genealogy informed by the duty of so-called benevolent assimilation to teach the savage to become civilized. Sarita See reminds us that the presence of Filipinos in the United States conveys a history of "violent inclusion rather than exclusion."[4] The rapid expansion of Filipino American hip hop dance culture presents an opportunity to uncover U.S. culture's permeation throughout U.S. empire, revealing that Filipinos and Filipino Americans are no strangers to U.S. culture and in fact have been critical contributors to it.

I begin this chapter by tracing an outline of the fundamental contributions of Filipino Americans to hip hop dance culture. As choreographers, dancers, and community leaders, Filipino Americans began in the early 1980s (and in the 1970s in the funk and disco era) performing in local dance crews and have since been at the forefront of large-scale hip hop dance institutions. As practitioners in a Filipino American hip hop vernacular, Filipino American dancers' influence in the dance scene points to the cultural mobility of this vernacular. Next, I investigate the historical background of so-called modern dance, especially the U.S. colonial moment during the advent of modern dance and, as a result of the racial crisis wrought by U.S. colonialism, the racial politics involved in the exhibiting of Filipino and African American bodies in the early twentieth century. This historical background sets up the cultural particularities of Filipino American hip hop dance performance—a vernacular culture inheriting the material conditions of colonialism. Then, I show such particularities are obscured as Asian American hip hop dancers ascend as celebrities. The "arrival" of Asian Americans in hip hop dance, evident in internet fans' exhortations of "Asian pride," has obscured the longer history of a Filipino American hip hop dance vernacular. Unpacking this obfuscation invites a critical inquiry into a more turbulent historical vantage of Filipino-U.S. cultural contact that should not be reduced to Asian American hip hop dance's preferred margins-to-mainstream discourse. The final sections discuss the transgressive queer forms of belonging and embodiments in hip hop "choreo" dance. In their unsettling of the traditional-versus-modern binary, alternative forms of community connectivity, and queer embodiments, Filipino American hip hop dancers re-author ethnicity, sexuality, and gender in hip hop culture. With these queer strategies of cultural identification, Filipino American hip hop dancers perform a cultural belonging that defies clean, linear national narratives. This chapter concludes by analyzing two videos featuring Samahang Modern, an "urban" dance group at the University of California, Los Angeles. The videos expertly illustrate the multiple and synergistic constructions of Filipinoness in PCN and its relationship to being modern.

It Started with a Crew

For Filipino Americans, especially those who went to college on the West Coast, Kaba Modern is a cultural vanguard of dance artistry. The crew takes its name from its institutional association to the larger Kababayan at UCI Filipino American student organization, where it first began performing at PCN. But, even if the group has been extremely influential, it cannot claim a historical monopoly in the Filipino American dance crew circuit. Before the advent of Kaba Modern in 1992, beginning in the late 1980s, short-lived but influential Filipino American dance groups such as Ladyz First, Protégé, Tribe, Funki Junction, and Johnny's Quest in Cerritos set the foundation for collegiate crews in Southern California, emerging out of local high schools and parishes where Filipino American youths gathered.[5] Today, PAC (Pilipino American Coalition) Modern at California State University, Long Beach, Samahang Modern at the University of California, Los Angeles (UCLA), and Team Millennia in Fullerton command a notable presence in the Southern California hip hop dance circuit. Filipino American–led breaking crews, rooted in California's unique funk sounds and movements, greatly influenced the Filipino American dance crew infrastructure. For example, inheriting San Francisco Bay Area funk legacies of the prior decade, Filipino American breaking crews developed as early as the early 1980s, such as the Rock Force Crew and the Renegade Rockers.[6]

Although supremely influential, the West Coast is not the only region that has fostered a vibrant Filipino American choreographed dance culture. Played by Filipino American actor Manny Jacinto, the Jason Mendoza character in the popular comedic TV series *The Good Place* hyperbolizes the presence of Filipino American hip hop dancers' in Jacksonville, Florida. In one episode, Jason, who habitually refers to his sixty-person dance crew throughout the series, must return to Jacksonville to assist a rival crew leader, who we find out is Jason's father. Many Filipino Americans who came of age in the 1980s to today understand the significance of the hip hop dance crew in their local communities. In small cliques and in large armies, Filipino American hip hop dance crews have been ubiquitous sights in many cities with a critical presence of young Filipino Americans. I played the role of a dancer and witness to these various scenes as a former hip hop dancer and an active participant in nationwide faith- and activist-based Filipino American organizations. From New Jersey to Seattle to Florida, I recognize the prominence of hip hop dance crews for young Filipino American youths, for both the "good" Catholic kids and the "angry" activists. I remember one moment in college when the choreographers for my dance crew, the Filipino Student

FIGURE 17. Renegade Rockers, 1984, performing at the San Francisco 49ers home game opener halftime show. Photo courtesy of Alfred David.

Association at the University of Florida, snickered while we sat in my living room and watched a VHS tape of a Catholic dance crew from another city. That moment of skepticism quickly gave way to awe as the Catholic kids expertly blended hip hop with Filipino traditional dance, code-switching between so-called traditional and modern dance forms. I concluded that those churchgoing dancers must also be a part of their respective Filipino American college organization.

Before there were professional dance competitions, TV shows, and You-Tube channels, there was the local dance crew. However ephemeral they were, crews were important forms of social organizing for young Filipino Americans. Paralleling the Filipino American mobile DJ scene in the Bay Area carefully documented by Oliver Wang, hip hop dance crews not only emerged out of a Filipino American community, the crews became integral components to shaping the Filipino American community at large.[7] Young Filipino Americans in high school clubs, community groups, and church organizations have spent endless hours practicing, coordinating, and perfecting their dance moves in garages, living rooms, basketball courts, and church halls. Recalling her days practicing with her crew for church talent shows, Filipino associations, high school PCN, garage/house parties, and debuts (eighteenth-birthday celebrations), early Kaba Modern member Cheryl Cambay describes the humble rehearsal settings before the MTV glitz and the rise of the hip hop dance studio industry:

I remember rehearsals well—we'd end up at someone's house and practice in the garages, front yard or the street. At one of the girls' houses—without the mirrors like you see in dance studios—the way we viewed our progress was literally to video tape rehearsals on a camera that was propped up on a tripod and view the footage and make adjustments, corrections, blocking as needed. When we rehearsed at Emil's house, I remember his mother had a glass-mirrored wall that we used to rehearse in front of and it was small so you couldn't see the whole group in the reflection! Oh the joy of practices at our parents' houses after school! And whenever we needed to rehearse or perform at a gig we literally had to call each other at home (no cell phones or email) or page each other to make sure we scheduled rehearsals and made ourselves available for the gigs we were asked to perform at. We also went shopping for performance outfits, which consisted throughout the years of overalls, paisley shirts, timberland boots, embroidered hats, parachute pants—what we considered cool and hip at the time![8]

Graduating from cramped living room rehearsals, Filipino American hip hop dance crews in colleges across the nation cemented their reputations as the most rigorous and competitive dance organizations on campus.[9] These college crews regularly attract non-Filipino dancers who want to learn new, creative movements. As I discuss below, the controversy surrounding the appearance of only non-Filipino representatives of Kaba Modern on MTV's *ABDC* points to the racial and ethnic diversity in Filipino American–led crews. The motivations for non-Filipinos to join vary. Often, students who majored in dance would join Filipino American hip hop dance crews in order to capitalize on the free training and the team's premiere reputation. This was the case for my dance crew at the University of Florida. For students on some campuses, having been a member of a Filipino American hip hop dance crew even provides a pathway to careers in the dance profession.[10]

Even though some formal community infrastructures have provided suitable conditions for the success of dance crews—for example, a network of Filipino American high school and college organizations, church associations, and nonprofit community groups that recruit and train young dancers—I suggest that there are other preconditions to explain the emergence of Filipino American hip hop dance crews stemming from an assemblage of historical and cultural phenomena. For example, it was about timing: a critical mass of Filipino Americans came of age and built collegiate and community infrastructures alongside the cultural rise of hip hop in the late 1980s and early 1990s.[11] The tendency to author a Filipino American ethnic identity via a coded Black Americanness plays a significant role here, a tendency shared by many U.S. youths regardless of ethnicity. However, the macro quality of the phenomenon—in its geographic spread, historical longevity, and the sheer number of practitioners—makes Filipino American hip hop dance crews a singular Filipino occurrence, as witnessed at the FPAC dance battles. Again, the Filipinoness of some hip hop dance scenes resembles the mobile DJ scene in the Bay Area, if only in regard to their large Filipino presences and the key contributions of Filipino leaders. Of the mobile DJ scene, Wang states, "it was as if the scene's ethnic composition was so ordinary as to be unworthy of note or reflection, even though it could not be sheer coincidence that so many Filipino American teenagers formed into mobile crews *with one another*" (original emphasis).[12] As in the mobile DJ scene, young Filipino Americans across the country were building both enduring organizations like Kaba Modern and more ephemeral affiliations, such as assembling impromptu dance crews among friends to perform at debuts, graduation parties, and other events.

The bourgeoning of a Filipino American dance community has grown to the extent that a number of their choreographers have broadened their talents to non–Filipino American spaces. Led by Filipino American choreographers, Boogiezone, Culture Shock, and Team Millennia Dance Studio are centered in Southern California, and some have international branches.[13] Boogiezone, founded by Elm Pizarro in 2003, is a pioneering online social network of dancers whose successful global presence helped inaugurate Boogiezone Utopia dance studios in Southern California and Japan.[14] Arnel Calvario, founder of Kaba Modern, serves as board president of both Culture Shock Los Angeles and Culture Shock International. Various chapters of Culture Shock are led by a whole host of talented Filipino Americans whose own stories and contributions deserve a research project on their own. Team Millennia founder Danny V. Batimana has choreographed the routines of several NBA cheerleader teams and has directed and managed several crews that appeared on *ABDC*. Batimana directs his nonprofit organization, Happiness is NOW Inc., which uses dance to promote youth wellness. Filipino American leadership in hip hop dance communities across the country for the past twenty or so years is incalculable. But without doubt the aforementioned choreographers and their respective organizations have been key contributors to the foundation of choreographed hip hop dance culture on a global scale. It must be noted that although they overlap especially in light of the professionalization of crews in the entertainment industry, the choreographed hip hop dance scene differs in many ways from the format and historical development of early competitive b-boy circuits, such as Battle of the Year, B-Boy Summit, Freestyle Session, Mighty 4, and Miami Pro-Am. Filipino American dancers were undoubtedly also dominant in the b-boy circuits as organizers, promoters, and competition champions. The vibrant b-boy scene deserves dedicated research and documentation well beyond this chapter. Appreciated together, choreographed hip hop dance and b-boy communities were foundational in shaping today's global hip hop dance industry.

Within the broader Asian American community, Filipino Americans have been instrumental in fostering a nationally recognized Asian American hip hop dance scene.[15] Before Asian Americans began to appear regularly on reality TV hip hop dance competitions in the few years before 2010, Filipino Americans led the way in organizing dance scene networks, as mentioned earlier. Anna Sarao, a Filipina American who was the artistic director of Culture Shock San Diego, organized Bustagroove in 2000, which later became the mega competition Body Rock in 2005.[16] In a 2005 interview, Sarao discussed the dominance of Filipino Americans in the Southern California hip hop dance scene, alluding to how Filipino Americans blend with an Asian American scene:

> Since I've been in Culture Shock, I would say its members were 80% Filipino descent. There's a couple Blacks, a couple whites, one Mexican. But you know, it's so funny, a lot of the dance crews are mostly Filipino! I never really thought about why there are so many Filipinos in dance crews. I don't think that networking strategies are just catered to Filipinos, but for some reason, we still are the majority. And I've been looking for so long, because I coordinate this competition called Bustagroove, but I haven't found any crew that isn't mostly Filipino or Asian. There just aren't any like all Blacks, or all Mexican, dance crews.[17]

The annual Vibe dance competition—"THE premier West Coast hip hop dance competition"—hosted by the Asian American fraternity Lambda Theta Delta at UCI, is credited as the first hip hop dance competition in Southern California (in 1995) and for popularizing hip hop dance among Asian Americans.[18] Joseph Lising, roommate of Arnel Calvario at the time and a member of Kaba Modern and Kababayan at UCI, first organized Vibe in 1995 as a fund-raiser for his fraternity.[19] Vibe has been an important Asian American hip hop dance institution, providing a space where young people can project and produce a type of Asian American social acceptability to combat commonly held and well-documented stereotypes that portray Asians as awkward, nerdy, and passive.[20]

The commercial success and cultural blossoming of hip hop dance scenes have thrived in large part thanks to the creative and organizational labor of Filipino Americans already active in the cultural spaces of a Filipino American hip hop vernacular. Yet, the contributions of their labor and bodies seem forsaken. Still subjected to the aftereffects of Spanish and U.S. imperialism, Filipino Americans are haunted by an unresolvable postcolonial positionality, which renders mobile and fleeting the status of "Filipino." In hip hop dance, this status informs Filipinos' presence in the scene, shaping dancers' narrations of their bodies on stage and in community.

From the Cakewalk to Hip Hop:
Modern Dance and Colonialism

The front page of the March 5, 1899, edition of the *Boston Sunday Globe* features a cartoon titled "Expansion, Before and After" satirizing U.S. colonial administrators' ambitions to assimilate newly annexed Filipino subjects into U.S. culture. Printed at the outbreak of the Philippine-American War, the cartoon presents a series of "before-and-after" panels visualizing primitive Filipinos' compatibility to U.S. activities such as sports, carriage riding, and dancing. The panels surround a dark-skinned, wide-grinning fashionable fellow sporting a top hat, high-collared fancy shirt, and a walking cane. The caption under this gentleman reads, "The Filipino after expansion," juxtaposing the adjacent image of him "before expansion" wearing only a grass skirt and grasping a bow and arrows in one hand and a spear in the other. The dancing panel at the bottom right corner shows him transitioning from grass skirted to smartly dressed: from clenching a spear and shield to elegantly tipping his top hat, his posture upright with chest out, and holding a walking cane. "From the war dance to the cake walk is but a step," the panel's caption reads.[21] The cakewalk was a popular American dance form that developed in the nineteenth century among enslaved African people who openly mocked the posturing, grandeur, and fashion of white people. Popularized through minstrel shows and establishing its own form of music, the cakewalk became an iconic part of mainstream entertainment. Although "cakewalk" has come to describe something easy, the dance required intense concentration and difficult maneuvers, executed to make it seem effortless.[22]

The *Boston Sunday Globe* cartoon and the cakewalk allegorize U.S. racial uplift, colonial evolution from the primitive to the modern, and embodied subversion and resignification. White fascination with the movements of the Black body is storied, with the cakewalk and hip hop being two examples of U.S. popular culture's indebtedness to Black vernacular culture. The cartoon and dance narrate the parallelisms of African American and Filipino relationships to U.S. modernity through the dancing racialized body. The cartoon would prophesy Filipino colonial subjects' fluency in the latest American dance moves; it is prescient in its depiction of embodied Blackness as a symbol of Filipinos' modernization through U.S. culture. The cartoon, however caricaturing and distasteful, inadvertently portrays the history of race and racism into the development of U.S. dance. As earlier chapters discuss, several scholars and documentarians have commented on the connected themes of empire, eugenics, labor, and antimiscegenation as they appeared in migrant Filipino agricultural workers' exceptional and infamous dance moves flexed in U.S. taxi dance halls from the 1920s to the end of the U.S. colonial period. What is less documented, but nonetheless significant, is Filipino Americans' dance culture after World War II to the late 1960s during the so-called bridge generation and the succeeding generation's participation in the funk and disco scenes in the 1970s. Since U.S. colonization of the Philippines, Filipinos and Filipino Americans have always been intimate partners with American dance. Hip hop dance, a realization of layers, samplings, and lineages of Black vernacular movements, became popularized among post-1965 Filipino American youths, who for the most part were not descended from earlier agricultural worker generations. The cartoon's exaggerated before-and-after time jump works as a metaphor to understand the rapidity with which Filipino Americans excelled in hip hop dance despite being mainly the children of more recent immigrants. The cartoon's time jump can be interpreted as Filipino American hip hop dancers' swift ascent in the global dance industry even if their decades of hard work in helping to build the scene is left largely unrecognized.

The 1899 cartoon is a grotesque yet useful resource to critique Filipino racial belonging in the aftermath of U.S. conquest. In its multiple and unstable stances and gestures, the dancing Filipino body envisioned from the cakewalk to hip hop reveals an ongoing struggle to choreograph Filipino subjectivity. Filipino American hip hop dancers' negotiations of "Filipino" illustrate the ways in which their hip hop vernacular culture develops from colonialism's structural and imagined inheritances. These dancers provide what Lucy Mae San Pablo Burns calls in her analysis of early twentieth-century Filipino taxi hall patrons an "archival embodiment" that "gestures to the corpus of Filipino American history and records, choreographed by and onto the Filipino body."[23] Archival embodiment inspires my investigation of the knowledge imbued by Filipino American hip hop dancers who seek voice and representation in the shadow of U.S. imperialism and in the ferment of U.S. liberal multiculturalism. Aptly constructing themselves as explicitly modern (e.g., Kaba Modern, PAC Modern, and Samahang Modern), these dancers choreograph both a pursuit of civic recognition in the United States today and colonial disciplining in earlier episodes. These dancers' forms of modernity provide a convoluted vocabulary to make intelligible an other-

FIGURE 18. Front cover of the *Boston Sunday Globe*, March 5, 1899. Public domain, "File:Racist Newspaper Clipping Filipino.Jpg," Wikimedia Commons, 2015.

wise inarticulable position of Filipino postcoloniality in the United States. In this sense, then, for these Filipino American hip hop dancers, claiming to be modern is a posture: it is an inhabitation, an expression, a presentation. Ultimately, these strategies speak to the unrelenting presence of colonialism in their racial and ethnic expressions.

Filipino American hip hop dancers' modern postures both resonate with and diverge from the aesthetic and cultural priorities of the conventionally understandings of modern dance. A versatile genre, modern dance is traditionally regarded as originating in the late 1890s and is deemed on par with jazz as a "truly American" art. Arriving at the time of mechanization and swift urbanization, modern dance often sees itself as liberating the body's movements. Often credited as pioneered by white U.S. women dancers, it is considered a rebellious response to corporeal restrictions placed on women, championing individual forms of freedom in light of the disciplined formalism of traditional ballet.[24] Filipino American hip hop dancers, as important cultural contributors to hip hop's postmodern attributes—its popular practices "from below"—blur the boundaries between modern and postmodern, a familiar compulsion reflected in modern dance. As Jack Anderson shows, "'Modern dance' can imply something merely transient. Nevertheless, the term has stuck. And attempts by some recent critics to devise a separate category for a type of dance that has developed from it have resulted in nothing more than a new and even more awkward term: 'postmodern dance.'"[25] Anderson's reluctance to separate modern and postmodern dance affords Filipino American hip hop dancers a linguistic bridge between the postmodern kinetics of hip hop and the modern ambitions of staged U.S. dance. For groups like Kaba Modern, hip hop's postmodernism and dancers' simultaneous modern postures presents no obvious awkwardness.

Much more than provoking the transient qualities of modern dance, Filipino American hip hop dance culture enacts the otherwise erased racial genealogies in the formation of modern dance. The dancing Filipino body, whether during the early twentieth century as documented by Lucy Burns or more currently on the stages of MTV, dramatizes a U.S. colonial preoccupation with a white universality through the simultaneous abjection and incorporation of racialized bodies, a preoccupation restaged in the traditions of modern dance. The idealization of the modern white body necessitated subordinating the nonwhite Other, including Filipino colonial subjects who were treated as clinical specimens by the white public at the moment of U.S. overseas expansion. Jayna Brown illustrates the racial exchange occurring in the formation of the "modern." "Performing race had everything to do with articulating the modern world," she writes. Brown considers the process of fragmentation and dislocation in the mechanized modern age and the responses represented in the dancing body: "Dance was the lexicon reflecting the dialectic process of modern transformation: the modern body continually reinventing itself, in and against its environment, at the same time as the environment made its claims upon the body." In this fragmented condition, "black expressive forms, miscoded as signatures for a timed and timeless past and separated from actual black subjects, were used as the source by which the modern (white) body could re-member itself."[26] Brown shows modernity was not limited to white universalist responses to mechanization and urban alienation and their search for "newness"; modernity emanated from Black performers' mobile, sexual, and multivalent bodies that defied national boundaries.[27]

Similarly, Susan Manning outlines the racial exchange occurring at the time: "Negro dance and modern dance were mutually constitutive categories, and their interdependent representations of blackness and whiteness shifted in tandem over time."²⁸ Both Brown and Manning recognize the ways in which modern sensibilities and modern dance owe much to Blackness and Black people, an indebtedness revisited among Filipino American hip hop dancers. Reading Brown's text as a guidepost to contemporary Filipino American hip hop dance scenes traces Filipino American culture to earlier episodes of shared Filipino and African American racial formation. With acts named "A Filipino Misfit," formerly called "A Darktown Frolic," among other orientalized and race-conscious acts, the cultural vocabulary of early twenti-eth-century African American performers' spoke to the geopolitical expan-siveness of imperialism at the same moment the United States was attempting to discipline Filipinos. Filipinos, along with other colonized and orientalized bodies, were featured in Black dance performers' racial vocabularies. Light-skinned Black performers especially participated in racial "passing" for vari-ous racialized subjects on stage. *The Creole Show*, which became a hit in 1890, and the chorus shows that followed "demonstrated that the city and colony (territories occupied by European and U.S. national and business interests) were intertwined spectacles." Brown turns to the Black women's "practices of racial delineation, alternately Cubana, Filipina, Chinese, Egyptian, as their acts mediated between and revealed the artifice of 'modern' and 'primitive' ideas of the feminine. These acts both celebrated and called into question the boundaries between colony and metropole and drew parallels between geog-raphies of imperial annexation and the sexualized, racialized zoning of city spaces, the lines of which were being drawn at the same time." As embodied archives, the multivalent embodiments of Black women performers issue a "critique of modernity" in that they "create forms of consciousness and re-sistance against a plethora of strategies that have barred them from inclusion in both dominant and resistant collective political-cultural bodies."²⁹ Brown unpacks a convoluted set of exchanges by which Blackness becomes mobile and multidirectional for early Black performers. Like Brown, Burns recalls the processes of African American and Filipino co-constitution on stage. Burns also notes African Americans' "brownface performance" of Filipinos occurring during this time as transgressive and defiant, even if the efforts of African American brownface promoted heroic Black American patriotism invested in U.S. empire building.³⁰ Ultimately, circa-1900 U.S. expansionism provided the structural and cultural conditions for the exploration of Black performative subjectivity via the colonized Filipino body.

Brown redeems the central role of Black women performers in the shaping of modern culture staged by white women's simultaneous incorporation and erasure of Black women's contributions to dance.[31] Ironically, the historical account of Filipino and Filipino American dance culture redirects modern dance to the colonial influence of white women in the Philippines. Studying early twentieth-century photographs that show white women teaching indigenous Filipinos popular American dance numbers, Burns examines "the pivotal role white women and performance played in the American civilizing mission."[32] The routing of Black vernacular dance through the tutelage of colonizing, liberal white women poses an irony in that the very fear of white America and its attached laws calling for Filipino exclusionary and antimiscegenation were grounded in the taboo of Filipino men's "splendid dancing" with white women. The "exceptionality" of Filipino men's skills is always linked to the exceptionality of U.S. empire.

As representatives of the afterlife of the very colonized subjects who were supposedly civilized by white women, Filipino American hip hop dancers reembody their African American dance predecessors' protean corporeality. Filipino American hip hop dancers signify the multiplicity of the politics of their racialized and gendered performances: as (largely) non-Black people, they engage Black expressive forms while recalling the "splendid dancing" of Filipino bodies that threatened early twentieth century whiteness. Said another way, Filipino Americans perform Blackness as hip hop dancers, but they are also performing Filipinoness as diasporic, Americanized postcolonials. In this instance, as this book repeatedly suggests, Filipinoness in hip hop is impure and mobile, traveling across a multitude of racial circuits.

The African American, white American, and Filipino racial intersections of the early twentieth century reemerge in hip hop dance culture in the contemporary period, except now Asian American dancers dominate both the spoken and unspoken racial discourse of hip hop dance. Filipino American hip hop dancers labor as unheralded teachers to the more visible and commodifiable Asian American hip hop dancer. Dance cultures in both beginnings of the twentieth and twenty-first centuries enact an erasure when it asserts its legibility either as art or as commercial product. Similar to early African American dancers who made a distinct yet largely unattributed imprint on modern dance and other forms of modern embodiments, Filipino American hip hop dancers, whose vernacular culture thrived decades before the emergence of Asian American hip hop dancers on a global scale, continue to be overlooked for their key contributions to hip hop dance, as I demonstrate in the next section; the visibility of Filipino American hip hop dance vernacular culture seems to be inversely proportional to the commercial rise of the Asian American hip hop dance scene.

Asian Pride, Anti-Blackness,
and Obscured Intermediaries

Since the premiere of MTV's *America's Best Dance Crew* in 2008, Asian Americans have had a noticeable presence on reality dance TV competitions. Their faces and bodies have graced the stages on shows such as *So You Think You Can Dance*, *Step It Up and Dance*, and *America's Got Talent*. Creating a niche entertainment career by hosting their own live shows in Las Vegas and performing backup for today's hottest pop stars, Filipino Americans particularly have fostered several generations of amateur dancers, some of whom are entering into the professional entertainment world. Bailey "Bailrok" Muñoz, the Rock Steady Crew member and young Filipino American b-boy prodigy, won the sixteenth season of *So You Think You Can Dance* (Fox, 2019), succeeding Filipina American virtuoso Hannahlei Cabanilla, who triumphed the previous season.[33] More than a decade earlier, the first season of *ABDC* set the stage for the cultural and commercial success of hip hop choreographed dance not just among Asian Americans but for the larger viewing public. The season also dramatized the politics of Filipino Americans' racial membership as fans and critics celebrated and debated the contributions and talents of Asian American and Filipino American dancers. *ABDC*'s inaugural season represented a "finally!" moment of mainstream recognition of Filipino and Asian Americans' cultural labor.

Season 1, perhaps the show's most iconic season in its four-year run, both reflects and contributes to the epistemology of Filipino American postcolonial erasure, whereby Asian Americans' debut in hip hop dance culture necessitates the subsuming and obscuring of Filipino Americans in the formation of that culture. In particular, I show that *ABDC* fans' exhortations of "Asian pride" elide years of Filipino American hip hop dancers' creative labor. Importantly, requisite Filipino American erasure that enables a larger Asian American cultural triumph locates the dissonant relationship between Filipino and U.S. national and cultural belonging. In identifying hegemonic U.S. narratives that reinforce U.S. exceptionalism in film, literature, and spoken-word poetry performances, Faye Caronan scrutinizes the U.S. cultural market's proclivity to contain, obscure, and marginalize Filipino American (and Puerto Rican) cultural critiques. The multiple and broad evacuation of imperial critique rife in Filipino American hip hop dance discourse waged by the general public, Asian Americans, and Filipino Americans themselves parallels Caronan's multi-genre observations. Echoing Caronan, I identify U.S. hegemonic narratives and its engine, the cultural market, as erasing Filipino American bodies in hip hop dance. Gesturing to Lisa Lowe's critiques of complicity in the hegemonic narratives of liberal multiculturalism prevalent in Asian American literature, Caronan writes that "the difficulty of reading beyond the hegemonic narratives of Asian American culture and multiculturalism lies in Asian American identification with these narratives."[34] My task, too, is to "read beyond" the hegemonic narratives and unpack critical ways to understanding Filipino American hip hop dance performances and embodiments. As I discuss later in this chapter, the dissonant relationship in Filipino-U.S. national and cultural belonging can be excavated in Filipino American dancers' queer strategies of community formation and counter-memory.

The popularity of Asian Americans in hip hop dance reached a fever pitch after the success of Kaba Modern and the Jabbawockeez crews on *ABDC*'s premiere season. After studying the big hip hop dance competitions over the years—Vibe, Body Rock, Fusion, and Prelude—the producers of the U.S. Aerobics Championships consulted leaders in the dance community, including Filipino American dance leaders Arnel Calvario, Anna Sarao, and Elm Pizarro, on how to establish a television show akin to *American Idol* but based on the hip hop dance scene. Soon Hip Hop International was created, which achieved its goal in creating the show *ABDC*.[35] Arnel Calvario relinquished his role as a consultant to *ABDC* in order to manage the Kaba Modern team that competed on the show. Out of twelve crews, Kaba Modern and the Jabbawockeez made it to the top three. Predominantly Asian American (particularly Filipino American) dance crews appeared on later seasons of the show (as well as in similar dance shows on other channels), such as Team Millennia, the Massive Monkees, Supreme Soul, and Super Cr3w, the last winning first place in the second season. The regularity of Asian Americans in earlier seasons of *ABDC* and their gradual decline had prompted the suspicion that the show was intentionally limiting the number of Asian American dancers on the show. Calvario discloses that he has "heard of casting directors turning away dance crews comprised of Asian-Americans in efforts to diversify the faces of their show and optimize ratings."[36] It seems that Asian American representation in hip hop dance had become so saturated that it stoked fears of Asian domination.

On season 1's episode 7, titled "Evolution of Street Dance," the remaining crews were presented with the challenge of devising a dance set for what *ABDC* host Mario Lopez called "the most iconic styles in past twenty years of street dancing."[37] Serving as a lesson of the recent history of popular dance, the episode prompted teams to exhibit a linear history of dance styles, starting with funk and ending with krumping. The episode was also the final standoff between crowd favorites Kaba Modern and the Jabbawockeez in what Lopez declared as the "most intense head to head clash on this stage." The Jabbawockeez, the all-male, mostly Asian American crew known for their "foundational" hip hop dance techniques, hit the stage first in the head-to-head battle. In a backstage interview, Jabbawockeez member Ben Chung acknowledged that their goal was to "tell the timeline of hip hop." Dressed in apocalyptic b-boy attire, they take to the stage in sinister-looking, expressionless, blood-red masks, ski goggles, snow hats, and brown vests. They breezed through the "timeline of hip hop," showing particular precision in flips, swipes, and footwork in their b-boy routine set to the b-boy canon Jimmy Castor Bunch's "It's Just Begun." The crew topped off their routine with Rynan Paguio's toe-touching three-minute head spin. The Jabbawockeez's routine set exemplified the crew's faithfulness to fundamental b-boy moves, which characterized the members' pre-*ABDC* repertoire, while also exhibiting a flair for crowd-pleasing acrobatics.

Could Kaba Modern compete with the intimidating masked men? "The judges have said that Kaba Modern is the future of dance. So let's see how they took on the styles of the past," Lopez stated before the video montage glimpsed at the mixed-gender group's preparation for the week's challenge. Kaba Modern took to the stage dressed in comfortable matching Adidas athletic gear. After the voice sample inspired by Jimmy Castor Bunch's song "Troglodyte (Cave Man)" bellowed—"Right about now, we're gonna go back into time"—Kaba Modern waved their Kangol caps and began to do their locking styles to Lipps INC's "Funkytown." Next, they donned black wide-brimmed hats in their nod to Run DMC, then red and blue beanies for the b-boy set. The women lost their pants to expose knee-high socks and very short red shorts for the Salt-N-Pepa "Push-It" routine. Unzipping their jackets to brandish their Kaba Modern–branded black hooded sweatshirts, they ended with a moderately aggressive krumping set. At the routine's climax, they crossed their arms, with their hoods up and backs to the audience. *ABDC* judge Lil Mama commended the group: "the walk-through . . . the evolution, was crazy." Likewise, judge Shane Sparks, an African American hip hop dance choreographer, applauded: "Ya'll bring back memories for me. I know a lot of old school brothers that are watching this show are like, 'Dang! They doin' all our dances!'" The third judge, former N'SYNC member JC Chasez, remarked to the Kaba Modern women: "You're like the last girls here, man. And you represented girls so well."

Despite the accolades given to Kaba Modern, the Jabbawockeez would win the episode's face-off and, eventually, take the crown for *ABDC*'s debut season. Of the Jabbawockeez's set, Sparks accurately prophesied in episode 7, "Y'all just set the standard for the next ten seasons. Look, if the crews that are watching at home don't come at that level, they need to stay home." That episode's lesson of popular dance styles highlights an attempt to ground the show as a legitimate and informed forum for popular Black dance (sprinkled with white boy band N'SYNC moves). Truly multiracial in its composition, for seven seasons *ABDC* sought to represent various competitors' colors, geographical regions, genders, and sexualities. Episode 7 of season 1, though, gave perhaps the most epic Asian American crew showdown never seen again on *ABDC*, cementing Asian Americans' competence in flexing Black popular dance. Ultimately, though, MTV's objective of deracination through a commodified and choreographed multiculturalism amplified and even calcified racial difference. Despite the color-blind utopia exhibited on the show, to repeat Jayna Brown's words, "performing race had everything to do with articulating the modern world."

Calvario's leadership in fostering hip hop dance both as a local, Filipino American expression and as an entertainment product on MTV encapsulates Filipino Americans' multiple roles in the development of the scene. In both their absence and presence on *ABDC*, Filipino Americans bridged a localized cultural dance vernacular to a virtual, global, and thoroughly commercialized cultural arena. The lights on more humble stages since the early 1990s were outshined by the digitized and dazzling glitz of telecommunications and globalized exchange represented by MTV. Magnifying the stakes of their craft, competitors became hypermobile, flocking to New York, Houston, Chicago, and other regional metropolises hoping to win an audition and, perhaps, freeze life plans for a few months to live in Hollywood and prove to the world that they are the best the nation has to offer. The pleasure of labor in building local dance communities is greatly indebted to the craft and vision of Filipino Americans. Yet, *ABDC*, as the supposed "debut" of choreographed hip hop to the world, arrested Filipino representation in modern hip hop dance culture while making hypervisible a "modern" Asian American hip hop constituency uplifted as fully capable to compete with the best.

For many Filipino American dancers, the Jabbawockeez's win made a lot of sense because the mostly Filipino American members came out of the competitive West Coast b-boy battle scene.[38] In short, the Jabbawockeez members, Filipino American or not, were party to the dance spaces in which Filipino Americans were already immersed. That Kaba Modern lost on *ABDC* even though it won the overall popularity contest online prompted a more mixed reaction among Filipino Americans. Many Filipino American netizens begrudged the fact that Kaba Modern, as a historically Filipino American group that maintains strong ties to PCN and Kababayan, had no Filipino Americans on the MTV show. Where many Filipino American dancers intuitively recognized that they have been highly involved in hip hop dance—from b-boying to choreographed dance—their absence on the show was yet another instance of their seemingly perpetual mainstream erasure. Expressing concern about the disconnect between the Kaba Modern name and its non-Filipino representatives on MTV, a Kaba Modern fan posted on the message board of the popular Asian American culture website www.8asians.com, which holds a rich archive of *ABDC* fan reactions, the following:

> As much I am a fan of kaba modern . . . I feel there is a sense of disappointment personally as a Filipino because there is not even at least just ONE filipino member. Kaba Modern was based on a filipino tradition and I feel like yes I am glad that we opened the doors to other cultures to participate in a great dance troupe. . . . BUT why is it they couldn't at least have the decency to allow a filipino member to be apart or the show. . . . If not[,] the people who are watching might not know where their name came from. And I feel that is it important to let the people of America know how it all really started . . . and it's simple. It start with filipinos. So why can't we get the recognition that we should be getting?[39]

Via Kaba Modern on *ABDC*, Filipino Americans may not have gotten the recognition that some feel they deserved. That none of the six members of the MTV Kaba Modern crew was Filipino signifies a manifestation of a Filipino American hip hop dance vernacular that weaves into a larger Asian American dance scene. Non-Filipino Asian Americans excelling on a world stage recalibrates the developmental linearity of episode 7's clean and simplified "Evolution of Street Dance." Central but unacknowledged in the story of street dance—and built into the conception of *ABDC*—is the creative labor of Filipino Americans who for years have defied the neat linearity of dance in their simultaneous absorption of multiple styles. The MTV Kaba Modern team, as what Lil Mama referred to as the "future of dance," signaled the "we-made-it moment" for Asian Americans tired of being seen as outside of street dance. Lil Mama's "future" comment was prescient indeed, as Asian American–majority dance teams exploded across the nation after 2008, concomitant to the overlooking of the core contributions of Filipino American dancers who directly or indirectly made the MTV Kaba Modern team possible.

For Asian Americans, being accepted as legitimate participants in U.S. culture has always proved vexing. Until the recent global dominance of state-supported Korean pop culture, Asians were categorically excluded from being hip and cool (in this book I use these terms interchangeably) in a U.S.

setting.[40] Of hip's insider/outsider dynamics, John Leland writes that "hip begins . . . as a subversive intelligence that outsiders developed under the eye of insiders." To be Asian and "hip" in U.S. culture—in this case Black American culture—implies being "in the know" despite being chronically castigated as "perpetual foreigners" to the United States. Further, the white imaginary continues to stereotype Asians as nerdy, having superior mental and spiritual capabilities but lacking corporeal power, and, for Asian men, being effete.[41] Laying out the racially dichotomous nature of hip, Leland continues: "hip tells a story of black and white America, and the dance of conflict and curiosity that binds it." Hip is constituted by white Americans' realizations of alternative whiteness through their appropriation of Blackness, where white rebelliousness can come to exemplify a "signature American style."[42]

Asian American coolness reveals ideological crevices presented by a Black/white cultural binary. As racialized minorities in U.S. society, Asian Americans exert a complex set of racial powers. For one, they have been accused of inhabiting many traits of whiteness, including class and propriety conceits and dominance in educational advancement. As such, a constellation of social and economic privileges that creates the dubious honor of "Asian American whiteness" certainly casts suspicion on Asian American cool culture, as some African Americans question whether Asian Americans are on their side or are more like whites.[43] But Asian Americans are also racialized minorities who have been historically targeted by extralegal and state-sanctioned exclusion precisely because of their unassimilability to the "white race."[44] They continue to be marked as Other in the U.S. racial scheme and quite conspicuously outside the decided attributes of U.S. culture, thus situating their civic belonging as never racially unmarked (i.e., white). To be regarded as cool and hip, though, ultimately harkens the masculine codes in African American vernacular culture linked to strategies of control, dignity, and awareness in the face of everyday crisis and racism.[45] To be a "cool" Asian American in hip hop, however, may connote a variety of gender expressions, experiences, aesthetics, and embodiments according to context. But, in hip hop especially, being cool necessitates a glancing toward the historical trajectory of Blackness that helps form the aesthetics and politics in Black music and dance, cultural forms that constitute a "signature American style."

Even if Asian Americans are minoritized as nonwhite, the hegemonic narrative exalting their inauguration into a "signature American style" in their success on *ABDC* uncovers the pernicious favorability attached to Asian American racial privilege. Examining Asian American representations on *ABDC*'s season 1, Brian Su-Jen Chung critiques Asian American media writers' tendency to universalize hip hop dance and promote a neoliberal narrative that privileges entrepreneurship, professionalism, and commercialism in hip hop. According to Chung, this neoliberal narrative advantages and celebrates Asian American bodies on *ABDC* while criminalizing African American dancers' supposed lack of professionalism. For these media writers, in order to justify Asian American triumphalism, hip hop's roots in leisure culture emerging from African American urban blight must be downplayed while *hip hop as industry*—as a professionalized and universalized capitalistic enterprise—is aggrandized. Chung states: "As these stories go, writers mention that Asian Americans gravitate toward hip-hop dance because they believe that Asian Americans, like African Americans, experience forms of disenfranchisement and social marginalization on an everyday basis. But these writers then make the leap to say that hip-hop dance provides a common ground for Asian Americans, African Americans, and the rest of the country to 'move beyond race.' The 'Americanness' of blackness lies in its signification of professionalism that holds the promise for Asian Americans to 'move beyond race.'" These discourses around Asian American hip hop dancers' success on TV extend a polite gesture to hip hop's Black origins, but they place Asian American arrival as one of liberal beneficiaries whereby African American gatekeepers have relinquished their power to allow disciplined, family-oriented, but historically shunned Asian bodies to participate in hip hop dance's cultural and material wealth. Chung continues: These writers frame liberal multiculturalism as resolving an unofficially regulated dance industry favoring black bodies. . . . In these instances, these writers identify with hip-hop's blackness only as a neoliberal, 'post-welfare' discourse when it constitutes Asian Americans as good citizens by virtue of their resourcefulness, entrepreneurship, work ethic, and Asian cultures of 'respect' in their approach to hip-hop dance cultures as a career ('premier entertainment)."[46] As Chung demonstrates, Asian Americans' mainstream arrival to a "signature American style" in hip hop involves a series of erasures. Blackness, in the case of the *ABDC* episode, is both celebrated yet somehow "evolved" to include Asian faces as the "future" of hip hop dance. Here, Asian Americans enter a field of power in hip hop in which the historical status of Blackness become vulnerable as non-Blacks arrive in hip hop. The most notorious incident of Asian Americans' assertion of power over Black bodies and culture through hip hop occurred through the very real—not figurative—practice of blackface performance in 2013. New members of the Asian American fraternity Lambda Theta Delta (LTD) at UCI (the same fraternity that has organized the Vibe dance competition) posted a YouTube video of members lip-synching to Justin Timberlake's song "Suit and Tie." In the video, one of the young men, in his role as the African American rapper Jay-Z, wears blackface paint. As the story goes, the video was intended to advertise an upcoming event and "did not intend racism," as noted in the YouTube video's description by the members. The video was soon taken down, but an outraged public calling the video racist and anti-Black had already reposted the video for the world to see and criticize. Given backlash aired on local and national news, LTD, which advertises itself as UCI's first and largest Asian American interest fraternity, suspended its activities for the academic year and jeopardized the cherished Vibe hip hop dance competition.[47]

The video depicts the class mobility, racial privilege, and male heterosexuality epitomized by Asian American fraternity culture, and it contorts the cultural work of Filipino American students at UCI. In the two-minute video, the anti-Black messaging casually objectifies Black people and obliterates their role as hip hop's primary cultural, political, and historical constituency. The incident provides a stark example of the historical power of non-Blacks to abuse—however intentionally and in whatever degree of admiration—the dignity of Black people through minstrelsy.[48] The LTD members who bore the brunt of the fallout were the fraternity's president at the time and the young man in blackface, both of whom are Filipino American. As the public spokesman for the organization, the president represented the face of the Asian American fraternity, and in effect, Asian American Greek culture in general. The blackface performer, his name displayed in captions in the original video, symbolized the willful ignorance usually attached to campus Greek life (the stereotypical "frat boy") and the cultural power of UCI Asian American students, who, in 2011, constituted half of the undergraduate body, while African American students stood at 2 percent.[49] During a protest led by African American students after the release of the video, protestors called out Asian American students' penchant for choreographed hip hop dance.[50] For the Filipino American LTD members, their particular ethnicity and any supposed historical relationship to Blackness, hip hop, and pre–hip hop collaborations (in funk, boogaloo, strutting, and popping) became moot. As members of a pan–Asian American fraternity that touts a mission of Asian American–oriented community service, Filipino American members effectively "became" Asian American, along with its attendant racial privileges. Coupled with the Greek system's association with upper-middle-class social power, members of LTD and other Asian American Greek organizations at UCI can be seen as attempting to achieve Asian American racial autonomy and distinction in the name of liberal multiculturalism and middle-class assimilation.

The preferred neoliberal facets of commodification, entrepreneurship, and universalism of hip hop dance that aid Asian American visibility in hip hop dance point to the literal and figurative obscuring of Filipino bodies in Kaba Modern. According to accounts familiar among Kababayan and Kaba Modern members, before the six *ABDC* members were chosen to appear on the show, two Filipino American coordinators were in the original lineup. However, the two were also committed to preparing the larger Kaba Modern group for the Vibe competition and ultimately could not participate in *ABDC*. So, with the strong embrace of the MTV Kaba Modern team as generically Asian American, to observers Kaba Modern virtually became a non-Filipino team.

Taking the controversy in another direction, some observers seized on Filipino absence to tout the virtue of Kaba Modern's multiracial composition. Another user on www.8asians.com, claiming to be a current dancer of the larger Kaba Modern group, wrote:

> our team is in fact CRAZY DIVERSE . . . we have pretty much every asian race, black, white and indian on the team . . . please realize that just because we began from our filipino culture club that we are not limited to just a certain type of people . . . as dancers OUR MAIN GOAL is to inspire through our passion and break the boundaries of narrow mindedness . . . we have been so successful throughout the years because of this very reason: we learn from each other and are constantly growing and absorbing backgrounds from cultures in not only dance but life as well!

The user suggests that a preoccupation with Filipino representation signals "narrow mindedness." A YouTube user commenting on a now-removed Kaba Modern *ABDC* clip also defends the idea that Kaba Modern's racial and ethnic heterogeneity contributes to the group's overall success, stating that "truth is only about half of our team is oriental . . . the other half is a combination of people from many other ethnicities . . . our choreographers are of many races as well. It is this diversity and respect for all people that allows us to innovate and display our love for dance =D." According to the two commenters above, Filipino centricity denotes ethnic parochialism, which inhibits the development of their craft. Instead, as implied, a liberal multicultural mantra of "respect for all people" propels the organization. Yet, even if both the larger Kaba Modern family and the six-member *ABDC* group are extremely diverse, clearly the organization is composed predominantly of Asian Americans, reflecting UCI's student demographics. So, apparently, Kaba Modern is multicultural in that its members are of different Asian ethnic backgrounds. Using the Tagalog term *kababayan* (countrymen) to account for all Asians, another commenter on the same YouTube video writes: "I'm filipino and it doesn't matter if there is no pinoy on the crew I'm still proud of them as asian and they carry the name kaba modern as the group. KABA mean kababayan right, group of asian country we can call them our kababayan because we are from asia." Like this user, many Filipino Americans claimed a sense of ethnic and racial legibility through the mainstream valorization of non-Filipino Asian Americans.

The tendency to de-prioritize Filipino American membership in the larger Kaba Modern organization over the years became a "solution" for a larger Asian American cultural gain. The chronic nature of Filipino American erasure in the American imaginary is well-discussed and theorized.[51] Furthermore, the concerns over Filipino American non-representation on *ABDC* also points to the erasure of Filipinos within the Asian category. As Kaba Modern continued to climb in *ABDC* season 1, ahistorical exhortations of "Asian pride" quickly flooded internet chat rooms and YouTube comment sections. One user on www.8asians.com proclaims, "Yo KaBa ModErN Is sOMe TiGHt AZN BreAkerS! I hOPE TheY MakE IT aLL thE WaY BABy! AZIAN PRIDE!!!!!!!!!!" As if "AZN" (Asian) recognition comes only when Filipino American gatekeepers "accept" non-Filipinos into their fold, one www.8asians.com user comments: "Kaba Modern is one of the BEST 'California AZN Collegiate' hip hop crews around. They're so notorious and they've accepted non-filipino's into their crew . . . just like all the other Chinese and Japanese crews do at other schools. If you wanna dance with the best, then you join the best! ^_^" Another, whose comment that his/her "peeps" are not on the show and suggests he/she is Filipino, dismisses the controversy surrounding the lack of Filipinos on the crew and instead praises "us asians" for competing at a high level: "who cares if theres any filipinos in kaba modern. They don't have my peeps in there but they are still representing for the azians. Kaba modern isnt the best asian crew compared to others but I hope they win so the world could see how us asians do it. One day im gonna go to UCI too and become one of them(but better) and I hope I meet YURI TANG!! =)"

This recent iteration of Asian pride is especially evident in the fandom surrounding Korean American dancer Yuri Tag, the starlet of the *ABDC* Kaba Modern team who characterizes the narratives of an Asian American cultural triumph story.[52] Fans' sexualization of and fascination with Tag is reminiscent of Rachael Miyung Joo's thesis on the "arrival" of the Korean female body in the Korean public sphere as athletes and fans, signifying a "modern" Korean nation able to compete in a globalized economy.[53] Tag's fandom points to an Asian American cultural desire for an Asian female who is sexy, hip, educated, and talented: a modern Asian American woman. Her teary-eyed biographical vignette on the first episode of *ABDC*, which introduced Kaba Modern to the world, featured her parents, who, according to the show's narration, initially only reluctantly approved of her dance career. The image of immigrant parental support is an important story for some Asian American viewers. Whereas Asian American members of the Jabbawockeez were certainly sexualized and celebrated for their Asian masculinity, the particular debut of the parentally supported, modern Asian American woman indicates an Asian American achievement that focuses on Asian femininity capable of competing kinesthetically with other racialized (especially Black) people.

Tag's appeal gave a younger community of dance fans a cause to celebrate Asian Americans' competence in hip hop dance. Yet, fans' exhortations of "Asian pride" are ahistorical because they do not reference the several generations of the Filipino American choreographed dance scene, the broader Filipino American hip hop and b-boy dance networks, nor the non-Filipino Asian Americans that later joined these overlapping communities. In short, "Asian pride" does not harken to the local, community-based Filipino American hip hop dance movement. Of course, *ABDC* and YouTube opened the world to younger generations of hip hop dance enthusiasts, bringing in a much larger audience to an already existing Asian American dance community in Southern California.

ABDC enthusiasts' naïveté was compounded by Filipinos' historical defiance of racial categorization. The mainstream success of non-Filipino Asian Americans in the hip hop dance world sparked debate about the contested claim of Filipino Americans' membership in a broader, imagined Asian American community. Their different racial memberships follow the interests of various, sometimes unclear, political stakes. For example, Asian pride incorporated the history of Filipino Americans in hip hop as a testament to a longer history of Asian American dominance in the scene. Here, non-Filipino Asian Americans and Filipino Americans alike can point to the longer arc of Kaba Modern's reign as evidence of Asian Americans' legitimate place in hip hop dance. In this case, as demonstrated by the previously cited message board user, "the best" started off with Filipinos but has now become bona fide "AZN" territory. Regardless of any distancing other Asian Americans had from Filipinos, Filipino Americans are welcomed into the fold as long as it benefits Asian America writ large. In another scenario illuminating the debate of Filipino Americans' racial membership, observers will distinguish Filipinos as Pacific Islanders. In a clumsily filmed YouTube interview, Yuri Tag is asked whether she thinks Filipinos are Asian or Pacific Islanders. Amid whispers of "Asian" from the person next her, she answers somewhat innocuously (as if she is uncomfortably put on the spot): "Actually, preferably, I'd have to pick Pacific Islander because they are always running the show and they have really good food and Kaba Modern." At that moment she pulls a Pinay dancer toward her and says, "Look, she's Pacific Islander, and I like her a lot."[54] The language of differentiation ("*they* are always running the show") does not in any way place Filipinos into the category of Pacific Islander, but Tag's response to somehow justify Filipinos' racial distance from "Asian" (as if she really believes non-Filipino Asians don't have good food) exhibits Tag's effort to distinguish Filipinos' roles in Kaba Modern relative to other Asian American dancers. Although these roles are unclear, Tag's response marks an anxiety some people—whether Filipino or not—have in identifying Filipinos as Asian. Among internet users, Filipino Americans' preferred identification with "Pacific Islander" became a hot point of contention. A vocal user on www.8asians.com sardonically states:

> THE IRONY OUT OF ALL THIS ARE THE FILIPINO-AMERICANS WHO DON'T WANT TO BE LABELED AS "ASIANS" RATHER "PACIFIC ISLANDERS." FOR ALL THE PEOPLE WHO SAYING "ASIAN PRIDE" NOT TO MENTION THE ASIANS WHO ARE REPRESENTING A FILI-PINO GROUP, THIS MUST REALLY PISS OFF THE FIL-AMS WHO DON'T LIKE TO BE KNOWN AS "ASIAN."
> ROFL! SO FUNNY!

This user, who later gives a pedantic discourse on why Filipinos are indeed Asian and calls those "Fil-Ams" who identify as Pacific Islanders "unedu-cated," further evidences Filipinos' disputed racial memberships. The user's point is well-taken in supposing some Filipino Americans' chagrin to being interpellated as Asian. However erudite the user may be in enumerating the political identification Filipinos in the Philippines have with Asia—especially as the Philippines was an original founder of the Association of Southeast Asian Nations—the user, who admits to being Filipino and not Filipino American, scoffs at the possibility of Filipino American cultural incommen-surability within the category "Asian." Whatever the case, the mainstreaming of Asian Americans in hip hop dance has put front and center the contested territory of Asian America, where Filipino Americans are simultaneously accepted and disavowed, and where Filipino Americans themselves find Asian America as a contradictory space of shared community and dissonant coalition. Here, Filipino Americans embody the holes in the unifying claims of Asian American panethnicity.[55]

Amid the controversy of Filipino absence in Kaba Modern, the Jabba-wockeez's win gave limited satisfaction for the calls of Filipino American recognition in hip hop dance, even if the crew did not give overt or even subtle references to their ethnicity. As a result of the Jabbawockeez's fame due to the show, the masked champions began hosting a lucrative theatrical show in Las Vegas.[56] Half of the crew's members were known by astute observers to be Filipino, with Rynan Paguio leading as an already popular Southern California Filipino American breaker. Without any references to Filipino ethnicity, the enigmatic, masked, all-male performers competed without the burden to demonstrate their connection to Filipino ethnicity, something Kaba Modern had to shoulder because of their namesake. The Jabbawockeez's win reflects the triumph more of a Filipino American *male* b-boy tradition going back to the early 1980s. For Filipino American fans, the Jabbawockeez spotlighted the "real hip hop" that Filipino Americans had been performing for a long time, a hip hop scene that developed outside of a college setting.[57]

Although they were often placed alongside Kaba Modern's "Asian pride" success story, the maleness and hip hop "realness" of the Jabbawockeez on MTV solicited a varied gaze: only two other non-Filipino Asian Americans filled the roster, with one African American dancer rounding out the six-member team. I contend that Kaba Modern's ethnic and gender diversity and its being composed of *all* Asian American dancers who are university-educated are significant assets to a circulating "Asian pride" discourse, particularly for Asian Americans who identify with safe, middle-class, model-minority aspirations where the proletarian idea of *street* dance can be innocuously transported into the elite university environment. The Jabbawockeez's "street" style did attract many Asian American fans, but for the reasons above, I suggest Kaba Modern garnered more "Asian pride" appeal.[58]

With the Jabbawockeez, Filipino Americans were on the U.S. stage but without having to *be* Filipino: their faces were actually obscured by their signature masks during their dance performances. Filipino representation on the show revealed itself when a member of Super Cr3w (another all-male crew) waved a Philippine flag when they were announced as champions of season 2. In season 3, Kristine Bueta of Team Millennia shouted out "Filipino!" and spoke on camera about traditional Filipino dancing. *ABDC* host Mario Lopez then hollered, "Pinay in the house!"[59] These brief eruptions of Filipino legibility on the show produced what Kaba Modern and the Jabbawockeez could not do: give overt credit to Filipino American dancers who helped build the hip hop dance scene.

In hip hop dance, the Asian American body has been constituted by ongoing Filipino American cultural negotiations and strategies. Borrowing a term from chapter 1 on the circulation of hip hop culture among Filipino Americans and the role of militarized geographies, choreographed dance has functioned as a "contact zone" for Asian Americans in hip hop.[60] Resonating with U.S. empire's spaces of colonial interaction, this particular contact zone involves a complex field of power relationships and identity formations. As such, Filipino Americans' articulations of their own historical, cultural, and racial affinities in these zones include but also exceed Asian American cultural politics. In their excess, whether they are regarded as Filipino, Asian American, Pacific Islander, or something else, Filipino Americans have worked as intermediaries for Asian Americans' success in the mainstream realm of hip hop dance.

Being modern signals varying forms of encounters for Filipino Americans and Asian Americans: the former harkens to centuries-long racial domination occurring in Asia and the latter involves the knocking on the door of American culture. Where Asian Americans triumph as legitimate players equivalent to the many racial categories in the patchwork of a liberal multicultural American society, Filipino Americans follow the determinations of U.S. empire: they disappear.

Queering Modern: Staging Tradition with Exceptional Form

So far this chapter unpacks Filipino American hip hop dancers' messy discourses of being modern in the world. These discourses, I contend, encounter friction when modernity meets U.S.-Philippine colonial history, the racialized development of modern dance, and the triumphalism of liberal multiculturalism as seen on MTV's *America's Best Dance Crew*. I suggest that a critical consideration of empire in Filipino American hip hop dance culture reorients power vertically, allowing for history-rich analyses of culture and representation. As unruly political actors, Filipino American hip hop dancers often resist their vernacular culture's articulation of racial domination in exchange for the safety of horizontally ordered racial differences. But as embodied archives of their own history, they "speak" otherwise: they unknowingly pun the concept of "modern."

The multigenerational and locally rooted vernacular culture of Filipino American hip hop dance remains one of the casualties of multicultural spectacle. I seek to recuperate Filipino American hip hop dance vernacular's important emergence out of the processes of Filipino American community building and belonging. In this section, I examine the productive friction occurring in Filipino American hip hop dancers' negotiations of "modern" and "traditional" as they relate to the representations of their bodies on stage and in community with each other. Dancers' mixed narrations of their participation in PCN and Kaba Modern exemplify a nonlinear and uncategorizable queer counter-memory of Filipino racial performances and belonging. I argue that experiencing modernity via the encounter of the United States' civilizational mission in the Philippines produces queer forms of affiliation for Filipino Americans whereby ethnicity and family become pliable signifiers of belonging.

In order to further appreciate the multifaceted discourses of modern and its association with Filipino American hip hop dancers, including in what I call their queer responses to their modern/traditional binary, it is essential to understand their dance crews' emergence from PCN and, more recently, from Pilipino American Culture Night. As a powerful cultural authority of Filipino ethnic identity, PCN demonstrates the cultural stakes involved in the processes of Filipino American postcolonial subjectivity that mixes orientalized and parochial visions of Filipino tradition into hip hop dance. In its blending, PCN points to both the Philippine cultural regime's postcolonial resolve of inhabiting principles of sovereignty (modernity) and hip hop dance's supposed promise of unchaining subjects from the stiffness of ethnic "tradition."

PCNs have typically endorsed a type of liberal multiculturalism that has been popularized since the 1980s.[61] PCN has served as an outlet for many Filipino American youths to make a spectacle of their imagined difference, where their staged Filipinoness pines for an authentic Filipino past and their aestheticized ethnicity deflects from material inequalities and social injustices perpetrated among different groups. J. Lorenzo Perillo observes instrumental U.S. colonial–era, Philippine-based dance texts from the early 1900s that instructed the lineage of Filipino and Filipino American "folk" dance. Laden with what he calls "choreographic whiteness," these texts reflected aspirations of Philippine nation building and the disciplining of Filipino children through physical education. Adopting a postcolonial intervention in reading these texts, Perillo contends, "provides a crucial lens to viewing the choreography of embodied modernism and for the rethinking the invention of 'folk' in Filipino dance." "A closer look at these embodied modernisms," he continues, "helps us understand how white dance is inscribed problematically onto brown bodies."[62] Filipino brown bodies would soon be put on display through formalized Philippine folk dance troupes. Since the 1930s, in an attempt to construct a national identity based on the archipelago's heterogeneity, Philippine state initiatives utilized tools of dance and performance such as the Bayanihan Dance Company to project to the world Philippine national unity despite its ethnic diversity and internal strife.[63] Bayanihan provided a durable and reproducible template for PCNs by staging various dance "suites" that showcased the range of regions and races of the Philippines. At the end of the twentieth-century, U.S. multiculturalism would mirror the Philippines's version of multiculturalism, and these paired national discourses would shape the stated motivations and formal elements of PCNs.

Between 1982 and 1992, when the number of Filipino American graduates from the University of California quadrupled, PCNs served as a main venue for students to recognize themselves as Filipino.[64] PCNs have since filled an ethnic void for second-generation Filipino Americans with only a symbolic connection to the Philippines.[65] As such, PCN organizers have worked as ordained recuperators of "lost" culture by formalizing and making rigid the ritualization of PCN. Theodore S. Gonzalves states: "In a patrimonial sense, the organizers are the inevitable inheritors and stewards of enduring, if beleaguered, cultural practices. To forestall the 'loss,' the custodians renew that patrimony every year, reminding themselves of tradition's vitality."[66] The "culture" of PCN for many Filipino American students suffices for Filipino culture writ large.[67] Participation in PCN to authenticate their Filipinoness has for many Filipino American students sanctified the PCN as an orthodox rite of passage to Filipino ethnic realization. Gonzalves continues: "like the other invented traditions that have dubious roots in an 'authentic past,' the Pilipino Culture Night has become a static and seemingly unchanging and unchangeable artifact."[68]

The irony of embodying an "authentic past" on the stage of modern theater that echoes the state-driven project of Philippine modernity is further seen in PCN students' acceding to the problematic representations of their bodies. In pursuit of their "lost culture," many PCN dancers reproduce discourses of Orientalism, as shown in their privileging of the Moro (Muslim) dance suite. "The modern theatricality of the Bayanihan genre," explains Barbara Gaerlan, "gave [students] a venue for expressing Filipino culture in the United States of which they could be proud. They seemed unaware that, in addition to theatricality, the Bayanihan included another 'modern' feature, Orientalism, highlighted in their presentation of the 'Muslim' as exotic, autocratic, slave holding and patriarchal."[69] The tenets of Filipinoness, however, would reach beyond the fabricated authenticity showcased in PCN traditional suites in order to accommodate a more U.S.-based cultural form with which young Filipino Americans aligned themselves: hip hop dance. The paradoxical accommodation of rigid Filipino tradition with hip hop's modernity characterizes the constant reinventing of Filipino cultural identity.[70] Not surprisingly, the newness of what was called the "modern suite" threatened PCN traditionalists. According to early organizers of PCN, other organizers resisted incorporating hip hop into the event, especially in the early days when concerns included "losing" Filipino cultural authenticity within the folklore of PCN to the ruin of hip hop's modernity.[71] Despite that early resistance, hip hop dance's eventual union into PCN's standard repertoire quickly became championed, due in large part to the modern dance suites' ability to draw sizable, screaming audiences. This union offers a critique of PCN's ethnic absolutism by demonstrating the capacity of diaspora to highlight the constant reconfiguring of culture.

Hip hop dance's legitimate placement into PCN's repertoire signals the flexibility of Filipino diasporic identity and the ease with which performers are willing to re-form the staged and formalized tenets of a supposed Philippine nationality. For PCN dancers who unflinchingly wed traditional and modern suites, their multiple manifestations of modern draws on the irony of their Filipino auto-orientalism and the betrayal of such orientalism through U.S.-based hip hop. As the modern dance suite became staple in Filipino American youths' performance, what was labeled modern became a Filipino American "tradition." The perceived binary between modern and traditional becomes muddied, troubling the rules governing Filipino ethnic authenticity.

For the most part, PCN fulfills multiculturalism's promise to equally include various national, ethnic, and racial groups within the U.S. national body by paradoxically flattening differences.[72] PCN during the late 1980s and early 1990s, therefore, functioned conservatively amid the racial rage erupting especially in Los Angeles. Kaba Modern's appearance in the spring quarter of 1992, around the same time as the buildup and aftermath of the LA riots, parallels the multiculturalism of PCN, where Filipino American ethnicity on stage is "updated" from the "backwardness" of traditional PCN suites to the modern, U.S.-based embodiment of cool. Such an embodiment, however indebted to Black dance, excused itself from Black protest.[73] In this way, the staged difference of PCN and Kaba Modern are more alike in their political posture of exhibiting the Filipino body as self-determining, respectable, and modern.

Emerging from and mirroring the parochial ethnic traditionalism of PCNs, Filipino American hip hop dance crews' resounding and resolute discourse of "family" signifies the syncretizing of traditional values of ethnic kinship and lateral or queer forms of community. In as much as KM 20's honoring of "Kaba Modern Family" represents a celebration of an intimate dance community, it signals a revised version of PCN's practice of ritualistic ethnic kinship. The tight membership in a Filipino American dance family allegorizes a postcolonial strategy of ethnic belonging. Where PCN helps realize an imagined Filipino ethnic identity through a rigid system of performances, Kaba Modern embraces unifying practices to foster a more amorphous and flexible feeling of belonging. Kaba Modern promotes family as a mode of communal identity so much that dancers credit their crew's strong familial bond to Kaba Modern's exceptional talent. For example, in the spring 2013 issue of *UC Irvine Magazine*, Kaba Modern's 2011 artistic director states: "The thing that sets us apart is that we're a big family. We know how to work together."[74] Likewise, in the Kaba Modern anniversary documentary, *Kaba Modern: The First 20 Years*, the centrality of family resonates throughout, with current and former dancers testifying to the importance of the group as a loving family. Arnel Calvario, still an active leader and in the dance company, says in the documentary: "Kaba Modern first and foremost is a family. So you have to be part of a family, contribute to the family, and just grow within the family."[75]

Interestingly, while highlighting the tightness in community-formation among dancers over a twenty-year span, the documentary elides references to Filipinos or any other ethnicity. While there is brief recognition of Kaba Modern's link to the Kababayan club, there is no explanation of what "kababayan" means, the club's history, or its purpose. Clues to interviewees' ethnic backgrounds can be inferred by their captioned surnames. The silence in the documentary's treatment of ethnicity can be symptomatic of a larger effort to downplay Kaba Modern's Filipino American roots. Simply put, it makes more sense to de-ethnicize Kaba Modern in order to promote its universal idea of family. Given this, the de-ethnicized family rhetoric pervading Kaba Modern's community mythology can be called post-Filipino. Regardless if the group comes out of PCN, continues to perform at PCN, and its dancers are dues-paying members of Kababayan, the family will supposedly be constrained, alienating non-Filipinos, if Filipinoness is afforded too much attention. Even if their very bodies dramatize the complexities of Filipino historical formation, the dance crew has attempted to transcend its Filipinoness.

Even if Kaba Modern de-emphasizes Filipinoness in its brand, the traces of distinct Filipino American traits are hard to shake. Kaba Modern parallels PCN's patrimonial culture of passing on "tradition" (discussed later in this chapter) revealing a "culture of Kaba Modern" that scaffolds the idea of family. In the documentary, Leej Razalan, a dancer from 1997–2000, states that "there's this continuation of the same essence that the forefathers placed as a foundation for the rest of the generations to come." Similarly, Alex Nguyen, dancer from 2002–2006, mentions that "the traditions that had been passed on from generation to generation—I think that's probably the most important thing."[76] One such tradition, as shown in the film, involves bringing one's toothbrush to dance practice in order to stay and feel fresh. Another Kaba Modern ritual is the "soul in the hole" rallying cry in which dancers link hands in a circle and commit positive energy to the group.[77] In true PCN fashion, Kaba Modern stresses a generational unity through the repetition of cemented practices.

Welcoming of dancers of varying gender and sexual identities in recent years, the emphasis on family in Kaba Modern not only offers dancers a loving space of belonging, it also imparts a particularly queer space of community formation. Similar to gay and lesbian "chosen families" that confound genealogically defined relationships yet are never really apart from the symbols of traditional kinships, the intense commitments formed in dance crew families can be read as queer.[78] In his ethnography of ballroom culture, Marlon M. Bailey comments on alternative kinship. In the Black queer space of ballroom culture, which includes house and vogue dance, dancers develop "houses" as forms of social structure, complete with mothers and fathers. Bailey writes that "houses are family-like structures that are configured socially rather than biologically."[79] The kinesthetic of ballroom culture is embraced in choreographed hip hop dance but often disavowed in more traditional b-boy spaces. Whether intentional or not, Kaba Modern's alternative kinships parallel ballroom culture's queer sociality, pointing to a desire for these various practitioners to create more desirable connectivities that respond to hegemonic social structures.

I read Kaba Modern's idea of family as queer in both the crew's gendered formations and in dancers' casual de-prioritization of Filipino ethnicity in their expansive understanding of community. The complex ways in which Filipino American hip hop dancers imagine their alternative family of belongings borrows from Fiona I. B. Ngô's analysis of Black artists' queer modernities produced through empire. Like subjects of Ngô's exploration, in their queer community formations, Filipino American hip hop dancers exhibit a "crisis of referentiality that occurs when bodies that are meant to signify certain relationships within national discourse take on multiple and unstable meanings brought about by the changes—often produced through empire—in geographical and ideological borders."[80] Through their defiance of tradition and modern, cemented rituals, narrations of family, and irreverence to conventional rules of ethnicity, these dancers foster queer counter-memories emerging out of empire's "crisis of referentiality." In the Kaba Modern documentary, Calvario, who came out at thirty-two, expresses the meaningfulness of his dance crew: "It's a place you can call home. Not just physically, but just a state of mind. Somewhere down the road, you feel connected. You feel related to, it's that kind of thing."[81] Here, Calvario sums up succinctly the "state of mind" put forth by young Filipino American hip hop dancers who have been forming new modes of connectivity. The queer modernities created in PCN and dance crew culture enable unique and often liberating community bonds.

The alternative families Filipino American hip hop dancers conjure to feel connected are symptomatic of the cognitive expansiveness met in Filipino American postcoloniality that imagines its boundaries of belonging beyond Filipino ethnicity or nationality. Multiracial and queer families become relatable proxies for "Filipino," even if the origin of their dance crews is indebted to PCN and their social spaces are largely that with other Filipinos.

As Filipino American–dominant crews like Kaba Modern create alternative modes of connectivity, dancers of these crews are also presenting gender expressions that challenge the hypermasculine styles typically associated with hip hop culture. Exhibiting more diversity in gender and sexuality than in other elements of hip hop, the hip hop dance scene in general unsettles the long-held notion that hip hop can only be led by heterosexual males and can only be expressed in a hypermasculine or "hard" manner. The demographics of the scene, including its queer male fandom, help to reimagine hip hop's gender and sexual identity. Choreographed hip hop dance, affectionately (and sometimes derogatorily) called "choreo," offers a more egalitarian alternative in hip hop dance, in which b-boy culture espouses predominantly male practitioners and heterosexual masculinity.[82] Staging the drama between b-boy culture and choreo rehearses the trope of tradition versus modern in Kaba Modern's contested incorporation into PCN. Like Kaba Modern dancers' syncretizing their notions of "ethnic" Filipino dances with hip hop, b-boy culture must negotiate its values of "tradition" given the rise of choreo. Filipino Americans' affinity for and avant-garde leadership in the choreo scene scandalizes the masculinized posturing in hip hop.

B-boying, with its acrobatics, machismo, overwhelmingly male constituency, and "burns" or violent gestures to diss and humiliate your opponent (the most popular being "throwing cock" or mimicking ejaculating on your opponent), has been widely designated as representing "real" hip hop culture compared to choreo's supposedly simplified, robotic movements. In light of b-boy culture's tendency to define hip hop's cultural boundaries, I redeem choreo's place in hip hop while at the same time foregrounding choreo's ability to flex different styles, including breaking. In effect, choreo's ability to transgress style and play with masculine and feminine movements contribute to the varied dimensions of hip hop: choreo queers hip hop's cultural expectations. Choreo is regarded as part of a family of dances under street dance, which Alan David defines as "an umbrella term for dances that have been created by people usually from low-economic backgrounds outside of traditional studio or professional setting. It refers to dancing in the streets

due to lack of access to other more formal venues."[83] Choreo is the synchro-
nized movements of several performers on stage as popularized by music
videos (such as those featuring Michael and Janet Jackson) and by the Fly
Girls dance segments on the TV show *In Living Color.* Early leaders of Kaba
Modern were fans of this dance genre and became vanguards in teaching
choreo skills to younger Filipino American women and men. By featuring the
talent of women and gay men, choreo's capacity to queer hip hop offers the
possibility to renegotiate hip hop's sexual embodiments.[84] The rise in Kaba
Modern's global and certainly national stardom, thanks in large part to the
coinciding of the premiere of *ABDC* and the boom in social media cyber
culture, demonstrates choreo's firm footing in the world of hip hop writ large.

The rise of choreo within the larger cultural imaginary of hip hop, however,
has inevitably met resistance from those who seek to preserve the gender and
sexual codes of a more "true" hip hop. In his ethnography on b-boy culture
in New York, Joseph G. Schloss recounts dancers' strict upholding of a "core
b-boy philosophy," or a "foundation": "*Foundation* is a term used by b-boys
and b-girls to refer to an almost mystical set of notions about b-boying that is
passed from teacher to student. In addition to the actual physical movements,
it includes the history of the movements and the form in general, strategies for
how to improvise, philosophy about dance in general, musical associations,
and a variety of other subjects."[85] Schloss neglects to examine the gender
and sexual codes in his study, but I contend that this b-boy "foundation"
has been structured by preferences for masculine and male heteronormative
bodies and embodiments. In an almost PCN manner, as Schloss evidences
in his study, b-boy culture perpetuates an ethos of "authenticity" that must
be passed down. This ethos, importantly, excludes (and demeans) femininity
and queerness.

Attached to b-boy culture's upholding of "foundation," it seems, is the abhorrence of any deviance from this ethos. B-boy culture's aversion to choreo,
for example, can be witnessed in internet discourse. During *ABDC*'s reign,
a fear of choreo became evident in the chatter on hip hop forums on the
internet and commentary on YouTube videos featuring various choreo performances. Whereas the more improvised and masculine form of b-boy
dance is often sanctified as "real" hip hop, in many hip hop circles, choreo is
frequently sidelined as inauthentic hip hop and seen as requiring "less skill"
because of the genre's rehearsed nature. For example, on the popular website
Bboyworld.com, users debated the merits of choreo dancers and whether they
should be considered inside or outside of hip hop culture. Not discounting
choreo's artistic value, but rather choreo dancers' knowledge of hip hop, one
user states that "im not BASHING the dance im talking about how upsetting

it is that 'hip hop dancers' are NOT educated on what hip hop is." Continuing the nebulous prioritization of "hip hop knowledge" as a prerequisite to hip hop membership, another user writes: "I don't hate on the choreo dancers that know their shit and are respectful, but there are a lot of posers who don't know shit. It's mostly people who are new to dancing . . . they watch you got served or bring it on [mainstream hip hop dance movies] and want to learn some moves."[86] These attitudes beg the question: how much and what kind of knowledge makes one deserving of respect in "real" hip hop culture?

Hip hop enthusiasts' resistance to choreo is symptomatic of a larger fear of women and gay men in hip hop. For purists, choreo hip hop dancers are "posers" who have no business claiming to "be" hip hop. Where the masculinized "genius" of b-boys' supposed improvisation is championed as the epitome of hip hop's cultural essence, choreo dancers are seen as "passive" and feminine bodies: they are simply taking orders from a choreographer rather than showcasing their individuality. Despite the notoriety and success of traditional b-boy crews on *ABDC*, such as the Jabbawockeez, the Massive Monkeys, Super Cr3w, Quest Crew, and Supreme Soul—all of whom performed choreo for the show—it seems that many foundation purists are intent on preserving an unsullied hip hop past.

But, change is inevitable, even in hip hop. Since the mainstreaming of choreo, to the chagrin of b-boy purists, the expectations of street dance have shifted to elevate choreo and, consequently, much more queer expressions. Gaining wide attention in social media, choreo and queer forms of movement is now dominating street dance fandom. For example, in September 2014, a video of two male Kaba Modern dancers, Jeffrey Caluag and Dimitri Mendez, rehearsing at the California State University, Fullerton campus, went viral on the internet, making rounds on several blogs and pop culture sites. The duo's masterfully feminine dance ("fem-dance") interpretation of Nicki Minaj's "Anaconda," a song that reinterprets Sir-Mix-A-Lot's early rap hit "Baby Got Back," left netizens in a fan frenzy.[87] The duo's routine, one pop culture website writer commented, "has more intense hip movements and attitude than the rapper's herself. . . . Minaj has a history of giving her fans a moment in the spotlight, so hopefully she'll see this fierce 'Anaconda' routine and call these boys to the stage. . . . Mind. Blown." As champions of numerous international hip hop dance battles before and after their MTV appearance, Kaba Modern dancers are veterans of cyber world publicity. The "Anaconda" routine, though, put into the greater universe of celebrity, gossip, and pop culture an endorsed and celebrated queerness not meant to scandalize, as Minaj's unsubtly pornographic "Anaconda" music video provokes, but to revel in such vivacious sexuality.

A celebrated male queerness in Kaba Modern was not always a staple in the crew's repertoire. Like any other cultural community, hip hop dancers' attitudes generally reflect the greater cultural climate from which it came. The Filipino American hip hop dance scene has not been any different, either perpetuating sexual roles or foregrounding radical changes in their rigid assignments. Whatever the case, Filipino Americans' creative labor in hip hop dance foregrounds the political terrain of sexual expression in hip hop. Similar to hip hop dance repertoire in general, including the crews I belonged to and observed over the years, Kaba Modern used to align male and female roles with their respective gender-assigned movements. Kimmy Maniquis, a choreographer for Kaba Modern in the early 1990s, reflects on the role playing of male and female dancers in Kaba Modern and the gendered movements of hip hop dance. During her time as a choreographer, she explains, Kaba Modern's dancers were segregated neatly to fit the "appropriate" gender for either masculine or feminine dance genres: "I think it's very interesting that back in the day, we portrayed a very heterosexual front on stage: the traditional 'nasty' part that was like a guy/girl dance, and maybe one guy doing the more 'feminine' pieces like the other traditional 'jazz' part."[88] Indicating changes in cultural expectations regarding the "proper" roles of men and women in dance, and perhaps generational changes in the broader acceptance of queer people, the gendered roles played by these dancers have become less regimented. Maniquis continues:

> What was striking when I judged the last Kaba auditions a few years back was how much that has transformed. There were entirely male groups that could perform what is perceived as "feminine" styles of dance and it being integrated within the team's performances seamlessly. In other words, it wasn't like "that's the gay piece, and this is the rest of the routine." Similarly, women are performing pieces that I would think would be performed by men back in the day. Women are b-girling, tutting, popping, doing all the stuff that the guys are doing and doing it well.[89]

The "Anaconda" duo and Maniquis testify to the cultural shifts in hip hop dance. Being more diverse in its gender composition, the choreo scene challenges the assumption that hip hop as a larger culture strictly adheres to "foundational" codes of masculinity with heterosexual males heralded as its main cultural agents. The embracing of queer movements (e.g., waacking, also called punking) frequent in choreographed hip hop dance repertoire exemplifies choreo's gender fluidity. One can even argue that some hip hop party dances, such as seen in the Dougie and the Nae Nae, contain queer movements popularized by Black heterosexual men, particularly sports celebrities.[90] Embracing a broader spectrum in Black vernacular dance can disrupt the gender traditionalism and parochialism of purist b-boy culture.

Choreo allows for a deeper dive into an embodied dance archive denied by b-boy dogma. The choreo dance scene recalibrates racial and gender power in Black vernacular dance, which encompasses a universe beyond hip hop. Non-Black dancers' affirmation of Black vernacular dance's larger and more fluid cultural repertoire invites practitioners to remember the Black and Latino gay disco spaces often disavowed in hip hop historiography, despite hip hop's early material indebtedness to gay dance scenes. Focusing on waacking/punking forms, Naomi Bragin discusses the practice of "corporeal drag," which is "a process of queer play in which performers try on and refashion movement as sensory-kinesthetic material for experiencing and presenting the body anew."[91] As movement and feeling, Bragin suggests, waacking/punking can potentially transform dancers' kinesthetic consciousness. Here, the newness of the body is a playful and pleasurable choreography of racial and gender power.

In choreo, the queering of gender roles has become a sign of dancers' virtuosity. This fluidity of skill holds particularly true for male dancers who can play feminine roles. In his interviews with gay male hip hop dancers, Joseph Ramirez shows the prestige attached to males (gay or straight) who can master feminine gestures. Describing the experience of Teri (one of his interviewees) in performing a gay male role, Ramirez writes of the authority queer male performance has in choreographed hip hop dance:

> Fem-dances incorporate moves that are hypersexual and draws from dance moves from famous hip hop and pop singers. Teri explains that these types of dances are usually reserved for gay-identified males and females (regardless of sexual orientation), but is received differently by audience members if a known heterosexual-identified male performs it. For heterosexual males, this form of performances excites the audiences and, according to Teri, boosts the respect of the dancers for their versatility. Yet, it is also known by dancers that such performances are done with the approval of female dancers and queer male dancers. This power dynamic between heterosexual males and queer males is unique to choreographed hip hop dance scene.[92]

The approval of straight male dancers' fem-dance skills by female and queer male dancers runs against the normative approval of hip hop skills prized in more heterosexually male-dominated genres of hip hop culture. This example of gender variance opens possibilities to push the boundaries of hip hop's conventional gender dynamics.

The authority and power of fem-dance skills performed by straight and queer male dancers expand the expected gender roles of the group. As already discussed, choreo dance scenes cultivate queer modernities in which queer members build trust and family—a queer form of affiliation. The relationship between the transgression of gender boundaries and the increase in numerical and authoritative representation of gay male dancers is symbiotic: the flexibility of form in choreographed hip hop dance has attracted more queer dancers, which in turn transforms the dances' form, or vice versa. Ramirez compares the more stringent rules of gender and sexuality in "traditional pillars of hip hop" to the openness of differences in choreographed hip hop. He claims that choreographed hip hop has been for gay males "a venue to not only express their sexuality, but also find community and camaraderie where they will not be judged because of their sexuality."[93] Similarly, in the documentary, openly gay former Kaba Modern dancer Miguel Zarate, who competed on the TV show *Step It Up and Dance*, notes the crew's notable capacity to embrace his queerness: "Kaba Modern literally gave me the first forum to completely be myself. It was the one place where I didn't have to censor myself."[94]

In broadening the scope of hip hop's form by diversifying its gender composition and its inclusion of queer movement, many adherents of hip hop culture would benefit from dismantling their own parochialisms of hip hop authenticity. For one, the idea that b-boys do not need to rehearse could and should be debunked. Rather than celebrating a supposed improvisation, breaking could be seen as a different kind of rehearsing that can inspire inventive and "spontaneous" movements. Also, b-boy battles around the world regularly include routines in which members of a crew synchronize movements to tell stories through dance. As part of the arsenal in battles between opposing crews, these routines are essentially short choreo dance sets. Recognizing the blurred lines between choreo and b-boying dance can help to reimagine the terms of membership in a hip hop community, where feminine and queer bodies not only perform as dancers in this community but also shape the expectations of what hip hop expressions could look like.

Calvario currently manages several world-touring dance crews who have gained mainstream popularity through reality TV dance competition shows, including MTV's *America's Best Dancer Crew* and NBC's *World of Dance*. He continues to be a leader in what has become a global hip hop dance industry, with movies, music videos, concerts, and sporting event contracts at stake. Since Kaba Modern's now-fabled MTV appearance, hip hop choreo dance has become a powerhouse multinational enterprise with a particularly strong presence in Asia, whose young people crave learning from professional dancers from the United States, many who happen to be Asian Americans who benefited from the hip hop dance scenes described throughout this chapter. One of Calvario's most prolific crews, the Kinjaz, commands a sophisticated online presence and whose thirty-eight male, nearly all-Asian American members boast top-notch résumés, including participation in the MTV Kaba Modern crew.[95] Affirming the added value of non-Filipino Asian difference as discussed in prior sections, the Kinjaz embrace Japanese ninja personae in fashion and in their martial arts postures. The Kinjaz capitalize on Asian difference, exemplified in their 2018 performance with Nicki Minaj for her song "Chun Li" on *Saturday Night Live.*

In honor of LGBTQ Pride Month 2019, the Kinjaz led an online #MantraKampaign to support LGBTQ nonprofit organizations.[96] Thanks to the diversity of voices in social media, the elevation of LGBTQ people and celebration of queer hip hop dancers was unimaginable in b-boy social circles a decade earlier. To be sure, the b-boy scene is still incredibly unfriendly to LGBTQ people and retains antigay and misogynistic practices. However, Calvario and other LGBTQ hip hop visionaries are contesting the otherwise obdurate terms of hip hop acceptability. The Kinjaz's Pride Month campaign could be read as the domestication of LGBTQ politics into a neoliberal and color-blind cultural regime. After all, the company enhances its brand by selling more merchandise to a wider audience. The rise of the Kinjaz best clearly evidences the circulation of global capital (especially from Asia), the professionalization of hip hop dance as a lucrative industry, and the democratization of the scene with greater LGBTQ representation.[97] At its highest representational pinnacle in recent years, the repercussions of Filipino American hip hop dance vernacular culture invites a critical understanding of modern dance's racialized legacy. The modern posture of Filipino American hip hop dance culture has proven exceptional through its encounter with empire and through the cultural leaders building community in empire's aftermath.

Conclusion: Modern Memory

One Down's video "Innovating Cultural Dance" begins with breakers doing top-rock moves between tinikling bamboo sticks before getting down on their hands to do a side-swipe.[98] Next, the camera zooms out from a closeup of dancers waltzing the Spanish "Valse Vieja: Maria Clara Suite." Lasting nearly two minutes, the elaborate, expertly choreographed video was posted on Facebook in early 2019 by Samahang Modern dancers. Staged in front of the iconic UCLA Pauley Pavilion, where the school's powerhouse basketball and gymnastics teams compete, the camera swings the viewer rapidly through various PCN dance suites that represent disparate regional, religious, and linguistic groups in the Philippines. A minimalist, percussive instrumental threads together each dance routine throughout the unedited, single-cut video. The camera acts as a roaming, dazzled bystander, like a witness to the controlled chaos of a PCN rehearsal, with some dancers looking confidently and directly into the lens. The "Urban Choreography: Modern Suite" is the video's grand finale: the camera zooms out as dancers have already arranged in static stage placement to flex hip hop moves. The hip hop dancers, some of whom remain barefoot or in folk costume from participating in other suites, are staged conspicuously at the front while folk dancers assemble in the background, clapping, waving fans, and otherwise gesturing according to their suite's theme.

With its trajectory from folk to hip hop and its neatly categorized suites, the Samahang Modern video choreographs the invented linear progress of the "modern," a concept discussed as rife with racial power and nation-building ideology. This chapter unpacks the various usages of "modern" among Filipino American hip hop dancers and their audiences. The concepts of modern and traditional collapse as a critical reading of Filipino American dance culture accounts for the constructed nature of each. On one hand, in reproducing the suites repertoire, the video reiterates the tendency to separate "urban" or hip hop dance from folk dance, where the former is seen as new and the latter as primordial or authentic. In other words, the newness of the modern suite juxtaposes the supposedly backward or traditional in a way that the *Boston Sunday Globe* cartoon allegorizes Filipino assimilation. On the other hand, the video playfully redistributes temporality by defying the boundaries that separate categories as dancers intermix movement repertoires and fashion, centering dancers' direct gazes that intimate their sense of agency and that they are not just passive bodies on display, and reveling in the sampling and layering aesthetic exemplified in the hip hop finale.

An accompanying One Down video, titled "The History of Pilipino Cultural Night," provides a vocal narration of the historical significance of PCN. It mixes documentary footage, still images, portraits of dancers featured in the first video, and direct address by the narrator, Sarah Albea. She begins by voicing the ambitious pedagogical challenge facing PCNs: "Can you fit six hundred years of Filipino culture into one night? Probably not, but every year, Filipino stores are told on Filipino terms. And this phenomenon is called 'PCN.'" Albea relays the erasure of Filipino people in the American popular imaginary: "Let's face it, Filipino history and culture is often forgotten and erased." After describing the elements expected in a conventional PCN and recalling the history of Filipino American cultural networking in California and the emergence of PCN, she closes by describing how PCNs "have become the gateway for most Filipino millennials to discover their own culture and continue to challenge the narrative of what it means to be

Filipino."[99] I would argue that, instead, PCN is merely a small part of Filipino Americans' "discovery" of their own culture. Only a fraction of Filipino Americans over several generations have had the privilege of attending a prestigious West Coast school with a sizable Filipino American population like UCLA or UCI. This chapter demonstrates that, rather than something to be discovered, Filipinoness is fluid, flexible, and mobile. It can be queer in its sexual expressions, gendered representations, and unorthodox modes of community. The larger universe of a Filipino American hip hop vernacular, incomplete without its talented dancers, has offered a larger vocabulary as well as a broader spatial reach for practitioners to express complex and ongoing narrations of Filipinoness.

One Down's videos exhibit the continuation of PCN traditions by a new generation of Filipino American college students. They are the beneficiaries of thirty years of hip hop's integration into PCN's choreographed cultural imaginary. As we well know, the foregrounding of hip hop repertoire in the PCN dance suites is not new and has in fact, as I have argued, become a PCN staple: the modern suite is traditional. The videos effectively normalize this contradictory synergism. Choreo crews' institutionalization, networking, competition, and professionalization—along with the thriving competitive b-boy circuits—helped foster what is today the global spectacle of choreographed hip hop dance shows and championships. This chapter explores the various ways hip hop dancers inventively shape what it means to be Filipino, amid U.S. exceptionalism and its liberal multicultural logic. Rather than advocate a remedy or redress to Filipino American erasure, this chapter suggests a better way of thinking, one that does not seek to obfuscate the power of race and racism in the development of modern dance history that made the emergence of hip hop possible. Kaba Modern, the Jabbawockeez, Samahang Modern, and countless other Filipino American hip hop dance crews are not simply modern manifestations of continental American culture. Rather, they are archival embodiments to the coterminous networks of U.S. empire. As experts in kinetic illusion, Filipino American hip hop dancers reveal a form of knowledge in their expressive gestures. They pun with their postures; performing history through repertoire, their bodies are conscious, their movements articulate. They prove that the body can be intelligent and thinking in its movement of limbs and twists of torsos in repeated practice so much so that movements are rehearsed in dancers' dreams. Revealing vernacular culture's material inheritances, their moves become a permanent imprint in memory. The Filipino American hip hop dancer, in the fluency of their repertoire, expertly remembers the past: to dance is to manifest intelligence in the synapses.

CONCLUSION

Work I Manifest

Memory is work. While my students learn for the first time about the Universal Zulu Nation, cities across the country are establishing holidays to honor hip hop icons, such as Phife Dawg Day in Oakland, California, on May 17 to recognize the late A Tribe Called Quest member who spent the last fifteen years of his life in the East Bay region.[1] At the same time that my students look clueless at the mention of Missy Elliot, Lauryn Hill, and the Beastie Boys, Staten Island renamed a section of its borough the Wu-Tang Clan District to celebrate its hometown heroes.[2] Three years before the 2019 NBA draft class would struggle to identify photos of Outkast and Destiny's Child, "Hip Hop Boulevard" was ordained in the South Bronx to memorialize the "birthplace of hip hop."[3] Filipino Americans are not exempt from the struggle between forgetting and memory work. My experience teaching college students in California and Pennsylvania in recent years suggests that, sadly, it is unlikely that a young Filipino American would be able to name one kindred hip hop recording artist or dancer.

I illustrate this series of forgetting not to make the obvious points that people inevitably age, that generation Z is different from generation X, or that the demographic composition of Filipino Americans invariably changes. Instead, I am interested in the labor involved in shaping memory; the labor this book focuses on are diverse forms of Filipino Americans' hip hop cultural productions. Rather than dismissing these cultural productions as a prosaic reflection of what many communities were involved in at the time, I appreciate the uniqueness of Filipino Americans' postcolonial memory work through hip hop.

My purpose is not to catalog the contributions of Filipino Americans in hip hop nor to make a case for their authentic membership in hip hop. Given limited space, time, and resources, one can understand the impossibility of giving a shout-out to every known Filipino American artist; it is my hope that this book sparks more efforts of documentation, curation, and commentary. In the preceding chapters, I show a Filipino American hip hop vernacular's manifestations in military culture, political and spiritual redemptions through Islam, funky memorializations and abstractions, and modern postures in dance. Understood as an everyday, bottom-up language inheriting the materiality of history, a Filipino American hip hop vernacular communicates postcolonial culture. Typically, such expressions have either been loathed as color-blind and apolitical or been revered as leftist and anticolonial. I frame Filipino American hip hop performances as more multifaceted than either of these polarities; in their unruly, contradictory, and queer political expressions, they testify to empire's enacting of colonial/neocolonial migration, racialization, and erasure. Spanish colonialism upended the spiritual worldviews of people from the archipelago since the sixteenth century, as I discuss when unpacking Filipino American hip hop artists' valorization of Moros (chapter 2). The U.S. form of colonialism in the Philippines, however, was more pernicious in its amnesia: the United States is seen as somehow innocent of military expansion, occupation, and genocide, a problem compounded by the presence of built monuments and tales that perpetuate conceits of the white man's burden and manifest destiny. As a popular, geographically capacious, and loosely networked mode of knowledge transference, a Filipino American hip hop vernacular resists American forgetting not in spite of but because of gaps in historical memory: the synapses are the conduits. As I have observed in the abstracted works in Afro-Filipino futurism and in the counterintuitive racial discourses in choreographed hip hop dance culture, Filipino American sonics, aesthetics, and postures speak from an archive of embodied knowledge. Their expressions deconstruct U.S. exceptionalism: they are articulate subjects of empire, breaking rules in their encounter with modernity.

While a Filipino American hip hop vernacular has labored to generate memory, efforts in recent years have sought to preserve the fragile history of Filipino Americans in hip hop; the history of Filipino Americans in hip hop can be admired in museums, exhibits, and legacy events. Filipino Americans are also claiming public space and asserting civic recognition. In 2018, a section of the Oakland Museum of California's special exhibition "Respect: Hip-Hop Style and Wisdom" featured the works of Filipino American artists, including the graffiti art of the late Oakland native Mike "Dream" Francisco.[4]

In 2019, the Cerritos Public Library in Southern California displayed the futuristic visual art and fashion designs of hometown innovator Ricardo "Rich One" Cofinco.[5] In 2018, Union City, California, officially recognized the community service of the b-boy crew the Rock Force Crew, which was celebrating its thirty-fifth anniversary.[6] Dream Day, which started in 2010 to honor Mike "Dream," has developed into an annual Oakland hip hop music and arts festival.[7] In addition to these public preservation efforts, Filipino American hip hop veterans are capitalizing on their unique wealth of knowledge in establishing "schools": DJ Qbert instructs his online Qbert Skratch University, the Massive Monkees run their dance studio the Beacon in the heart of the International District in Seattle, and the Beat Junkies operate their Beat Junkie Institute of Sound.[8] Students of hip hop dance can pay for lessons with an expert from Kaba Modern, PAC Modern, or Culture Shock in what has become a global industry of in-studio and online dance tutorials.

As more established generations of Filipino Americans embrace nostalgia, establish legacy spaces, and professionalize their expertise, we must also recognize that the 2010s and early 2020s have been defined by the work of Ruby Ibarra. Ibarra, along with Bambu, Rocky Rivera, and Geologic (aka Prometheus Brown), is associated with the Beatrock Music label. She independently released her first project, the *Lost in Translation* mixtape, in 2012 and dropped her first full album, *Circa91*, in 2017 under Beatrock Music. The emcee has commanded a broad reach on television and in social media, having starred in a Mastercard music video commercial with popular R&B singer-songwriter SZA.[9] Ibarra offers a strident voice during a moment of candid white supremacy and blatant American fascism. I see her craft as building from the late 1990s Filipino American spoken-word and hip hop aesthetics, seen in the Balagtasan Collective, isangmahal arts kollective, 8th Wonder, and L.A. Enkanto. In her work, Ibarra is adding to a rich legacy of Filipino American lyrical craft.

Ibarra's music represents the postcolonial anxiety of recent generations of Filipino Americans who migrated to the United States in the 1990s. As the first chapter suggests, militarized Filipino Americans migrated the circuit of navy bases and helped cultivate hip hop among Filipino American communities. Navy bases as hometowns stand as material evidence of Filipino Americans' "special relationship" with the United States. Professional preferences, family reunification, and clandestine migration to the United States continued after the cessation of military recruitment in the early 1980s. Thanks to her mother's accounting degree, Ibarra and her family migrated to the San Francisco Bay Area in 1991, hence the title of her album *Circa91*. The unifying themes of her music recount her migration story and reflect a larger narrative of Filipino migrants who constitute a laboring Filipino global diaspora now even more concentrated in the Middle East, East Asia, Australia, and Europe due to export policies with roots in the U.S. colonial era.[10] Further removed from the Philippines' formal colonial and militarized neocolonial eras, Ibarra's music sustains the aesthetic and politics of her artistic forebears.

In 2019, Ibarra received special recognition from National Public Radio's annual Tiny Desk Contest, which received over six thousand video submissions.[11] Ibarra and her band, the Balikbayans (Filipino for "returners to home"), submitted a live video recording titled "Someday," which blends her songs "Someday" and "The Other Side" from *Circa91*. "Someday" is a cautionary tale of migration to the "greener place" of the United States. A dedication to her mother, who experienced downward social mobility in the United States, Ibarra paints a picture of migration as a process of loss. Textured with sad notes and melancholic background vocals, the track denaturalizes the assumption of migration to the United States as a guaranteed pathway to upward mobility. The song's chants of "someday" aspires to a better life, a future yet realized; yet, this promise symbolized by crossing the Pacific Ocean is conditioned by necessary loss, pain, and displacement. In the first verse she raps, "the day we rode the ocean was the day I learned to nose dive," and in the second verse she concludes, "after all, the stolen lands are always greener places." After the Balikbayans take a short instrumental break, the song transitions to "The Other Side." In the chorus, Ibarra takes on a cautionary voice that tempts the listener to take a "ride" across the Pacific:

> The grass is greener on the other side
> Forget your dreams, is you down to ride?
> The grass is greener on the other side
> Come fuck with me, is you down to ride?
> The grass is greener on the other side
> Follow me, they'll eat you alive
> The grass is greener on the other side
> Now I'm feeling a lesser brown inside.

She does not adopt a voice that merely highlights the "positive" aspects of migration to the United States to hide its difficulties from relatives in the Philippines. Analyzing the letters written by early Filipino migrants, historian Dawn Mabalon notes that, "preferring to pepper their letters with exaggerated stories of success rather than tales of failure, the earliest emigrants encouraged thousands of others to follow."[12] Rather, "The Other Side" prompts the listener to reconsider following, especially if it means living with the violence of whiteness in the United States.

Ibarra marks an amplification of women's voices among Filipino American recording hip hop artists. In an interview with NPR, she says: "I am what I talk about in my music. I am *Pinay*, I'm powerful, I'm fearless, I'm unfiltered. And I like to hope that there's young women out there who feel the same way. Or even if they don't feel the same way, I hope to inspire young women out there to want to use their voice, to claim who they are and to embrace their identity."[13] Preceded by the leadership of artists like Hopie, Rocky Rivera, and Rivera's former group the Rhapsodistas, Ibarra assembles an illustrious cast of Pinay artists in her music. "Us" from *Circa91* best symbolizes Ibarra's Pinay feminism.[14] Emcees Rocky Rivera and Klassy together with spoken-word poet Faith Santilla join Ibarra in crafting the lyrical content of the song. The "Us" music video, directed by Ibarra and featuring a Pinay-only cast, is a playful visual sampling and layering of a PCN dress rehearsal, West Coast low-rider rap video, and activist rally. A giant crowd of multigenerational Pinays—artists, dancers, educators, community members, and activists—gaze defiantly into the camera, some dressed in gloriously heterogeneous PCN costumes. Hopie makes a cameo appearance, stylizing a traditional Maria Clara dress with her tattoos while brandishing a Filipino balisong knife. Harmonizing intergenerational lyrical sensibilities, the emcees syncretize different lyrical cadences: they bounce between the quick 3/4 cadence preferred in today's trap music and the more traditional 4/4 rap cadence, flowing together over a 4/4 hip hop beat pattern. Further emphasizing intergenerational collaboration, Klassy, the youngest of the group, scaffolds the song's chorus, while Faith Santilla, who commanded the Filipino American spoken-word scene in its prime in the late 1990s, closes the song with a stirring poetic verse on Pinay resilience, resistance, and community building. This intergenerational exchange shows the resonant aesthetics that span multiple eras of Filipino American hip hop craft.

Many of the artists this book examines are contributing to the more recent Filipino American cultural expression making waves on a national scale: the Filipino food movement. Having anticipated this movement and adding to its growth, many artists have shifted their musical genius to the kitchen. Filipino American spoken-word artists and DJs have been involved with food for a long time; it seems, then, that the current cultural surge of the Filipino food movement, praised by celebrity chefs Andrew Zimmern and Anthony Bourdain and by the *New York Times* and *Bon Appétit*, benefited partly by the cultural foundation laid by Filipino American hip hop practitioners. Geologic and his wife Chera, a poet in the isangmahal arts kollective, are prominent chefs in the Seattle foodie scene, with Chera a semifinalist for a 2020 James Beard Award. Filipino American–owned Blu Monkey bar in Hollywood, which hosted a number hip hop jams over the years, morphed into Barkada, a

FIGURES 19 AND 20. *Top:* Ruby Ibarra stands before powerful Pinays. *Bottom:* Rocky Rivera, Ibarra, and Klassy warning the colonizers. Screenshots from Ruby Ibarra's music video "Us" (2018).

lauded boutique Filipino restaurant in Hollywood. Balagtasan Collective poet and vocalist Johneric Concordia celebrated more than ten years of his success with his barbecue joint, the Park's Finest (in L.A.'s Historic Filipinotown), one of the most well-reviewed Filipino food establishments. Concordia also opened a southern-inspired bar Thunderbolt next door. Non-Filipino hip hop artists are also contributing to the Filipino food movement: Bay Area rap mogul E-40, who is African American, co-owns the Lumpia Company, an innovative eatery in Oakland. Although the restaurants do not specialize in Filipino cuisine, Bambu was involved in marketing for chef Roy Choi's LocoL healthy fast food joints. Similarly, DJ Neil Armstrong had been hosting his global and mobile "Dinner and a Mixtape" pop-up dining events.

I hope this book prompts further research and writing in the subject area of Filipino Americans and hip hop. Future projects could consider Filipino Americans' significant (but overlooked) roles as the following: leaders in b-boy/b-girl competitions and communities, voices in broadcast radio, talent in beat making (e.g., Chad Hugo, !llmind, Mndsgn, and Free the Robots), members in gangs, fashion designers, and party promoters. Of further interest could be studies on the rise of Black Filipino American recording artists (e.g., Che, H.E.R., Saweetie, Danny Brown, and Toro y Moi).

The golden age of Filipino Americans' special hip hop community ferment has come and gone. Those decades were marked by an unprecedented expanse in Filipino American demographics and geography as well as artists' avant-garde expressivity, collaborative alliances, and epistemological explorations. Fortunately, new generations have taken up the hip hop mantle and are steering the craft in fresh directions. Through dance, DJ culture, music, visual art, and community formation, several generations of Filipino Americans have been "looking around" in remembering the past. Hip hop has provided a critical technique to manifest the beautiful, genuine, transformative ways of being Filipino, moving us toward a visionary, collective future.

Notes

Preface

1. Prometheus Brown, "Blue Scholars' Prometheus Brown Writes a Song for the City," *Seattle Times*, June 9, 2012, https://www.seattletimes.com/opinion/blue-scholars-prometheus-brown-writes-a-song-for-the-city.

Introduction

1. See the first note in chapter 4 for my explanation of my use of the term "hip hop dance."

2. In this book, I use the terms Filipino American hip hop cultural production, Filipino American hip hop performance, Filipino American hip hop dancer, Filipino American hip hop vernacular, etc., as "Filipino American" in these cases refers to specific participants or modifiers of a noun or concept. I avoid the term "Filipino American hip hop" as it implies an ethnic or language-based subgenre of hip hop, such as rap lyrics in Filipino. Rather than focus on a hip hop subgenre, my study is concerned with Filipino Americans' collaborations in the larger multiethnic and multiracial universe of hip hop.

3. Chang, "Foreword," xi.

4. Rosal, *Uprock Headspin Scramble*; Rosal, *Brooklyn Antediluvian*.

5. Cambay, "Filipino American Dance Culture," 22.

6. Kandi, "Introduction," xviii.

7. See Merk, *Manifest Destiny*.

8. See Brantlinger, "Kipling's 'The White Man's Burden.'"

9. Sharma, *Hip Hop Desis*, 2.

10. Cruz et al., *Forbidden Book*, 66.

11. Talusan, *Body Papers*.

12. Rae, *Misadventures of Awkward Black Girl*, 138.

13. Gilroy, *Black Atlantic*, 83.

14. Schleitwiler, *Strange Fruit*, 16.

15. Balce, *Body Parts*, 92.

16. Ibid., chapters 2 and 3.

17. Ibid., 92, 116. Here, Balce quotes Marks, *Black Press*.

18. Balce, *Body Parts*, chapter 3.

19. See Balce, *Body Parts*, chapter 2; Cruz et al., *Forbidden Book*.

20. Du Bois, *Souls of Black Folk*.

21. España-Maram, *Creating Masculinity*, 125.

22. Ibid., chapter 5.

23. See Allen, "Afro-Amerasians," for representations of Blackness in the Philippines in the context of U.S. colonialism.

24. "Filipino Americans," Pew Research Center, accessed March 22, 2017, http://www.pewsocialtrends.org/asianamericans-graphics/filipinos.

25. Rebecca Bodenheimer, "Bay Rising: Oakland Music's Moment in the Sun, 30 Years Later," *Ringer*, May 13, 2020, https://www.theringer.com/music/2020/5/13/21256521/oakland-hip-hop-r-b-too-short-hammer-en-vogue-digital-underground.

26. See David, "Funk Behind Bay Street Dance."

27. See Guzman-Sanchez, *Underground Dance Masters*.

28. HipHopLivesToday, "KRS-One & Marley Marl—Hip Hop Lives."

29. Burns, *Puro Arte*, 3.

30. Taylor, *Archive and the Repertoire*, 20, xvi.

31. Burns, *Puro Arte*, 7.

32. Gonzalves, *Day the Dancers Stayed*, 14.

33. Tiongson, "On the Politics," 121.

34. See, *Decolonized Eye*, 140.

35. Francia, *History of the Philippines*.

36. See, *Decolonized Eye*, xxxiii; See, *Filipino Primitive*.

37. For example, Christine Bacareza Balance's concept of disobedient listening proposes another way to understand Filipino representation and cultural production. See Balance, *Tropical Renditions*, 5.

38. Balance, *Tropical Renditions*, xxxiv.

39. Flores, *From Bomba to Hip-Hop*, 49.

40. Viesca, "Native Guns and Stray Bullets."

41. Wang, *Legions of Boom*.

42. Nasty, "Building Hip Hop."

43. Chang, "Foreword."

44. Wang, "Rapping and Repping Asian"; Chang, "Foreword."

45. "Pharrell Williams on Juxtaposition and Seeing Sounds," *NPR Music*, December 31, 2013, http://www.npr.org/sections/therecord/2013/12/31/258406317/pharrell-williams-on-juxtaposition-and-seeing-sounds?sc=17&f=3.

46. "Key Facts about Asian Americans, a Diverse and Growing Population," *Pew Research Center*, September 8, 2017, www.pewresearch.org/fact-tank/2017/09/08/key-facts-about-asian-americans.

47. Sam Slovick, "The Fil-Am Invasion: Embedded with the Hip-Hop Movement That's Taking Over Hollywood," *LA Weekly*, August 8, 2007, http://www.laweekly.com/music/the-fil-am-invasion-2149983.

48. Villegas, "Legend."

49. Ibid.

50. Sha Boogie in Bass, *B-Girling*.

51. Pisares, "Do You Mis(recognize) Me."

52. Potter, *Spectacular Vernaculars*, 6.

53. For more on hip hop "core" in the case of New York, see Rivera, *New York Ricans*, 13–16.

54. Gilroy, *Black Atlantic*, 133.

55. Of course, as evident in this book, the nature of this connectivity changes with the advent of a digital network, where artists and fans increasingly rely on virtual connectivity via AOL, Asian Avenue, Myspace, Facebook, YouTube, and Instagram.

56. Eric Arnold, "Afrika Bambaataa and the Universal Zulu Nation Scandal: The Secret History," *OkayPlayer*, June 10, 2016, http://www.okayplayer.com/news/afrika-bambaata-child-abuse-scandal-universal-zulu-nation.html; Justin Ivey, "Krs-One: 'Anyone Who Has a Problem with Afrika Bambaataa Should Quit Hip-Hop,'" *XXL*, July 19, 2016, http://www.xxlmag.com/news/2016/07/krs-one-problem-afrika-bambaataa-quit-hip-hop.

57. "About Zulu Nation," *Universal Zulu Nation*, accessed June 19, 2018, http://www.zulunation.com/about-zulunation.

58. Rosa Clemente, DJ Kuttin Kandi, and Julie-C, "Hip Hop Breaking the Silence: An Open Letter to Our Beloved Community," *R.E.A.C.H.: Representing Education, Activism, and Community through Hip-Hop* (blog), April 18, 2016, http://reachhiphop.tumblr.com/post/143067260386/hip-hop-breaking-the-silence-an-open-letter-to.

59. Adisa Banjoko, "#42 The Hip-Hop Vatican: Afrika Bambaataa and Betrayal Pt. 1," Bishop Chronicles, May 15, 2016, http://www.bishopchronicles.com/podcast/2016/5/15/42-the-hip-hop-vatian-afrika-bambaataa-betrayal.

60. Wang, *Legions of Boom*, 100–104.

61. Theodore Gonzalves quoted in Tiongson, "On the Politics," 121.

62. Tiongson, *Filipinos Represent*.

63. de Leon, "Filipinotown and the DJ Scene," 192, 205.

64. Mabalon, de Leon, and Ramos, *Beats, Rhymes, and Resistance*.

65. Viesca, "Native Guns and Stray Bullets," 135.

66. Viola, "Hip-Hop and Critical Revolutionary Pedagogy," 182.

67. Harrison, *Hip Hop Underground*, 134. For more on Filipino American emcees' postcolonial consciousness, see Harrison, "Post-Colonial Consciousness."

68. I address this type of Philippine nationalism in chapter 2. See also Aguilar, "Tracing Origins"; Salman, *Embarrassment of Slavery*; Mojares, "Claiming Malayness."

69. Roderick Labrador centralizes such complexity in political meanings in Bambu's musical autobiography. See Labrador, "Rock, Rock On."

70. See Maxwell, *Picture Imperfect*; Rafael, *White Love*; Vergara, *Displaying Filipinos*; McCoy, *Policing America's Empire*, 73.

71. Cruz, Baluyut, and Reyes, *Confrontations*, 6–7.

72. Ibid., 7.

73. For more on Philippine colonial statecraft and the creation of the Filipino racial subject, see D. Rodriguez, *Suspended Apocalypse*.

Chapter 1. Currents of Militarization, Flows of Hip Hop

1. Hillary Clinton, "America's Pacific Century," *Foreign Policy*, October 11, 2011, http://foreignpolicy.com/2011/10/11/americas-pacific-century/.

2. Ankita Panda, "US-Philippines Enhanced Defense Cooperation Agreement Bolsters 'Pivot to Asia,'" TheDiplomat.com, April 29, 2014, http://thediplomat.com/2014/04/us-philippines-enhanced-defense-cooperation-agreement-bolsters-pivot-to-asia/; Christi Parsons and David Cloud, "Philippines Agrees to Large-Scale Return of U.S. Military Forces," *Los Angeles Times*, April 27, 2014, http://latimes.com/world/worldnow/la-fg-wn-us-philippines-defense-cooperation-20140427,0,6497128.story.

3. Emily Rauhala, "Philippines' Duterte Called for a 'Separation from the U.S. He Is Now Backtracking," *Washington Post*, October 21, 2016, https://www.washingtonpost.com/news/worldviews/wp/2016/10/21/the-backtracking-begins-duterte-ally-softens-philippines-separation-from-u-s/?utm_term=.ec1e8281e87f.

4. Panos Mourdoukoutas, "South China Sea: Duterte Must Do the Right Thing," *Forbes*, June 29, 2019, https://www.forbes.com/sites/panosmourdoukoutas/2019/06/29/south-china-sea-duterte-must-do-the-right-thing/#1a2cabad2bc5.

5. Amee Chew, "Stop the $2 Billion Arms Sale to the Philippines" *Jacobin*, May 17, 2020, https://jacobinmag.com/2020/05/arms-sale-philippines-rodrigo-duterte; Elias Yousif, "Arms Sales and Security Aid in the Time of Duterte," *Security Assistance Monitor*, May 4, 2020, http://securityassistance.org/fact_sheet/arms-sales-and-security-aid-time-duterte.

6. Shigematsu and Camacho, *Militarized Currents*, xv.

7. Gonzalez, "Touring Military Masculinities," 71. Gonzalez studies what she calls the "tropical cartography of American desire" as it relates to the "mutual deployment of tourism and militarism" in *Securing Paradise*, 9.

8. Author's interview with Geologic, Irvine, California, May 23, 2014.

9. Labrador, "'Freaky' Asian Americans," 478.

10. Mohajerjasbi, "Blue Scholars."

11. See Ngô, *Imperial Blues*.

12. See Burns, *Puro Arte*, 22; see also Pratt, *Imperial Eyes*, 7.

13. DJ Kuya D et al., "Certain Style," 100, 101.

14. George Quibuyen, "Translocal Cultural Flows" (Empire of Funk Conference, University of California, Irvine, May 23, 2014).

15. George Quibuyen, personal communication, May 2014.

16. See Baldoz, *Third Asiatic Invasion*; Choy, *Empire of Care*; Espiritu, *Home Bound*.

17. See Espiritu, *Home Bound*, 28; Quinsaat, "Exercise," 102–3; Pomeroy, "Philippines."

18. Quinsaat, "Exercise," 108. For more on Filipinos' political status and military service during World War II, see Baldoz, *Third Asiatic Invasion*, 194–236.

19. Quinsaat, "Exercise," 102, 104, 105, 108; Maligat, "Study," 40.

20. Espiritu, *Home Bound*, 28–29; Schirmer and Shalom, *Philippines Reader*, 96–103.

21. Quinsaat, "Exercise," 96–97.

22. Espiritu, *Home Bound*, 28.

23. Manalansan, *Global Divas*, 12.

24. Espiritu, *Home Bound*, 106; Quinsaat, "Exercise," 106.

25. See Enloe, *Maneuvers*; Sturdevant and Stoltzfus, *Let the Good Times Roll*; Brocka, *Macho Dancer*.

26. See Perillo, "Empire State of Mind," 49; J. Wood, "Yellow Negro," 465; Condry, *Hip-Hop Japan*, 64.

27. D. Rodriguez, *Suspended Apocalypse*, 180.

28. See Cenidoza-Suarez, "Militarized Filipino Masculinity"; Pacleb, "Gender"; Oades, *Beyond the Mask*.

29. See Choy, *Empire of Care*; R. Rodriguez, *Migrants for Export*; Parreñas, *Force of Domesticity*; Parreñas, *Children of Global Migration*; Parreñas, *Servants of Globalization*.

30. See "Appendix 1: Captains of the Field: San Francisco Drill Teams," in Wang, *Legions of Boom*, 163–65. For the role of Junior Reserve Officers' Training Corps in the lives of Latina/o and African American youth, which can in ways apply to Filipino American youth, see Pérez, *Citizen, Student, Soldier*.

31. For a more robust and necessary examination of men and masculinity in Filipino American hip hop performance, see the study on DJ culture in Tiongson, *Filipinos Represent*.

32. Timothy Ingram quoted in Quinsaat, "Exercise on How to Join the Navy," 108.

33. Quinsaat, "Exercise on How to Join the Navy," 108.

34. Shore duty assignments also mentioned in Oades, *Beyond the Mask*, 15.

35. Cenidoza-Suarez, "Militarized Filipino Masculinity."

36. D. Rodriguez, *Suspended Apocalypse*, 33–34.

37. Clifford, "Traveling Cultures."

38. Espiritu, *Home Bound*, 107.

39. Quibuyen, "Translocal Cultural Flows."

40. Oades, *Beyond the Mask*, 118, 123, 120.

41. Ibid., 118.

42. *Navy MWR*, http://navymwr.org, accessed September 1, 2013; Oades, *Beyond the Mask*, 127, recounts these benefits for navy brats.

43. For more on the importance of the suburban garage in Filipino American DJ culture, see Balance, *Tropical Renditions*, and Wang, *Legions of Boom*.

44. In stating he was "minimum wage earning," Geo belies his earlier lyrics in

"Proletariat Blues," where he states that he worked for tips only. Tips, which can earn workers less than minimum wage, was a well-known form of payment for commissary baggers and cart collectors, to which countless former commissary workers, including me, can confidently testify.

45. Espiritu, *Home Bound*, 110.

46. In a racial and class context, one may call these resistant moments "infrapolitics" as described by James C. Scott and Robin D. G. Kelley. See Kelley, *Race Rebels*.

47. Brown, *Babylon Girls*, 102.

48. Espiritu, *Home Bound*, 47.

49. For more on hip hop's cultural stakes, see Kelley, *Yo' Mama's Disfunktional!*; Rose, *Black Noise*.

50. Daulatzai, "Rebel to America," 42, 44.

51. Nama, "It Was Signified."

52. See Black, *Maps and Politics*.

53. See Burnett and Marshall, *Foreign in a Domestic Sense*.

54. Shigematsu and Camacho, *Militarized Currents*, xxv–xxvi.

55. Quibuyen, "Translocal Cultural Flows."

56. Esclamado, "Y'all Want This Party," 95.

57. Viesca, "Native Guns and Stray Bullets," 133; "Nathan," "Q&A: Bambu, the Filipino Mos Def," *DadWagon*, February 17, 2010, http://www.dadwagon.com/2010/02/17/qa-bambu-the-filipino-mos-def; Dani Burlison, "From Gangs to Glory: Bambu's Political Hip-Hop for the People," *KQED Arts*, March 9, 2015, http://ww2.kqed.org/arts/2015/03/09/from-gangs-to-glory-bambus-political-hip-hop-for-the-people.

58. Viesca, "Native Guns and Stray Bullets," 133.

59. Shigematsu and Camacho, *Militarized Currents*, xxvi.

60. For more on the 1946 Rescission Act, see Baldoz, *Third Asiatic Invasion*, 231–32.

61. Mico Letargo, "Fil-Am Students Veterans Day Protest Closes Hollywood Blvd," *Inquirer-Global Nation*, November 17, 2013, http://globalnation.inquirer.net/91381/fil-am-students-veterans-day-protest-closes-hollywood-blvd#ixzz2kverR9Qn.

62. Buenavista and Gonzales, "DREAMs Deterred," 21.

63. Thomas Gibbons-Neff, "For U.S. Commandos in the Philippines, a Water Pump Is a New Weapon against ISIS," *New York Times*, April 27, 2019, https://www.nytimes.com/2019/04/27/world/asia/pentagon-philippines-isis.html.

64. Jeoffrey Maitem, "Amid Calls for Philippines to Seek US Help vs China, US Warship Docks in Duterte Home City for Port Call," *Inquirer-Global Nation*, June 29, 2019, https://globalnation.inquirer.net/177176/amid-calls-for-philippines-to-seek-us-help-vs-china-us-warship-docks-in-duterte-home-city-for-port-call.

65. Floyd Whaley, "Murder Charge Is Recommended for U.S. Marine in Death of Transgender Filipino," *New York Times*, December 15, 2014, http://www.nytimes.com/2014/12/16/world/asia/murder-charge-is-recommended-for-us-marine-in-death-of-transgender-filipino.html; Trefor Moss, "U.S. Role in Botched Philippines Raid Comes under Scrutiny," *Wall Street Journal*, http://www.wsj.com/articles/u-s-role-in-botched-philippines-raid-comes-under-scrutiny-1427435700.

Chapter 2. "Civilize the Savage"

The chapter title is a lyric from Grand Puba, "360° (What Goes Around)."

1. Walden Bello, "The U.S. Military Just Plunged Philippine Politics into Crisis," *Foreign Policy in Focus*, March 17, 2015, http://fpif.org/the-u-s-military-just-plunged-philippine-politics-into-crisis; Adam Hudson, "US Wages 'War on Terror' in the Philippines," *Truthout*, April 9, 2015, http://www.truth-out.org/news/item/30061-us-wages-war-on-terror-in-the-philippines; Marlon Ramos, "Police BOI Report Confirms US Role in 'Oplan Exodus,'" *Philippine Daily Inquirer*, March 13, 2015, http://globalnation.inquirer.net/119512/police-boi-report-confirms-us-role-in-oplan-exodus/#ixzz3VQXsDhgS; Associated Press, "Philippine Military Says 23 Muslim Rebels Killed in Clashes," *New York Times*, March 11, 2015, http://nyti.ms/1FKzz4A; Craig Whitlock, "Manila: U.S. Had Key Role in Deadly Counterterrorism Raid in Philippines," *Washington Post*, March 17, 2015, https://www.washingtonpost.com/world/national-security/us-had-role-in-deadly-counterterrorism-raid-in-philippines/2015/03/17/6ab42816-ccd6-11e4-8a46-b1dc9be5a8ff_story.html; Floyd Whaley, "Refugee Crisis in Philippines as Peace Deal Is at Risk," *New York Times*, March 10, 2015, http://nyti.ms/1C1iRP0; Arlyn de la Cruz, "US Drone Watched Mamasapano Debacle," *Philippine Daily Inquirer*, February 8th, 2015, http://newsinfo.inquirer.net/671237/us-drone-watched-mamasapano-debacle.

2. Neil Jerome Morales and Simon Lewis, "U.S. Joins Battle as Philippines Takes Losses in Besieged City," *Reuters*, June 10, 2017, https://www.reuters.com/article/us-philippines-militants/u-s-joins-battle-as-philippines-takes-losses-in-besieged-city-idUSKBN19107I.

3. Staff and agencies in Manila, "Philippines Reopens Subic Bay as Military Base to Cover South China Sea," *Guardian*, July 15, 2015, http://www.theguardian.com/world/2015/jul/16/philippines-reopens-subic-bay-as-military-base-to-cover-south-china-sea.

4. "Near East" and "Middle East" geopolitical descriptors are western-centric, but I've retained these phrasings for the ease of the reader.

5. Paulskee, "Mighty4 15th Year Anniversary: A R-evolution of Flyer Designs," *Master Culture*, September 30, 2013, www.themasterculture.com/?p=1869.

6. Quan Vu, "Real Recognize Real: Odessa Kane on the SDMAs," *Sound San Diego on NBC San Diego*, December 11, 2013, http://www.nbcsandiego.com/blogs/sounddiego/Real-Recognize-Real-Odessa-Kane-on-the-SDMAs-231374981.html.

7. See Aguilar, "Tracing Origins"; Salman, *Embarrassment of Slavery*.

8. See Mojares, "Claiming Malayness."

9. Paradoxically, as explored later in this chapter, hip hop often imagines Asia as the origin of Black Islam.

10. Khabeer, *Muslim Cool*.

11. Gilroy, *Black Atlantic*, 83.

12. Daulatzai, *Black Star*, 111.

13. See Daulatzai, *Black Star*.

14. Ibid., 97, 110–11.

15. McAlister, *Epic Encounters*, 104.

16. Deutsch, "Asiatic Black Man," 196.

17. Mullen, *Afro-Orientalism*, xvi.

18. Deutsch, "Asiatic Black Man," 203.

19. Turner, *Islam in the African-American Experience*, 450.

20. Miyakawa, *Five Percenter Rap*, 11.

21. Turner, *Islam in the African-American Experience*, 446–49; Daulatzai, *Black Star*, 102.

22. Daulatzai, *Black Star*.

23. James Baldwin quoted in McAlister, *Epic Encounters*, 95.

24. Daultazai, *Black Star*.

25. Ibid., 112.

26. Daulatzai, *Return of the Mecca*, 6.

27. Adam K. Raymond, "Why Did Islam Disappear From Hip-Hop?" *Vocativ*, October 27, 2014, http://www.vocativ.com/culture/religion/islam-hip-hop/?page=all.

28. Davis, *Deen Tight*; Daulatzai, *Return of the Mecca*.

29. Mustafa Davis, *Deen Tight*, online (Tabah Foundation, 2011), https://vimeo.com/27049587.

30. Daulatzai, *Return of the Mecca*, 6.

31. Siyam, "Knowledge of Self," 48.

32. Labrador, "Rock, Rock On," 256.

33. Aguilar, "Tracing Origins," 631; Salman, *Embarrassment of Slavery*, 144.

34. Salman, *Embarrassment of Slavery*, 151–52.

35. Abinales, *Making Mindanao*, 30–40.

36. Abinales, "American Colonial State," 90.

37. Brecht-Drouart, "Muslim Women Leaders," 208–9.

38. See Lara, "New Face of Mindanao's Strong Men"; Gil C. Cabacungan Jr., "WikiLeaks: US Backed MILF: Washington Favored MOA-AD, Cables Show," *Philippine Daily Inquirer*, September 8, 2011, http://newsinfo.inquirer.net/54889/wikileaks-us-backed-milf.

39. Abinales, *Making Mindanao*, 46.

40. Ibid., 45–68.

41. Rafael, *White Love*, 8.

42. See Abinales, *Making Mindanao*.

43. See Sadiq, *Paper Citizens*.

44. Aguilar, "Tracing Origins," 630.

45. Rafael, *White Love*, 7.

46. Siyam, "Knowledge of Self," 51–52.

47. Daulatzai, *Return of the Mecca*, 32.

48. Quan Vu, "The Wrath of Odessa Kane," *San Diego City Beat*, February 27, 2013, http://sdcitybeat.com/music/music-feature/wrath-odessa-kane.

49. Ibid.

50. Analyn Perez and TJ Dimacali, "The Ampatuan Massacre: A Map and Time-line," *GMA News Online*, November 25, 2009, http://www.gmanetwork.com/news/story/177821/news/specialreports/the-ampatuan-massacre-a-map-and-timeline.

51. Ryce, "Art as Political Weapon," 219.

52. See Smith, *Photography on the Color Line*.

53. Abinales, *Making Mindanao*, 47–52; Arnold, *Moro War*, 8–9.

54. Arnold, *Moro War*, 124–25.

55. See Abinales, *Making Mindanao*.

56. Rafael, "Parricides," 362.

57. Gonzalves, *Day the Dancers Stayed*, 10.

58. Daulatzai, *Black Star*, 109.

59. Mullen, *Afro-Orientalism*, 43.

60. Yasiin Bey quoted in Daulatzai, *Return of the Mecca*, 32–33.

61. Angeles, "From Catholic to Muslim," 184.

62. Digital Martyrs, personal communication, August 2012.

63. Rafael, "Parricides," 362.

64. See DeOcampo, "Hispanic Influences," 356; Fernández, *Palabas*.

65. Aguilar, "Tracing Origins."

66. Salman, *Embarrassment of Slavery*, 52.

67. Daulatzai, *Black Star*, xviii.

68. Nadeau and Barlow, *Story of Spanish*.

69. Aidi, "Let Us Be Moors," 36–37.

70. Ibid., 49.

71. See Tim Padgett, *WLRN*, "Why So Many Latinos Are Becoming Muslims," October 9, 2013, http://wlrn.org/post/why-so-many-latinos-are-becoming-muslims; Aidi, "Jihadis in the Hood."

72. Donoso, "Al-Andalus and Asia," 30, 29.

73. Gaerlan, "In the Court of the Sultan," 254.

74. Daulatzai, *Black Star*; Deutsch, "Asiatic Black Man."

75. Turner, *Islam in the African-American Experience*, 456.

76. Deutsch, "Asiatic Black Man," 197. Muhammad Ali quoted in Deutsch, "Asiatic Black Man," 194.

77. Miyakawa, *Five Percenter Rap*, 9, 15.

78. Ibid., 21, 35–37.

79. Daulatzai, *Black Star*, 102–3, 131.

80. Elijah Muhammad quoted in Deutsch, "Asiatic Black Man," 194.

81. Mullen, *Afro-Orientalism*; Turner, *Islam in the African-American Experience*.

82. Machida, *Unsettled Visions*, 58–61.

83. See Baldoz, *Third Asiatic Invasion*.

84. Ibid., 70–112.

85. True AsiatikTribe is a larger group of Filipino hip hop artists of different crafts

of which MastaPlann are core leaders. For more, see "MastaPlann: True Asiatic Legends," *Laking Hip Hop Music*, January 19, 2011, http://lakinghiphopmusic.blogspot.com/2011/01/mastaplanntrue-asiatic-legends.html.

86. Siyam, "Knowledge of Self," 48–49.

87. George Quibuyen, personal communication, February 2007.

88. See Caronan, *Legitimizing Empire*.

89. Villegas, "Redefined."

Chapter 3. Nation in the Universe

1. Ra, "Bambu || Comrades."

2. Akbar Ahmed, "Deadly Drone Strike on Muslims in the Southern Philippines," *Brookings*, March 5, 2012, http://www.brookings.edu/research/opinions/2012/03/05-drones-philippines-ahmed.

3. "Designer Turns Fantasies into Fashion," *Gadsden Times*, May 13, 1979, https://news.google.com/newspapers?nid=1891&dat=19790513&id=ynMpAAAAIBAJ&sjid=N9YEAAAAIBAJ&pg=2020,2342389.

4. Rose Eveleth, "The Subversive Science Fiction of Hip-Hop," *Motherboard*, July 7, 2015, http://motherboard.vice.com/read/the-subversive-science-fiction-of-hip-hop.

5. Stones Throw, "Mndsgn—Cosmic Perspective."

6. Womack, *Afrofuturism*, 9, 17.

7. Jamie Broadnax, "What The Heck Is Afrofuturism?," *Huffington Post*, February 16, 2018, https://www.huffingtonpost.com/entry/opinion-broadnax-afrofuturism-black-panther_us_5a85f1b9e4b004fc31903b95.

8. Eshun, "Further Considerations of Afrofuturism," 288, 298–99.

9. See Rafael, *White Love*; Salman, *Embarrassment of Slavery*; See, *Decolonized Eye*; See, *Filipino Primitive*.

10. See, *Decolonized Eye*, xxx.

11. See Balce, "Filipino Bodies"; Bascara, *Model-Minority Imperialism*; Schleitwiler, *Strange Fruit*; Chuh, *Imagine Otherwise*; Ngai, *Impossible Subjects*.

12. Mabalon, *Little Manila*, 144; Baldoz, *Third Asiatic Invasion*.

13. Special thanks to Leo Esclamado, Anna Alves, Thea Quiray, Barbara Jane Reyes, Oliver Wang, and Charles Tan for their electronic correspondences in helping me think through these concepts. For an article on Filipino American representation in science fiction, see Charles Tan, "Award-winning writers explore Filipino representation in fantasy and science fiction," *CNN Philippines*, September 9, 2016, http://cnnphilippines.com/life/culture/literature/2016/09/09/trota-and-wong-interview.html.

14. Wang quoted in Pisares, "Do You Mis(recognize) Me," 194.

15. Ibid., 194.

16. Tiongson, *Filipinos Represent*, 59.

17. Qbert and Labrador, "We're Up There Performing a Character," 10.

18. Vergara, *Displaying Filipinos*, 20.

19. "DJ Qbert Shows Off His Incredibly Diverse Record Collection," *FuseTV*, March 5, 2014, https://www.fuse.tv/2014/03/qbert-crate-diggers?campaign=ytb-cd-030514 -end#ooid=FzYm12azqEjYYV9qLaPCSHiQnPVdEC8V.

20. Eric Sanford, personal communication, February and July 2015.

21. Bea Lesaca, "Rooted TV Episode 1: Jmasta (Battlekrew)," *Boogie Down Manila* (blog), March 10, 2014, https://funkynastycrazyclassy.wordpress.com/2014/03/10/ rooted-tv-episode-1-jmasta-battlekrew.

22. "What Is the Universal Zulu Nation???????," Universal Zulu Nation, http://www .zulunation.com/about-zulunation/, accessed July 23, 2015.

23. Ibid.

24. Nelson, "Introduction," 8.

25. Ras G., public conversation with Nicole Mitchell (Black Urban Music Conference, University of California, Irvine, February 28, 2015).

26. Sylvan, "Rap Music," 418.

27. Chang, *Can't Stop Won't Stop*, 93.

28. Ibid., 92.

29. Ibid., 93.

30. Ibid., 94.

31. Ibid., 91.

32. McAlister, *Epic Encounters*, 104.

33. See Coney, *Space Is the Place*.

34. StreetTV, "Afrika Bambaataa Interview on Hip Hop, Street Gangs and the 5th Element of Hip-Hop," YouTube Video, August 5, 2006, https://youtu.be/563eLRk3lts.

35. Luv and Saphire, *Green Book*, 7.

36. Michael "Mikeydisko" Barairo, personal communication, January 2013.

37. Bishop Chronicles, "B-Boys in the Bay w/ Rob Nasty Rocker," September 2019, https://open.spotify.com/episode/4XhqLHW7RSLXI5Lsl75vRd?si=ol63OCkUQYqr Lng5KiFfqw&fbclid=IwARodbh76AmolKB8KQ2QKHSnLFgl6wh9hnkx1LHvmzBS gD6BuoBX5gs69NPA; Nasty, "Building Hip Hop."

38. See Eure and Spady, *Nation Conscious Rap*, 329.

39. Afrika Bambaataa, "Message to the Youth and Young Adults of the World," *Universal Zulu Nation*, http://www.zulunation.com/the-message, accessed July 23, 2015.

40. Chang, *Can't Stop Won't Stop*, 106.

41. George Quibuyen, personal communication, February 2007.

42. Deutsch, "Asiatic Black Man," 197.

43. For more on the politics of nation and diaspora, see Alim, Ibrahim, and Pennycook, *Global Linguistic Flows*; Hall, "Cultural Identity and Diaspora"; Gilroy, *Black Atlantic*.

44. Tiongson, *Filipinos Represent*, 97.

45. Conscious Youth Media, "2012 Reel Hood Hero: Gabriel Dela Cruz Aka The Mighty Delrokz," YouTube, July 24, 2012, https://www.youtube.com/watch?v=gk7wHQFhUsM.

46. For more on roots versus routes, see Gilroy, *Black Atlantic*, 19.

47. Adisa Banjoko, "The Hip-Hop Vatican: Afrika Bambaataa & Betrayal Pt. 1," *Bishop Chronicles,* May 5, 2016, http://www.bishopchronicles.com/podcast/2016/5/15/42-the-hip-hop-vatian-afrika-bambaataa-betrayal.

48. Balance, *Tropical Renditions,* 49.

49. Eshun, *More Brilliant than the Sun,* 43.

50. Ibid., 21.

51. "SXSW Film Winners: Winners of the SXSW 2001 Film Festival," *Austin Chronicle,* March 16, 2001, http://www.austinchronicle.com/screens/2001–03–16/sxsw-film-winners.

52. Balance, *Tropical Renditions,* 50.

53. Ibid., 42.

54. Ibid., 47.

55. Ibid., 40.

56. Coney, *Space Is the Place.*

57. Eshun, *More Brilliant than the Sun,* 192, 84.

58. James Tai, Dave Tompkins, and Brian "B+" Cross, "Science Friction," *URB,* February 1998. Special thanks to Sean Slusser for a copy of this article.

59. Balance, *Tropical Renditions,* 36–37.

60. See McAlister, *Epic Encounters.*

61. Hopie, "Writing Wrongs."

62. Hopie Baby, "Hopie Ft. Del."

63. Hopie, "Writing Wrongs," 163.

64. See Rydell, *All the World's a Fair.*

65. Dutton, "Hopie—Solar Systems."

66. Rafael, *White Love,* 34–35.

67. Hopie, "Writing Wrongs," 164.

Chapter 4. Postcolonial Bodies, Modern Postures

1. The term "hip hop dance" is hotly contested, especially among members of the dance community. Other preferred terms are "urban dance" and "street dance." Hip hop can even be regarded as a genre distinct from b-boying/breaking. For the purpose of consistency, however imperfect and debatable, I use "hip hop dance" to signify the cultural genre this book discusses. Furthermore, "hip hop dance" is more recognizable to a general public, even if dance communities acknowledge that various dance forms, traditions, and styles in "hip hop dance" have distinct roots, legacies, and regional significance. My use of "street dance" later in this chapter emphasizes this term's various racialized and gendered connotations.

2. See, *Decolonized Eye,* 103, 95.

3. Ngô, *Imperial Blues,* 76.

4. See, *Decolonized Eye,* 73.

5. A few members of these early crews would go on to become Kaba Modern leaders and hip hop cultural innovators in general. See Cambay, "Filipino American Dance Culture," and Calvario, "Soul in the Whole."

6. Leaño, "Rhythm of a Nation"; David, "Funk Behind Bay Street Dance." For more documentation of the origin and growth of California dancer crews, see Jessie Ma, "The Evolution of our Global Dance Community," *Steezy*, June 7, 2016, https://blog. steezy.co/evolution-of-our-dance-community/; Alvina Ng, "Bustin a Groove: Body Rock Dance Competition Origins with Anna Sarao," *Steezy*, June 11, 2014, https://blog .steezy.co/body-rock-dance-competition-origins-with-anna-sarao/; Jessie Ma, "Origin Stories of the Norcal and Socal Dance Communities," *Steezy*, June 8, 2016, https:// blog.steezy.co/origin-stories-of-the-norcal-and-socal-dance-communities/.

7. Wang, *Legions of Boom*.

8. Cambay, "Filipino American Dance Culture," 20.

9. David, "Funk Behind Bay Street Dance," 44, 56–57.

10. Kathryn Bold, "Majoring in Kaba Modern: Hip-Hop Crews Come of Age on Campus" and "The King of Tut: Alumnus Mike Song Has Everyone—and His Mother—Dancing 'Gangnam Style,'" both in *UC Irvine Magazine* 1, no. 3 (Spring 2013).

11. For Filipino American collegiate culture and demographics, see Gonzalves, *Day the Dancers Stayed*, esp. 95–96.

12. Wang, *Legions of Boom*, 19.

13. "Happiness Is Now Tour," Happiness Is Now, http://happinessisnow.org/happy man (dead), accessed July 27, 2015.

14. Michelle Woo, "Kaba Modern Created a Dance Dance Revolution," *OC Weekly*, January 12, 2012, http://www.ocweekly.com/2012–01–19/culture/kaba-modern-irvine.

15. Elizabeth Lee, "Asian Americans Break Stereotypes through Urban Dance," *Voice of America*, June 24, 2013, http://www.voanews.com/content/asian-american -break-sterotypes-through-urban-dance/1687837.html.

16. "Interview with Anna Sarao (Body Rock Dance Competition)," OneCypher: Street Dance, September 28, 2004, http://www.onecypher.com/2004/09/28/interview -with-anna-sarao.

17. Leaño, "Rhythm of a Nation," 41–42.

18. "Vibe Dance Competition," Facebook page, https://www.facebook.com/VIBE DanceComp/info, accessed July 27, 2015; "Vibe Dance Competition," http://vibe dancecomp.com, accessed July 27, 2015.

19. Calvario, "Soul in the Whole."

20. Lee, "Asian Americans Break Stereotypes."

21. Cruz, Baluyut, and Reyes, *Forbidden Book*, 66.

22. Baldwin, "Cakewalk."

23. Burns, *Puro Arte*, 54.

24. Anderson, *Art without Borders*; McDonagh, *Rise and Fall*.

25. Anderson, *Art without Borders*, 5.

26. Brown, *Babylon Girls*, 1, 16–17.

27. For more on the genealogy of modern dance, the breaking of form, progressivism, feminism, and Blackness, see Daly, *Done into Dance*; Franko, *Work of Dance*; Martin, *Modern Dance*.

28. Manning, *Modern Dance*, xiv.

29. Brown, *Babylon Girls*, 93, 95, 17.

30. Burns, *Puro Arte*, 40.

31. Brown, *Babylon Girls*, 169.

32. Burns, *Puro Arte*, 50.

33. Billy de la Cruz, "Fil-Am Bailey Munoz wins 'So You Think You Can Dance' Season 16," *Asian Journal*, September 17, 2019, https://www.asianjournal.com/features/people/fil-am-bailey-munoz-wins-so-you-think-you-can-dance-season-16.

34. Caronan, *Legitimizing Empire*, 16.

35. See Woo, "Kaba Modern"; Calvario, "Soul in the Whole."

36. Calvario, "Soul in the Whole," 27.

37. *America's Best Dance Crew*, season 1, episode 7, "Evolution of Street Dance," MTV, aired March 20, 2008. Unattributed quotations in this and the following paragraphs are also from this episode.

38. Bass, *B-Girling*.

39. Ernie, "Kaba Modern on America's Best Dance Crew," *8 Asians* (blog), January 29, 2008, http://www.8asians.com/2008/01/29/kaba-modern-on-americas-best-dance-crew. Later quotations from www.8asians.com are from this citation.

40. Hong, *Birth of Korean Cool*.

41. See Machida, *Unsettled Visions*, 58–61; Wang, "Rapping and Repping Asian."

42. Leland, *Hip*, 6, 13.

43. See Harrison, *Hip Hop Underground*.

44. Lowe, *Immigrant Acts*.

45. See Majors and Billson, *Cool Pose*.

46. Chung, "Started in the Streets," 133, 135.

47. Lisa Brenner Katz, "UCI Asian-American Fraternity Imposes Self-Suspension over Blackface Video," *89.3 KPCC*, May 3, 2013, http://www.scpr.org/blogs/news/2013/05/03/13530/uci-asian-american-fraternity-imposes-self-suspens.

48. See Lott, *Love and Theft*.

49. "Student Data Enrollment," University of California, Irvine, http://www.oir.uci.edu/enrollment.html, accessed July 28, 2015.

50. John Murillo III, "Op Ed: Defying Antiblackness at UC Irvine—and Everywhere," *Feminist Wire*, April 28, 2013, http://thefeministwire.com/2013/04/op-ed-defying-antiblackness-at-uc-irvine-and-everywhere.

51. See, for example, Pisares, "Do You Mis(recognize) Me."

52. "Yuri Tag of Kaba Modern," *Kineda* (blog), March 7, 2008, http://www.kineda.com/yuri-tag-of-kaba-modern/#.UdjOXj5ATvZ.

53. See Joo, *Transnational Sport*.

54. Filipinos4Islanders, "Kaba Modern—Filipinos Are PACIFIC ISLANDERS! Filipinos Are NOT Asian!," November 29, 2011, YouTube Video, http://www.youtube.com/watch?v=INiVQnwq1e0.

55. See this Fung Brothers episode for an instructive example: Fung Bros., "Pacific Islander or Asian: ARE FILIPINOS ASIAN OR PACIFIC ISLANDER?—Level: Asian—Fung Bros," YouTube Video, February 24, 2014, https://youtu.be/lEmsdHw6trM.

56. Chung, "Started in the Streets."

57. For more on the Jabbawockeez's discussion of the garage as the space of dance socialization, see Jabbawockeez Official, "The History of the Jabbawockeez: Garage and a Boombox," YouTube, May 18, 2012, https://youtu.be/zISskHpvo9c.

58. For more on the origins of the Jabbawockeez, see Jabbawockeez Official, "The History of the Jabbawockeez: Forming the Group," YouTube Video, May 31, 2012, https://youtu.be/bJOVeRiXsMA.

59. *America's Best Dance Crew*, season 3, episode 1, "Sudden Death Challenge," MTV, aired January 15, 2009.

60. For more on the term "contact zones," see Ngô, *Imperial Blues*.

61. See Gonzalves, *Day the Dancers Stayed*.

62. Perillo, "Embodying Modernism," 123, 143.

63. Gonzalves, *Day the Dancers Stayed*, 63–88.

64. Ibid., 114.

65. See Espiritu, *Home Bound*.

66. Ibid., 113.

67. See Hernandez, "Behind the Curtain."

68. See Gonzalves, *Day the Dancers Stayed*, 116.

69. See Gaerlan, "In the Court of the Sultan," 256.

70. Called the "modern suite" in PCN, the hip hop dance suite affirms Jack Anderson's attempt to describe the vision of modern dance: "Modern dancers have tended to use 'modern' as a synonym for 'new' or 'creative,' and they have prized experimentation" (Anderson, *Art without Borders*, 4).

71. For more on unsettling notions of modernity, see Clifford, "Traveling Cultures."

72. Lowe, *Immigrant Acts*.

73. Edgar Dormitorio (former PCN director), personal communication, June 24, 2013.

74. Bold, "Majoring in Kaba Modern."

75. *Kaba Modern: The First Twenty Years*.

76. Ibid.

77. Calvario, "Soul in the Whole," 23.

78. Weston, *Families We Choose*.

79. Bailey, *Butch Queens*, 5.

80. Ngô, *Imperial Blues*, 76.

81. *Kaba Modern: The First Twenty Years*.

82. LaBoskey, "Getting Off."

83. David, "Funk Behind Bay Street Dance," 6–7.

84. The centrality of women in hip hop dance can be seen in Leung, *Furious Beauty*.

85. Schloss, *Foundation*, 12.

86. "Thread: Fed Up with 'Hip Hop Choreo Dancers," *Bboyworld*, www.bboyworld.com/forum/showthread.php?91615-Fed-up-with-quot-Hip-Hop-quot-Choreo-Dancers/page3, accessed July 29, 2015.

87. Emily Arata, "These Guys Dancing to 'Anaconda' Could Give Nicki Minaj a Run for Her Money," *Elite Daily*, September 9, 2014, http://elitedaily.com/music/guys

-dancing-anaconda-nicki-minaj-video/746911; Tanya Chen, "These Two Guys Dancing to Nicki Minaj's 'Anaconda' Will Give You So Much Life," *BuzzFeed*, September 8,
2014, http://www.buzzfeed.com/tanyachen/two-guys-choreography-to-nicki-minajs-
anaconda#.bpQp68zwZ; Brandi Fowler, "Move Over Ellen DeGeneres: These Two
Guys Dancing to Nicki Minaj's 'Anaconda' Came to Win," *Cambio*, September 10,
2015, http://www.cambio.com/2014/09/10/move-over-ellen-degeneres-these-two
-guys-dancing-to-nicki-minaj.

88. Kimmy Maniquis, personal communication, May 1, 2013.

89. Ibid.

90. A whole host of college and professional sports players have "gone viral" in
their performances of said dances, at the time NBA player John Wall was the most
publicized. See Jason McIntyre, "John Wall Doing the Nae Nae with Paul George
Was Better than the Dunk Contest," *USA Today Sports*, February 17, 2014, http://
thebiglead.com/2014/02/17/john-wall-doing-the-nae-nae-with-paul-george-was
-better-than-the-dunk-contest.

91. Bragin, "Techniques of Black Male Re/dress," 62.

92. Ramirez, "Booty Pop Madness," 167.

93. Ibid., 165.

94. *Kaba Modern: The First Twenty Years.*

95. "Kinjaz," Kinjaz, https://www.kinjaz.com, accessed May 2, 2020.

96. Queen ShanShan, "Doctor Strikes a Pose," A Broad Cast, June 18, 2019, https://
www.iheart.com/podcast/263-a-broad-cast-podcast-30903499/episode/27-category
-is-doctor-strikes-a-46196869/?cmp=ios_share&pr=false&fbclid=IwAR0HOmoKo
gNUrPwZVLmfITZp12HqG8c4zZ8NkfNnofa4MkSXz9DURovCQfo.

97. To be fair, in 2020, Arnel Calvario and the Kinjaz were part of an ongoing
conversation on Blackness, racism, privilege, and power. This effort and openness
should be celebrated.

98. One Down, "Innovating Cultural Dance."

99. One Down, "History of Pilipino Cultural Night."

Conclusion

1. Kyle Eustice, "City of Oakland Declares May 17 'Phife Dawg Day,'" *HipHopDX*,
May 18, 2019, https://hiphopdx.com/news/id.51468/title.city-of-oakland-declares-
may-17-phife-dawg-day.

2. Harmeet Kaur, "New York City Now Has a Wu-Tang Clan District," *CNN*, May
5, 2019, https://www.cnn.com/2019/05/05/entertainment/wu-tang-clan-street-sign-
trnd/index.html.

3. Joe Price, "NBA Draftees Quizzed on '90s Pop Culture Couldn't Name OutKast or
Destiny's Child," *Complex*, June 22, 2019, https://www.complex.com/music/2019/06/
nba-draftees-outkast-destinys-child; Jackson Connor, "The Bronx's Hip-Hop Boulevard Connects the Borough's Past to Its Future," *Village Voice*, March 1, 2016, https://
www.villagevoice.com/2016/03/01/the-bronxs-hip-hop-boulevard-connects-the
-boroughs-past-to-its-future.

4. "Respect: Hip-Hop Style and Wisdom," exhibition, Oakland Museum of California, https://museumca.org/exhibit/respect-hip-hop-style-wisdom, accessed June 16, 2020.

5. "Displays," Cerritos Library, http://cerritoslibrary.us/cl_displays_MarApr19.htm, accessed June 16, 2020.

6. "Union City, CA Proclamation," Keep It Flowing, https://keepitflowingmedia .com/portfolio-item/union-city-ca-proclamation/, accessed June 16, 2020. An early example of civic recognition was in 2004, when the mayor of Seattle declared April 26 "Massive Monkees Day" to commend the historically Filipino American–led b-boy crew for their success in winning global championships. See Julie Pham, "Bboy Crew Massive Monkees Build a Break Dancing Business," *Forbes*, April 23, 2013, https://www.forbes.com/sites/juliepham/2013/04/23/bboy-crew-massive-monkees -build-a-break-dancing-business/#35fd35864273.

7. Nastia Voynovskaya, "Dream Day Pays Homage to a Beloved Figure in Oakland's Hip-Hop and Graffiti Scenes," *East Bay Express*, August 16, 2016, https://www .eastbayexpress.com/oakland/dream-day-pays-homage-to-a-beloved-figure-in -oaklands-hip-hop-and-graffiti-scenes/Content?oid=4940387&fbclid=IwAR19TL9i 3FhwJkv-qeG842taZpMdRe62C5tdFFayAZSd7NSEc20Oy6SaMxo.

8. Aidin Vaziri, "DJ Qbert Brings Turntable Skills to Second Season of Undiscovered SF," *San Francisco Chronicle*, July 20, 2018, https://www.sfchronicle.com/ music/article/DJ-QBert-brings-turntable-skills-to-second-season-13082751.php; Pham, "Bboy Crew Massive Monkees"; Oliver Wang, "The Beat Junkie Institute of Sound Gets DJ Hopefuls Up to Scratch," *KCET*, May 26, 2017, https://www.kcet.org/ shows/artbound/the-beat-junkie-institute-of-sound-gets-dj-hopefuls-up-to-scratch.

9. Lex Celera, "This Filipina-American Rapper's Heartfelt Song for Her Immigrant Mother Is Worth a Listen," *Vice*, June 27, 2019, https://www.vice.com/en_in/article/ d3njeq/filipina-american-rapper-ruby-ibarra-someday-npr.

10. See R. Rodriguez, *Migrants for Export*; Francisco, *Labor of Care*.

11. Denise Guerra and Rosalind Faulkner, "This Tiny Desk Contestant Rapped a Love Letter to Her Immigrant Mother," *NPR*, June 22, 2019, https://www.npr.org/ sections/allsongs/2019/06/22/734403197/this-tiny-desk-contestant-rapped-a-love -letter-to-her-immigrant-mother?fbclid=IwAR0Os4EqelRYp6amo5ZWsPY8q_upf xqHpIekNRGGrA5LuW9DakLAffEx5_s.

12. Mabalon, *Little Manila*, 56.

13. Guerra and Faulkner, "This Tiny Desk Contestant."

14. Ibarra, "Us"; Ibarra, "Ruby Ibarra Feat. Rocky Rivera, Klassy, & Faith Santilla."

Selected Bibliography

Multimedia

Ahearn, Charlie, dir. 1982. *Wild Style*. Video. 81 min. Rhino Home Video.

Baluyot, Pearlie Rose S., and Agnes A. Bertiz. 2009. "The (Dis)embodied Filipina: Fashioning Domesticity, Weaving Desire: Visions of the Filipina." Exhibit. USC Pacific Asia Museum, Pasadena, CA. October 14, 2009, to February 8, 2010.

Bambu. 2008. "Make Change." 1:40 min. On . . . *Exact Change* . . . CD. Bambu/Community Kitchen Recordings.

———. 2012. "Bronze Watch." 4:05 min. On . . . *One Rifle per Family* CD. Beatrock Music.

———. 2012. "Moms." 5:22 min. On . . . *One Rifle per Family* CD. Beatrock Music.

———. 2012. "So Many." 3:47 min. On . . . *One Rifle per Family* CD. Beatrock Music.

———. 2012. "Upset the Set Up (featuring Killer Mike)." 3:40 min. On . . . *One Rifle per Family* CD. Beatrock Music.

———. 2013. "Crosshairs (featuring DJ Qbert)." 2:30 min. On *Sun of a Gun* CD. Beatrock Music.

———. 2016. "Comrades." 3:08 min. On *Party Worker* CD. Beatrock Music.

Bass, Angela J. 2010. *B-Girling in a B-Boy's World*. Video. 2:34 min. https://vimeo.com/11516937.

Blue Scholars. 2004. "Burnt Offering." 5:07 min. On *Blue Scholars* CD. Blue Scholars.

———. 2004. "Motion Movement." 3:46 min. On *Blue Scholars* CD. Blue Scholars.

———. 2004. "No Rest for the Weary." 5:36 min. On *Blue Scholars* CD. Blue Scholars.

———. 2005. "Proletariat Blues." 3:56 min. On *The Long March* EP CD. Blue Scholars.

———. 2005. "Talk Story." 3:46 min. On *The Long March* EP CD. Blue Scholars.

———. 2005. "Wounded Eyes." 3:36 min. On *The Long March* EP CD. Blue Scholars.

———. 2007. "Back Home." 5:10 min. On *Bayani* CD. Massline Media.

———. 2007. "Opening Salvo." 3:13 min. On *Bayani* CD. Massline Media.

———. 2012. "May Day." Audio. 2:53 min. https://soundcloud.com/bluescholars/may-day-1.

Brocka, Lino, dir. 1988. *Macho Dancer*. DVD. 136 min. Viva Films.

Clearn, Harry, dir. 2014. "The Bar || Barkada || Produced by Bean One || Directed by Harry Clean." YouTube video, 3:50 min. March 18, 2014. https://youtu.be/tV-S083rIvTQ.

Coney, John, dir. 2003. *Space Is the Place*. Written by Sun Ra and Joshua Smith. 85 min. DVD. Plexifilm.

Davis, Mustafa, dir. 2011. *Deen Tight*. Video. 62:20 min. Tabah Foundation. https://vimeo.com/27049587.

Dutton, David, dir. 2014. "Hopie—Solar Systems." YouTube video, 2:34 min. October 16, 2014. https://youtu.be/FSfsp2PnVGs.

EyeASage [Rocky Rivera]. 2008. "Married to the Hustle." Audio. 3:00 min. On *Married to the Hustle Mixtape*. Mama Clothing. https://soundcloud.com/rocky-rivera-1/sets/married-to-the-hustle-mixtape-2008.

George, Nelson, dir. 2013. *Finding the Funk*. Video. 90 min. Finding the Funk Productions.

Grand Puba. 1992. "360° (What Goes Around)." 4:01 min. On *Reel to Reel* CD. Elektra.

HipHopLivesToday. 2009. "KRS-One & Marley Marl—Hip Hop Lives (I Come Back) [HD]." YouTube video, 3:49 min. December 12, 2009. https://youtu.be/ZRmbCa4FLnY.

Hopie. 2013. "Solar Systems." 2:29 min. On *Sugar Water* CD. Diamond Rooftops.

———. 2013. "Space Case (Feat. Del the Funky Homosapien)." 5:03 min. On *Raw Gems* CD. Diamond Rooftops.

Hopie Baby, dir. 2011. "Hopie Ft. Del the Funky Homosapien—Space Case." YouTube video, 5:15 min. August 23, 2011. https://youtu.be/kzD22MF4NJo.

Ibarra, Ruby. 2012. "Come on Y'All (featuring Prometheus Brown)." 2:59 min. On *Lost in Translation Mixtape* CD. Ruby Ibarra.

———. 2017. "Us." 4:28 min. On *Circa91* CD. Beatrock Music.

———, dir. 2018. "Ruby Ibarra Feat. Rocky Rivera, Klassy, & Faith Santilla || Us || Prod. by Nphared." YouTube video, 4:39 min. March 8, 2018. https://youtu.be/AUfNeCozJBw.

———, dir. 2019. "Ruby Ibarra & the Balikbayans—Someday [2019 NPR Tiny Desk]." YouTube video, 8:49 min. April 14, 2019. https://youtu.be/SCd3iSfnWSw.

Kaba Modern: The First 20 Years. 2012. DVD. 26:44 min. Red 5 Studios.

Kane, Odessa. 2012. "Olmec Mask (the Intro)." Audio. 2:13 min. Online. Odessa Kane. https://odessakane.bandcamp.com/album/odessa-kane.

———. 2012. "The Pen and the Gun." 4:11 min. On *Cuetes & Balisongs* EP CD. Red Lotus Klan.

Koroma, Salima, dir. 2016. *Bad Rap*. DVD. 62 min. FilmRise.

Leung, Calvin, dir. 2013. *Furious Beauty: A Hip-Hop Family*. DVD. 88 min. Cinema Libre Studio, Plixyl Studios INC.

Mabalon, Dawn, Lakandiwa de Leon, and Jonathan Ramos, dirs. 1997. *Beats, Rhymes, and Resistance: Pilipinos and Hip Hop in Los Angeles.* Video. 20 min. https://vimeo.com/3722157.

Mohajerjasbi, Zia, dir. 2007. "Blue Scholars—'Back Home' Music Video." YouTube video, 5:18 min. June 6, 2007. https://youtu.be/En8DwCeKa6M.

Native Guns. 2006. *Barrel Men.* CD. Native Guns.

———. 2006. "1995." 4:33 min. On *Barrel Men* CD. Native Guns.

———. 2010. "Handcuffs." Audio. 4:00 min. https://soundcloud.com/kiwizzo/handcuffs-native-guns-2010.

One Down. 2019. "The History of Pilipino Cultural Night | One Down." Facebook video, 2:21 min. March 31, 2019. —https://www.facebook.com/onedwnmedia/videos/439228303514664.

———. 2019. "Innovating Cultural Dance | One Down | Takes a Beat by Samahang Modern." Facebook video, 1:44 min. May 30, 2019. https://www.facebook.com/onedwnmedia/videos/425628944946714.

Pray, Doug, dir. 2001. *Scratch.* DVD. 92 min. Palm Pictures.

Ra. 2015. "Bambu || Comrades || Produced, Directed and Edited by Ra." YouTube video, 3:07 min. July 29, 2015. https://youtu.be/H2VDED—fi8.

Rivera, Rocky. 2010. "The Rundown." 3:48 min. On *Rocky Rivera* CD. Beatrock Music.

Stones Throw. 2016. "Mndsgn—Cosmic Perspective." YouTube video, 4:28 min. August 16, 2016. https://youtu.be/BGgaZ66-hPA.

Tandoc, Eric, dir. 2008. *Sounds of a New Hope.* Video. 40:13 min. https://vimeo.com/333833672.

The Bar. 2011. "Lookin' Up." 4:25 min. On *Prometheus Brown and Bambu Walk into a Bar* CD. Beatrock Music/In4mation.

———. 2014. "Barkada." 3:36 min. On *Barkada* CD. Beatrock Music.

Tony Touch. 2000. "Toca's Intro." 2:52 min. On *The Piece Maker* CD. Tommy Boy.

Villegas, Mark R. 2008. "Legend." Video. 5:00 min. https://vimeo.com/6393958.

Other Sources

Newspaper articles, articles in popular magazines, and websites are cited in full in the notes.

Abinales, Patricio N. 2000. *Making Mindanao: Cotabato and Davao in the Formation of the Philippine Nation-State.* Quezon City: Ateneo de Manila University Press.

———. 2002. "An American Colonial State: Authority and Structure in Southern Mindanao." In *Vestiges of War: The Philippine-American War and the Aftermath of an Imperial Dream, 1899–1999,* edited by Angel Velasco Shaw and Luis H. Francia, 89–117. New York: New York University Press.

Aguilar, Filomeno V., Jr. 2005. "Tracing Origins: 'Ilustrado' Nationalism and the Racial Science of Migration Waves." *Journal of Asian Studies* 64 (3): 605–37.

Aidi, Hisham D. 2002. "Jihadis in the Hood: Race, Urban Islam and the War on Terror." *Middle East Research and Information Project,* no. 224: 36–43.

———. 2005. "Let Us Be Moors: Islam, Race, and 'Connected Histories.'" *Souls* 7 (1): 36–51.

Alim, H. Samy, Awad Ibrahim, and Alastair Pennycook, eds. 2009. *Global Linguistic Flows: Hip Hop Cultures, Youth Identities, and the Politics of Language.* New York: Routledge.

Allen, Angelica. 2020. "Afro-Amerasians: Blackness in the Philippine Imaginary." PhD dissertation, University of Texas, Austin.

Anderson, Jack. 1997. *Art without Borders: The World of Modern Dance.* Iowa City: University of Iowa Press.

Angeles, Vivienne S. M. 2013. "From Catholic to Muslim: Changing Perceptions of Gender Roles in a Balik-Islam Movement in the Philippines." In *Gender and Islam in Southeast Asia,* edited by Susanne Schröter, 181–206. Leiden: Brill.

Arnold, James R. 2011. *The Moro War: How America Battled a Muslim Insurgency in the Philippine Jungle, 1902–1913.* New York: Bloomsbury.

Bailey, Marlon M. 2013. *Butch Queens Up in Pumps: Gender, Performance, and Ballroom Culture in Detroit.* Ann Arbor: University of Michigan Press.

Balance, Christine. 2016. *Tropical Renditions: Making Musical Scenes in Filipino America.* Durham, NC: Duke University Press.

Balce, Nerissa S. 2006. "Filipino Bodies, Lynching, and the Language of Empire." In Tiongson and Gutierrez, *Positively No Filipinos Allowed,* 43–60.

———. 2016. *Body Parts of Empire: Visual Abjection, Filipino Images, and the American Archive.* Ann Arbor: University of Michigan Press.

Baldoz, Rick. 2011. *The Third Asiatic Invasion: Migration and Empire in Filipino America, 1898–1946.* New York: New York University Press.

Baldwin, Brooke. 1981. "The Cakewalk: A Study in Stereotype and Reality." *Journal of Social History* 15 (2): 205–18.

Banjoko, Adisa. 2015. *Bobby, Bruce, and the Bronx: The Secrets of Hip-Hop Chess.* N.p.: Three Lions Press.

Bascara, Victor. 2006. *Model-Minority Imperialism.* Minneapolis: University of Minnesota Press.

Black, Jeremy. 2000. *Maps and Politics.* Chicago: University of Chicago Press.

Bragin, Naomi. 2014. "Techniques of Black Male Re/dress: Corporeal Drag and Kinesthetic Politics in the Rebirth of Waacking/Punkin.'" *Women and Performance: A Journal of Feminist Theory* 24 (1): 61–78.

Brantlinger, Patrick. 2007. "Kipling's 'The White Man's Burden' and Its Afterlives." *English Literature in Transition, 1880–1920* 50 (2): 172–91.

Brecht-Drouart, Birte. 2013. "Muslim Women Leaders in the Philippines." In *Gender and Islam in Southeast Asia,* edited by Susanne Schröter, 207–20. Leiden: Brill.

Brown, Jayna. 2008. *Babylon Girls: Black Women Performers and the Shaping of the Modern.* Durham, NC: Duke University Press.

Buenavista, Tracy Lachica, and Jordan Beltran Gonzales. 2010–11. "DREAMs Deterred: Filipino Experiences and an Anti-Militarization Critique of the Development, Relief, and Education for Alien Minors Act." *Harvard Journal of Asian American Policy Review* 21: 29–37.

Burnett, Christina Duffy, and Burke Marshall. 2001. *Foreign in a Domestic Sense: Puerto Rico, American Expansion, and the Constitution*. Durham, NC: Duke University Press.

Burns, Lucy Mae San Pablo. 2012. *Puro Arte: Filipinos on the Stages of Empire*. New York: New York University Press.

Calvario, Arnel. 2014. "Soul in the Whole: The Success and Challenges of Representation from Kaba Modern and Beyond." In Villegas, Kandi, and Labrador, *Empire of Funk*, 23–27.

Cambay, Cheryl. 2014. "Filipino American Dance Culture in Suburbia: The Story of Funki Junction." In Villegas, Kandi, and Labrador, *Empire of Funk*, 19–22.

Caronan, Faye. 2015. *Legitimizing Empire: Filipino American and U.S. Puerto Rican Cultural Critique*. Urbana: University of Illinois Press.

Cenidoza-Suarez, Theresa. 2010. "Militarized Filipino Masculinity and the Language of Citizenship in San Diego." In *Militarized Currents: Toward a Decolonized Future in Asia and the Pacific*, edited by Setsu Shigematsu and Keith L. Camacho, 181–202. Minneapolis: University of Minnesota Press.

Chang, Jeff. 2005. *Can't Stop Won't Stop: A History of the Hip-Hop Generation*. New York: St. Martin's.

———. 2014. "Foreword: For the Moment." In Villegas, Kandi, and Labrador, *Empire of Funk*, xi–xiii.

Choy, Catherine Ceniza. 2003. *Empire of Care: Nursing and Migration in Filipino American History*. Durham, NC: Duke University Press.

Chuh, Kandice. 2003. *Imagine Otherwise: On Asian Americanist Critique*. Durham, NC: Duke University Press.

Chung, Brian Su-Jen. 2016. "'Started in the Streets . . .' Criminalizing Blackness and the Performance of Asian American Entrepreneurship on America's Best Dance Crew, Season 1." In *Contemporary Directions in Asian American Dance*, edited by Yutian Wong. Madison: University of Wisconsin Press.

Clifford, James. 1992. "Traveling Cultures." In *Cultural Studies*, edited by Lawrence Grossberg, Cary Nelson, and Paula Treichler, 96–112. New York: Routledge.

Condry, Ian. 2006. *Hip-Hop Japan: Rap and the Paths of Cultural Globalization*. Durham, NC: Duke University Press.

Cruz, Enrique de la, Jorge Emmanuel, Abe Ignacio, and Helen Toribio, eds. 2004. *The Forbidden Book: The Philippine-American War in Political Cartoons*. San Francisco: T'boli Publishing.

Cruz, Enrique de la, Pearlie Rose S. Baluyut, and Rico J. Reyes, eds. 1998. *Confrontations, Crossings, and Convergence: Photographs of the Philippines and the United States, 1898–1998*. Los Angeles: UCLA Asian American Studies Center Press.

Daly, Ann. 2010. *Done into Dance: Isadora Duncan in America*. Middletown, CT: Wesleyan University Press.

Daulatzai, Sohail. 2009. "A Rebel to America: 'N.Y. State of Mind' after the Towers Fell." In *Born to Use Mics: Reading Nas's Illmatic*, edited by Michael Eric Dyson and Sohail Daulatzai, 33–60. New York: Basic Civitas Books.

———. 2012. *Black Star, Crescent Moon: The Muslim International and Black Freedom beyond America*. Minneapolis: University of Minnesota Press.

———. 2014. *Return of the Mecca: The Art of Islam and Hip-Hop*. Razor Step Media.

David, Alan Mar. 2012. "The Funk Behind Bay Street Dance." Master's thesis, San Francisco State University.

de Leon, Lakandiwa M. 2004. "Filipinotown and the DJ Scene: Cultural Expression and Identity Affirmation of Filipino American Youth in Los Angeles." In *Asian American Youth: Culture, Identity, and Ethnicity*, edited by Jennifer Lee and Min Zhou, 191–206. New York: Routledge.

DeOcampo, Nick. 2008. "Hispanic Influences on Tagalog Cinema: The Battle for Hegemony on the Native Screen." In Donoso, *More Hispanic than We Admit*, 345–62.

Deutsch, Nathaniel. 2001. "'The Asiatic Black Man': An African American Orientalism?" *Journal of Asian American Studies* 4 (3): 193–208.

DJ Kuya D, DJ Delinger, Martin Briones, and Kuttin Kandi. 2014. "A Certain Style: A Conversation on Virginia Beach." In Villegas, Kandi, and Labrador, *Empire of Funk*, 99–103.

DJ Qbert, and Labrador, Roderick N. 2014. "We're Up There Performing a Character." In Villegas, Kandi, and Labrador, *Empire of Funk*, 7–11.

Donoso, Isaac. 2008. "Al-Andalus and Asia: Ibero-Asian Relations Before Magellan." In Donoso, *More Hispanic than We Admit*, 9–35.

Donoso, Isaac, ed. 2008. *More Hispanic than We Admit: Insights into Philippine Cultural History*. Quezon City: Vibal Foundation.

Du Bois, W. E. B. 1994. *The Souls of Black Folk*. Mineola, NY: Dover.

Enloe, Cynthia. 2000. *Maneuvers: The International Politics of Militarizing Women's Lives*. Berkeley: University of California Press.

Esclamado, Leo. 2014. "Y'All Want This Party Started Right? Fil-Ams Getting Down in Jacksonville, Florida." In Villegas, Kandi, and Labrador, *Empire of Funk*, 91–97.

Eshun, Kodwo. 1999. *More Brilliant than the Sun: Adventures in Sonic Fiction*. London: Quartet Books.

———. 2003. "Further Considerations of Afrofuturism." *CR: The New Centennial Review* 3 (2): 287–302.

España-Maram, Linda. 2006. *Creating Masculinity in Los Angeles's Little Manila: Working-Class Filipinos and Popular Culture, 1920s-1950s*. New York: Columbia University Press.

Espiritu, Yen Le. 2003. *Home Bound: Filipino American Lives across Cultures, Communities, and Countries*. Berkeley: University of California Press.

Eure, Joseph D., and James G. Spady. 1991. *Nation Conscious Rap: The Hip Hop Vision*. New York: PC International Press.

Fajardo, Kale Bantigue. 2011. *Filipino Crosscurrents: Oceanographies of Seafaring, Masculinities, and Globalization*. Minneapolis: University of Minnesota Press.

Fernández, Doreen G. 1996. *Palabas: Essays on Philippine Theater History*. Manila: Ateneo de Manila University Press.

Flores, Juan. 2000. *From Bomba to Hip-Hop: Puerto Rican Culture and Latino Identity*. New York: Columbia University Press.

Folkmar, Daniel. 1904. *Album of Philippine Types (Found in Bilibid Prison in 1903), Christians and Moros (Including a Few Non-Christians), Eighty Plates, Representing Thirty-Seven Provinces and Islands*. Manila: Bureau of Public Printing.

Francia, Luis. 2013. *A History of the Philippines: From Indios Bravos to Filipinos*. New York: Overlook Press.

Francisco, Valerie. 2018. *The Labor of Care: Filipina Migrants and Transnational Families in the Digital Age*. Urbana: University of Illinois Press.

Franko, Mark. 2002. *The Work of Dance: Labor, Movement, and Identity in the 1930s*. Middletown, CT: Wesleyan University Press.

Gaerlan, Barbara. 1999. "In the Court of the Sultan: Orientalism, Nationalism, and Modernity in Philippine and Filipino American Dance." *Journal of Asian American Studies* 2 (3): 251–87.

Gilroy, Paul. 1993. *The Black Atlantic: Modernity and Double-Consciousness*. Cambridge, MA: Harvard University Press.

Gonzalez, Vernadette Vicuña. 2010. "Touring Military Masculinities: U.S.-Philippines Circuits of Sacrifice and Gratitude in Corregidor and Bataan." In *Militarized Currents: Toward a Decolonized Future in Asia and the Pacific*, edited by Setsu Shigematsu and Keith L. Camacho, 63–88. Minneapolis: University of Minnesota Press.

———. 2013. *Securing Paradise: Tourism and Militarism in Hawai'i and the Philippines*. Durham, NC: Duke University Press.

Gonzalves, Theodore S. 2010. *The Day the Dancers Stayed: Performing in the Filipino/American Diaspora*. Philadelphia: Temple University Press.

Guzman-Sanchez, Thomas. 2012. *Underground Dance Masters: Final History of a Forgotten Era*. Santa Barbara, CA: Praeger.

Hall, Stuart. 1990. "Cultural Identity and Diaspora." In *Identity, Community, Culture, Difference*, edited by Jonathan Rutherford, 222–37. London: Lawrence and Wishart.

Harrison, Anthony Kwame. 2009. *Hip Hop Underground: The Integrity and Ethics of Racial Identification*. Philadelphia: Temple University Press.

———. 2012. "Post-Colonial Consciousness, Knowledge Production, and Identity Inscription within Filipino American Hip Hop Music." *Perfect Beat* 13 (1): 29–48.

Hernandez, Xavier J. 2020. "Behind the Curtain: The Cultural Capital of Pilipino Cultural Nights." *Journal of Southeast Asian American Education and Advancement* 15 (1): 1–23.

Hong, Euny. 2014. *The Birth of Korean Cool: How One Nation Is Conquering the World through Pop Culture*. New York: Picador.

Hopie. 2014. "Writing Wrongs." In Villegas, Kandi, and Labrador, *Empire of Funk*, 159–64.

Jamero, Peter. 2011. *Vanishing Filipino Americans: The Bridge Generation*. Lanham, MD: University Press of America.

Joo, Rachael Miyung. 2012. *Transnational Sport: Gender, Media, and Global Korea.* Durham, NC: Duke University Press.

Kandi, Kuttin. 2014. "Introduction: A Hip Hop Story to Tell: It's Just Begun." In Villegas, Kandi, and Labrador, *Empire of Funk*, xv–xxiv.

Kelley, Robin D. G. 1994. *Race Rebels: Culture, Politics, and the Black Working Class.* New York: Free Press.

———. 1997. *Yo' Mama's Disfunktional! Fighting the Culture Wars in Urban America.* Boston: Beacon.

Khabeer, Su'ad Abdul. 2016. *Muslim Cool: Race, Religion, and Hip Hop in the United States.* New York: New York University Press.

Lara, Francisco, Jr. 2012. "The New Face of Mindanao's Strong Men: The Politico-Economic Foundations of Legitimacy in Muslim Mindanao." *Asian Studies* 48 (1–2): 55–68.

LaBoskey, Sara. 2001. "Getting Off: Portrayals of Masculinity in Hip Hop Dance in Film." *Dance Research Journal* 33 (2): 112–20.

Labrador, Roderick N. 2015. "'The Rock, Rock On': Musical Autobiography as National Counter-Story." *Popular Music and Society* 38 (2): 243–60.

———. 2018. "'Freaky' Asian Americans, Hip-Hop, and Musical Autobiography: An Introduction." *Biography* 41 (3): 473–83.

Leaño, Ryan Anthony. 2005. "The Rhythm of a Nation: The Filipin@ American Movement in Hiphop Dance." Master's thesis, San Francisco State University.

Leland, John. 2005. *Hip: The History.* New York: Harper Perennial.

Lott, Eric. 2013. *Love and Theft: Blackface Minstrelsy and the American Working Class.* Oxford: Oxford University Press.

Lowe, Lisa. 1996. *Immigrant Acts: On Asian American Cultural Politics.* Durham, NC: Duke University Press.

Luv, King Mark, and Malika Saphire. N.d. *The Green Book, Universal Zulu Nation Infinity Lessons Archive, 1973–2000, for the Masses: Book #1.* Comp. Queen Saphire. https://uznnoble9.files.wordpress.com/2015/01/green_book.pdf.

Mabalon, Dawn. 2013. *Little Manila Is in the Heart: The Making of the Filipina/o American Community in Stockton, California.* Durham, NC: Duke University Press.

Machida, Margo. 2009. *Unsettled Visions: Contemporary Asian American Artists and the Social Imaginary.* Durham, NC: Duke University Press.

Majors, Richard, and Janet Mancini Billson. 1993. *Cool Pose: The Dilemmas of Black Manhood in America.* New York: Touchstone.

Maligat, Luisito G. 2000. "Study of the U.S. Navy's Philippines Enlistment Program, 1981–1991." Master's thesis, Naval Postgraduate School.

Manalansan, Martin F. 2003. *Global Divas: Filipino Gay Men in the Diaspora.* Durham, NC: Duke University Press.

Manning, Susan. 2006. *Modern Dance, Negro Dance: Race in Motion.* Minneapolis: University of Minnesota Press.

Marks, George P., III. 1971. *The Black Press Views American Imperialism (1898–1900).* New York: Arno Press and the New York Times.

Martin, John. 1972. *The Modern Dance*. Trenton, NJ: Dance Horizons.

Maxwell, Anne. 2008. *Picture Imperfect: Photography and Eugenics, 1879–1940*. Eastbourne, UK: Sussex Academic Press.

McAlister, Melani. 2001. *Epic Encounters: Culture, Media, and U.S. Interests in the Middle East since 1945–2000*. Berkeley: University of California Press.

McCoy, Alfred W. 2009. *Policing America's Empire: The United States, the Philippines, and the Rise of the Surveillance State*. Madison: University of Wisconsin Press.

McDonagh, Don. 1990. *The Rise and Fall and Rise of Modern Dance*. Atlanta: A Cappella Books.

Merk, Frederick. 1995. *Manifest Destiny and Mission in American History: A Reinterpretation*. Cambridge, MA: Harvard University Press.

Miyakawa, Felicia. 2005. *Five Percenter Rap: God Hop's Music, Message, and Black Muslim Mission*. Bloomington: Indiana University Press.

Mojares, Resil B. 2008. "Claiming Malayness: Civilizational Discourse in Colonial Philippines." In Donoso, *More Hispanic than We Admit*, 303–26.

Mullen, Bill V. 2004. *Afro-Orientalism*. Minneapolis: University of Minnesota Press.

Nadeau, Jean-Benoit, and Julie Barlow. 2014. *The Story of Spanish*. New York: St. Martin's Griffin.

Nama, Adilifu. 2009. "It Was Signified: 'The Genesis.'" In *Born to Use Mics: Reading Nas's Illmatic*, edited by Michael Eric Dyson and Sohail Daulatzai, 13–31. New York: Basic Civitas Books.

Nasty, Rob. 2014. "Building Hip Hop from the Bay to the World." In Villegas, Kandi, and Labrador, *Empire of Funk*, 117–20.

Nelson, Alondra. 2002. "Introduction: Future Texts." *Social Text* 20 (2): 1–15.

Ngai, Mae. 2014. *Impossible Subjects: Illegal Aliens and the Making of Modern America*. Princeton, NJ: Princeton University Press.

Ngô, Fiona I. B. 2014. *Imperial Blues: Geographies of Race and Sex in Jazz Age New York*. Durham, NC: Duke University Press.

Oades, Riz A. 2004. *Beyond the Mask: Untold Stories of U.S. Navy Filipinos*. National City, CA: KCS Publishing.

Pacleb, Jocelyn. 2003. "Gender, Family Labor, and the United States Navy: The Post–World War II San Diego Filipina/o American Immigrant Navy Community." PhD dissertation, University of California, Irvine.

Parreñas, Rhacel Salazar. 2001. *Servants of Globalization: Women, Migration, and Domestic Work*. Stanford, CA: Stanford University Press.

———. 2005. *Children of Global Migration: Transnational Families and Gendered Woes*. Stanford, CA: Stanford University Press.

———. 2008. *The Force of Domesticity: Filipina Migrants and Globalization*. New York: New York University Press.

Pérez, Gina M. 2015. *Citizen, Student, Soldier: Latina/o Youth, JROTC, and the American Dream*. New York: New York University Press.

Perillo, J. Lorenzo. 2012. "An Empire State of Mind: Hip-Hop Dance in the Philippines." In *Hip-Hop(e): The Cultural Practice and Critical Pedagogy of International*

Hip-Hop, edited by Brad J. Porfilio and Michael J. Viola, 42–64. New York: Peter Lang.

———. 2017. "Embodying Modernism: A Postcolonial Intervention across Filipino Dance." *Amerasia Journal* 43 (2): 122–40.

Pisares, Elizabeth H. 2006. "Do You Mis(recognize) Me: Filipina Americans in Popular Music and the Problem of Invisibility." In Tiongson and Gutierrez, *Positively No Filipinos Allowed*, 172–98.

Pomeroy, William. 1974. "The Philippines—A Case History of Neo-Colonialism." In *Remaking Asia: Essays on the American Uses of Power*, edited by Mark Selden, 157–99. New York: Pantheon Books.

Potter, Russell A. 1995. *Spectacular Vernaculars: Hip-Hop and the Politics of Postmodernism*. New York: State University of New York Press.

Pratt, Mary Louise. 2007. *Imperial Eyes: Travel Writing and Transculturation*. New York: Routledge.

Quinsaat, Jesse. 1976. "An Exercise on How to Join the Navy and Still Not See the World." In *Letters in Exile: An Introductory Reader on the History of Pilipinos in America*, edited by Jesse Quinsaat, Henry Empeno, Vince Nafarrete, and Lourdes Pammit, 96–111. Los Angeles: UCLA Asian American Studies Center Press.

Rae, Issa. 2015. *The Misadventures of Awkward Black Girl*. New York: 37 Ink Atria.

Rafael, Vicente L. 2000. *White Love and Other Events in Filipino History*. Durham, NC: Duke University Press.

———. 2002. "Parricides, Bastards, and Counterrevolution: Reflections on the Philippine Centennial." In *Vestiges of War: The Philippine-American War and the Aftermath of an Imperial Dream, 1899–1999*, edited by Angel Velasco Shaw and Luis H. Francia, 361–75. New York: New York University Press.

Ramirez, Joseph. 2014. "Booty Pop Madness: The Negotiation of Space for Gay Pilipino American Males and Choreographed Hip Hop." In Villegas, Kandi, and Labrador, *Empire of Funk*, 165–68.

Rivera, Raquel Z. 2003. *New York Ricans from the Hip Hop Zone*. London: Palgrave Macmillan.

Rivera, Rocky. 2014. "Rap Out Loud." In Villegas, Kandi, and Labrador, *Empire of Funk*, 277–80.

Rodriguez, Dylan. 2010. *Suspended Apocalypse: White Supremacy, Genocide, and the Filipino Condition*. Minneapolis: University of Minnesota Press.

Rodriguez, Robyn. 2010. *Migrants for Export: How the Philippine State Brokers Labor to the World*. Minneapolis: University of Minnesota Press.

Rosal, Patrick. 2003. *Uprock Headspin Scramble and Dive: Poems*. New York: Persea Books.

———. 2016. *Brooklyn Antediluvian: Poems*. New York: Persea Books.

Rose, Tricia. 1994. *Black Noise: Rap Music and Black Culture in Contemporary America*. Middletown, CT: Wesleyan University Press.

Ryce, Manila. 2014. "Art as Political Weapon." In Villegas, Kandi, and Labrador, *Empire of Funk*, 217–19.

Rydell, Robert W. 1987. *All the World's a Fair: Visions of Empire at American International Expositions, 1876–1916*. Chicago: University of Chicago Press.

Sadiq, Kamal. 2000. *Paper Citizens: How Illegal Immigrants Acquire Citizenship in Developing Countries*. Oxford: Oxford University Press.

Salman, Michael. 2001. *The Embarrassment of Slavery: Controversies over Bondage and Nationalism in the American Colonial Philippines*. Berkeley: University of California Press.

Schirmer, Daniel B., and Stephen Rosskamm Shalom, eds. 1987. *The Philippines Reader: A History of Colonialism, Neocolonialism, Dictatorship, and Resistance*. Boston: South End Press.

Schleitwiler, Vince. 2017. *Strange Fruit of the Black Pacific: Imperialism's Racial Justice and Its Fugitives*. New York: New York University Press.

Schloss, Joseph G. 2009. *Foundation: B-Boys, B-Girls and Hip-Hop Culture in New York*. Oxford: Oxford University Press.

See, Sarita. 2009. *The Decolonized Eye: Filipino American Art and Performance*. Minneapolis: University of Minnesota Press.

———. 2017. *The Filipino Primitive: Accumulation and Resistance in the American Museum*. New York: New York University Press.

Sharma, Nitasha. 2010. *Hip Hop Desis: South Asian Americans, Blackness, and a Global Race Consciousness*. Durham, NC: Duke University Press.

Shigematsu, Setsu, and Keith L. Camacho, eds. 2010. *Militarized Currents: Toward a Decolonized Future in Asia and the Pacific*. Minneapolis: University of Minnesota Press.

Siyam, Freedom Allah. 2014. "Knowledge of Self: From Islam through Hip-Hop to Freedom." In Villegas, Kandi, and Labrador, *Empire of Funk*, 47–54.

Smith, Shawn Michelle. 2004. *Photography on the Color Line: W. E. B. Du Bois, Race, and Visual Culture*. Durham, NC: Duke University Press.

Sturdevant, Saundra Pollack, and Brenda Stoltzfus. 1993. *Let the Good Times Roll: Prostitution and the U.S. Military in Asia*. New York: New Press.

Sylvan, Robyn. 2014. "Rap Music, Hip-Hop Culture and 'the Future Religion of the World." In *The Hip Hop and Religion Reader*, edited by Monica R. Miller and Anthony B. Pinn, 407–20. New York: Routledge.

Talusan, Grace. 2019. *The Body Papers: A Memoir*. Brooklyn: Restless Books.

Taylor, Diana. *The Archive and the Repertoire: Performing Cultural Memory in the Americas*. Durham, NC: Duke University Press, 2003.

Tiongson, Antonio T., Jr. 2006. "On the Politics of (Filipino) Youth Culture: Interview with Theodore S. Gonzalves." In Tiongson and Gutierrez, *Positively No Filipinos Allowed*, 111–23.

———. 2013. *Filipinos Represent: DJs, Racial Authenticity, and the Hip-Hop Nation*. Minneapolis: University of Minnesota Press.

Tiongson, Antonio T., Jr., and Ricardo V. Gutierrez. 2006 *Positively No Filipinos Allowed: Building Communities and Discourse*. Philadelphia: Temple University Press.

Turner, Richard Brent. 2003. *Islam in the African-American Experience*. Bloomington: Indiana University Press.

Vergara, Benito M., Jr. 1995. *Displaying Filipinos: Photography and Colonialism in Early 20th Century Philippines*. Quezon City: University of the Philippines Press.

Viesca, Victor H. 2012. "Native Guns and Stray Bullets: Cultural Activism and Filipino American Rap Music in Post-Riot Los Angeles." *Amerasia Journal* 38 (1): 113–42.

Villegas, Mark R. 2018. "Redefined What Is Meant to Be Divine: Prayer and Protest in Blue Scholars." *Biography: An Interdisciplinary Quarterly* 41 (3): 509–26.

Villegas, Mark R., Kuttin' Kandi, and Roderick N. Labrador, eds. 2014. *Empire of Funk: Hip Hop and Representation in Filipina/o America*. San Diego: Cognella Academic Publishing.

Viola, Michael. 2006. "Hip-Hop and Critical Revolutionary Pedagogy: Blue Scholarship to Challenge 'The Miseducation of the Filipino.'" *Journal for Critical Education Policy Studies* 4 (2): 1–23.

Wang, Oliver. 2007. "Rapping and Repping Asian: Race, Authenticity, and the Asian American MC." In *Alien Encounters: Popular Culture in Asian America*, edited by Mimi Thi Nguyen and Thuy Linh Nguyen Tu, 35–68. Durham, NC: Duke University Press.

———. 2015. *Legions of Boom: Filipino American Mobile DJ Crews in the San Francisco Bay Area*. Durham, NC: Duke University Press.

Weston, Kath. 1997. *Families We Choose: Lesbians, Gays, Kinship*. New York: Columbia University Press.

Womack, Ytasha L. 2013. *Afrofuturism: The World of Black Sci-Fi and Fantasy Culture*. Chicago: Chicago Review Press.

Wood, Joe. 2006. "The Yellow Negro." In *Blacks and Asians: Crossings, Conflict and Commonality*, edited by Hazel M. McFerson, 463–83. Durham, NC: Carolina Academic Press.

Index

MARK R. VILLEGAS is an assistant professor of American studies at Franklin & Marshall College.

The Asian American Experience

The Hood River Issei: An Oral History of Japanese Settlers in Oregon's Hood
River Valley   *Linda Tamura*
Americanization, Acculturation, and Ethnic Identity: The Nisei Generation
in Hawaii   *Eileen H. Tamura*
Sui Sin Far/Edith Maude Eaton: A Literary Biography   *Annette White-Parks*
Mrs. Spring Fragrance and Other Writings   *Sui Sin Far; edited by Amy Ling
and Annette White-Parks*
The Golden Mountain: The Autobiography of a Korean Immigrant, 1895–1960
Easurk Emsen Charr; edited and with an introduction by Wayne Patterson
Race and Politics: Asian Americans, Latinos, and Whites in a Los Angeles Suburb
Leland T. Saito
Achieving the Impossible Dream: How Japanese Americans Obtained Redress
Mitchell T. Maki, Harry H. L. Kitano, and S. Megan Berthold
If They Don't Bring Their Women Here: Chinese Female Immigration
before Exclusion   *George Anthony Peffer*
Growing Up Nisei: Race, Generation, and Culture among Japanese Americans
of California, 1924–49   *David K. Yoo*
Chinese American Literature since the 1850s   *Xiao-huang Yin*
Pacific Pioneers: Japanese Journeys to America and Hawaii, 1850–80
John E. Van Sant
Holding Up More Than Half the Sky: Chinese Women Garment Workers in
New York City, 1948–92   *Xiaolan Bao*
Onoto Watanna: The Story of Winnifred Eaton   *Diana Birchall*
Edith and Winnifred Eaton: Chinatown Missions and Japanese
Romances   *Dominika Ferens*
Being Chinese, Becoming Chinese American   *Shehong Chen*
"A Half Caste" and Other Writings   *Onoto Watanna; edited by Linda Trinh Moser
and Elizabeth Rooney*
Chinese Immigrants, African Americans, and Racial Anxiety in the United States,
1848–82   *Najia Aarim-Heriot*
Not Just Victims: Conversations with Cambodian Community Leaders in the
United States   *Edited and with an introduction by Sucheng Chan;
interviews conducted by Audrey U. Kim*
The Japanese in Latin America   *Daniel M. Masterson with Sayaka Funada-Classen*
Survivors: Cambodian Refugees in the United States   *Sucheng Chan*
From Concentration Camp to Campus: Japanese American Students and
World War II   *Allan W. Austin*
Japanese American Midwives: Culture, Community, and Health Politics
Susan L. Smith
In Defense of Asian American Studies: The Politics of Teaching and
Program Building   *Sucheng Chan*

Lost and Found: Reclaiming the Japanese American Incarceration
  Karen L. Ishizuka
Religion and Spirituality in Korean America   *Edited by David K. Yoo and
  Ruth H. Chung*
Moving Images: Photography and the Japanese American Incarceration
  Jasmine Alinder
Camp Harmony: Seattle's Japanese Americans and the Puyallup
  Assembly Center   *Louis Fiset*
Chinese American Transnational Politics   *Him Mark Lai; edited and with
  an introduction by Madeline Y. Hsu*
Issei Buddhism in the Americas   *Edited by Duncan Ryūken Williams and
  Tomoe Moriya*
Hmong America: Reconstructing Community in Diaspora   *Chia Youyee Vang*
In Pursuit of Gold: Chinese American Miners and Merchants in the
  American West   *Sue Fawn Chung*
Pacific Citizens: Larry and Guyo Tajiri and Japanese American Journalism in
  the World War II Era   *Edited by Greg Robinson*
Indian Accents: Brown Voice and Racial Performance in American Television
  and Film   *Shilpa S. Davé*
Yellow Power, Yellow Soul: The Radical Art of Fred Ho   *Edited by Roger N. Buckley
  and Tamara Roberts*
Fighting from a Distance: How Filipino Exiles Helped Topple a Dictator
  Jose V. Fuentecilla
In Defense of Justice: Joseph Kurihara and the Japanese American Struggle
  for Equality   *Eileen H. Tamura*
Asian Americans in Dixie: Race and Migration in the South   *Edited by Jigna Desai
  and Khyati Y. Joshi*
Undercover Asian: Multiracial Asian Americans in Visual Culture
  Leilani Nishime
Islanders in the Empire: Filipino and Puerto Rican Laborers in Hawai'i
  JoAnna Poblete
Virtual Homelands: Indian Immigrants and Online Cultures in the United States
  Madhavi Mallapragada
Building Filipino Hawai'i   *Roderick N. Labrador*
Legitimizing Empire: Filipino American and U.S. Puerto Rican Cultural Critique
  Faye Caronan
Chinese in the Woods: Logging and Lumbering in the American West
  Sue Fawn Chung
The Minor Intimacies of Race: Asian Publics in North America   *Christine Kim*
Reading Together, Reading Apart: Identity, Belonging, and South Asian
  American Community   *Tamara Bhalla*
Chino: Anti-Chinese Racism in Mexico, 1880–1940   *Jason Oliver Chang*

The University of Illinois Press
is a founding member of the
Association of University Presses.

———————————————————

University of Illinois Press
1325 South Oak Street
Champaign, IL 61820-6903
www.press.uillinois.edu